Parsloes to Pompeii
Wedding Tour 1844

Parsloes to Pompeii
Wedding Tour 1844

Letters of Helen Fanshawe and Edward Hanson Denison

Transcribed and researched
by Deirdre Marculescu
Prepared for publication by Derek Alexander
and Rosalind Alexander

VALENCE HOUSE
a place of discovery

Valence House Publications

Published in 2023 by Valence House Publications
Valence House, Becontree Avenue
Dagenham, Essex RM8 3HT

www.valencehousecollections.co.uk

ISBN 978-1-911391-10-4

Introduction and all editorial material copyright ©Valence House Publications 2023

All rights reserved. No part of this book may be reproduced or transmitted in any form or by any means, electronic or mechanical, including photocopying, recording or by any information storage or retrieval system, without permission from the Publisher in writing

Previous Fanshawe Publications
Sebastopol to Dagenham (978-1-911391-02-9)
Abyssinia 1868 (978-1-911391-04-3)
Fanshawe's Indian Summer (978-1-911391-050)
The Life of Sir Richard Fanshawe (978-1-911391-00-5)

Cover Images :
Courtesy of The Archives and Local Studies Centre
Valence House Museum - Dagenham :
Parsloes Manor House Sketch (1780)
Scanned letters with letterhead of Lake Lucerne - Helen Fanshawe Denison (1844).

Dagenham Village

The old Essex village of Dagenham has almost disappeared, but a quiet undisturbed corner still remains and although surrounded by modern housing, it proudly displays the sign 'Dagenham Village'. There the old parish church stands and across a narrow street, despite many periods of dilapidation, the vicarage sits inside the garden that was once nurtured by the Revd Thomas Lewis Fanshawe.

The ancient public house, The Cross Keys has survived and a few steps away, the national village school building sits close to the full churchyard where weathered memorials cluster together and remind us of families well-known in Dagenham's story.

Sadly, nothing is left of the village houses that gave shelter in centuries past, but if you stroll among the wild flowers of the churchyard and hear quiet chatter and domestic bustle drifting from nearby modern homes or the public house gardens, those sounds blend seamlessly with all that linger from the past.

You will not find the old manor house of Parsloes - it was demolished a hundred years ago and only the parklands are left to remind us of the scale and site of the Fanshawe family estate.

Fortunately, memories of Parsloes and the history of Dagenham village have been kept alive by past and present local historians and in Valence House Museum & Archives there is a store of documents, maps and images – that tell for Dagenham's past inhabitants and reveal the patterns of village days.

Sometimes, we want to probe a little further and discover the finer, more subtle aspects of past personal worlds and it is then that we look for family letters, diaries and notes; items rarely donated, as they are especially treasured and usually kept within families.

Conscious of this, we remain always grateful to John Gordon[1] for making his gift to the Fanshawe Collection at Valence House when he generously donated many items passed down to him from his grandmother, Violet Fanshawe. Included was a unique collection of 19th century private letters with pages of well-formed sentences, which since have taken us down a pathway to a period of Fanshawe family history, until now much overlooked.

The letters create a bridge to voices not very distant from our time, who speak as the last generation of the family who lived at Parsloes and Dagenham Vicarage. Although they too are now all beyond reach, their words have ensured their family emerges from the shade of their illustrious Tudor and Stuart ancestors who until recently have occupied most of our attention.

This is a collection of letters written by Helen Fanshawe who is able to draw us back to the time when her family were still central in Dagenham's community. While focusing on local points of interest, she expresses contemporary opinions and attitudes that could also interest researchers of other 19th century families, both local and elsewhere.

Captured in Helen's words, written in her early maturity, is the fashionable 'Grand Bridal Tour'. We learn her experiences of using early modern transport links, as she shares stories of the art treasures seen and vivid descriptions of touristic sights. Interwoven are her comments on customs and history with her reports often coloured by local or national events as witnessed. All was told to delight and include her family for this was how Helen kept her family close when she was so far from home. How she succeeded

---

[1] Grandson of Violet Gordon née Fanshawe – youngest daughter of Helen's older brother John Gaspard Fanshawe.

will become clear as you read – but don't be surprised if you slip into her forgotten, gentle world.

The bride

Helen Fanshawe enjoyed a privileged life, greater even than most could experience today, since the opportunity to take an extensive European bridal tour would still remain beyond all but the very rich. Nevertheless, many of us have travelled to the cities she visited and perhaps taken similar routes, so her words will possibly evoke your own memories. Her comments and thoughts are interesting and mostly relatable, even to a modern reader…

Despite apparent maturity, Helen was only eighteen when the letters were written. When she was born in 1826 her ancestors had occupied Parsloes for more than two centuries. Many Fanshawe daughters before her had left Parsloes on their wedding day but Helen's unique distinction was to be the last bride of Parsloes.

The marriage took place at Dagenham village church on Tuesday 7th May 1844 and days later, she and her husband Edward Hanson Denison set off on a bridal tour of Europe with the plan to return at Christmas or early the following year.

Throughout their journey, Helen constantly wrote to her family and in almost journal-style she told them all she saw and heard. She asked in return for their family news and gossip and through this 'conversation' she reveals the activities of the Fanshawe family at home.

Often including in the letters are comments about friends, family and neighbours who were, previously not known to be connected. Helen had grown up in Dagenham but knew a village vastly different from today. Our post-industrialised world follows decades of changes, leaving Dagenham's present community living and working in a hinterland of the River Thames almost unaware of the river's close proximity. This was not how it was in Helen's time as the people lived closer to the marsh and river, and knew the seasonal tides and the history of flooding. They vigilantly monitored the sea defences and as they moved by foot all were aware and thankful for the natural gradient rising slowly from the Thames. They knew the old tales of early settlers by the river, but the 'Dagenham Idol' still lay dormant in the Ripple Marsh - it was many decades later when that proof of Bronze Age habitation was discovered.

Despite being only a dozen miles downstream from London this southern part of Essex remained rural long after Helen's childhood. Modern inventions arrived slowly and with most families being dependant on land and river, few needed to travel further than Romford, the thriving market town two miles away and easily reached by well-trodden lanes. Decades later, as heavy industrialization began along the river, the village passed through many periods of change as it became an urban town, but that was far in the future…

Helen's family, having 'society' connections would often travel away from Dagenham yet they still played a central role in village life. Helen's father, Thomas Lewis Fanshawe was a major landowner but he was more important to the parish as Dagenham's vicar. Helen's letters imply all his family took interest in his pastoral duties and despite social differences, the letters also reveal she and her brothers were friendly with the young people whose families owned the larger local farms. Her girlish gossip about their friends 'pairings' was very natural but how might they have viewed her marriage and extended bridal tour? Differences in opportunities must have been obvious to all.

Helen's Family at Parsloes

Undoubtedly, Helen's family at Parsloes were privileged but despite their substantial land and property holding they were not wealthy by 19th century standards. However, money was still not paramount in British society and the family's ancient pedigree assured them a place among the gentry.

Nevertheless, Helen's young life was appreciably more than 'comfortable' for she and her siblings were brought up with servants and placed in small schools or tutored at home from an early age. As her brothers grew older, they boarded at top public schools and a place at Oxford was always available. These family traditions and educational institutions formed characters with assurance, independence and self-confidence – the assets Helen demonstrates even as a young woman. A similar style was displayed by her brothers John Gaspard, Basil and Richard[1], and naturally, as would be expected, by her husband.

Separation and distance from their parents never affected unity in this family, surely a situation to the merit of their mother. From their earliest years Mrs Catherine Fanshawe wrote regularly to each of her children and her reassuring letters continued all her life. She was probably a very talented correspondent, but it must have been the regularity and diplomacy of her despatches which kept them united. She was informed by her own experience of similar education and understood the need of children to feel included when apart from family.

Unfortunately, despite all we know of Mrs Fanshawe she remains frustratingly a shadow. We cannot fix her image as neither a portrait or photograph has been discovered, and sadly none of her own

---

[1] Valence House Publications – collected letters of Thomas Basil Fanshawe (3 vols).

letters are in the collections. She was 'the collector' so naturally had no interest in her own letters.

Anybody reading letters addressed to Mrs Fanshawe from her children will almost certainly conclude her replies must have been packed with intelligent advice and interest. This mother, not only enjoyed a special relationship with each of her children, but also had that special 'agility' of being able to adapt when they matured. This flexibility, essential when an adult child marries can be seen when Edward Hanson Denison writes so confidently to her soon after his marriage. Their relationship, obviously already informal, enjoyed report and even a shared 'quirky' sense of humour – yet she was still calling him 'Mr Denison'.

When Catherine Fanshawe died in 1881 she had outlived all her brothers and sisters and was helping her children until the last of her eighty-four years. She had proudly held to the traditions of her own family and passed on the education received from her father, Major General John Gaspard Le Marchant who was killed at the Battle of Salamanca in 1812. It is the pride of his descendants that the British Army acknowledges him as the founder of the first Royal Military College, the precursor to the 'Royal Military Academy' at Sandhurst. Upon his inspiration for exceptional standards of good education and rigorous self-discipline the college has built a world class reputation.

That refinement of education and style, passed by Mrs Fanshawe to her children, is reflected in their letters.

Parsloes

The family at Parsloes understood the ways of the British countryside and how by working together all could thrive. It was experience learnt and passed to successive Fanshawe sons since the property was first purchased in 1619 by Helen's five times great grandfather William Fanshawe (1583 – 1634).

John Fanshawe was the eldest of Helen's uncles who succeeded his father in 1822, and when he died without children in 1843, Henry, the next elderly bachelor brother did not inherit to allow the estate to pass directly to their younger brother, Thomas Lewis Fanshawe.

The eldest of the three sons of Helen's father was John Gaspard who was just finishing his education at Eton. Although he needed to learn the management of the estate, first he had to settle on a career. Income from Parsloes would not be sufficient so paid employment was essential, but this was far from unusual by that time when even gentleman with larger fortunes often preferred to have a 'useful occupation'. Career choices were still limited and most chose to enter 'the professions' of law, medicine, the church or the military – as all came with a level of personal status. Banking and insurance were becoming acceptable and potentially more lucrative, although risky – the magnets that always attract young men!

Obviously not interested in going to Oxford as had his father, John Gaspard was as we learn from Helen, waiting to take a place in the merchant bank of his widowed uncle-in-law, Henry Shaw Lefevre... *'What is John doing now? I suppose he's waiting with you, if Uncle Henry Lefevre's plans come to anything'*. Such good connections have always 'opened doors' so we must assume that when later John took up a career at Westminster, he was assisted again by another of his uncles, Denis Le Marchant. Their confidence in John Gaspard was justified as he eventually became a Cabinet Secretary at the Board of Trade.

Helen wrote often to her brother and began by focusing on his 20th birthday and his holiday after leaving Eton and before starting work. Whilst keeping contact and visiting his school friend, Oswald Smith, his diary was full of the major 'Society' events of the 1844 season – the last Montem at Eton, Royal Ascot, cricket and weekend parties at country houses with sporting events.

Helen liked receiving John's news of his sporting successes along with the gossip of country houses. They got on well together and she particularly enjoyed his love of music, singing and dance - eager to know if he had learnt to polka. Both enjoyed the company of 'Annie', a young cousin who was obviously full of life and often accompanied John on family visits. Anna-Maria Tupper had an amusing talent for mimicry and was a lively regular visitor to Parsloes that all enjoyed – which is why it was sad to find record of her death just two years after these letters…

Whilst away, Helen was very pleased to hear news of the people John had met and the social and royal occasions he had attended by invitation. She understood this was not idling away time, but by meeting well-connected people he might shape his adult life.

A young girl's social circle

Compared to a young man, a girl's social life was restricted but opportunities to meet 'vetted' young men of good background through a brother could lead to friendship and even marriage. Introducing friends to sisters was often part of a brother's role and it was one shared with many aunts, uncles and others in their extended families.

With this in mind it is impossible not to consider how Helen and Edward might have been introduced. Details have not been recorded and family connections are not obvious so although details of their meeting are not essential to the enjoyment of Helen's letters, the background to her story is worth exploring.

We know Helen did not grow up as the only daughter of her family - her sister Catherine, older by three years, died at the age of eighteen in 1841. From scant information available about the unfortunate girl's death, it appears to have been quite sudden. Comments made about the health and weight of Mrs Fanshawe, might indicate how profoundly her daughter's death had affected her to the detriment of her health. Perhaps those circumstances brought Helen exceptionally close to her mother and explain Helen's early maturity and marriage. She was so young and newly married and yet so at ease with Edward, twelve years older and socially sophisticated.

All readers of history, romantic or otherwise will know that until the 20th century, marriages among society's upper classes were rarely a matter of chance, and a degree of careful timing, vetting, and even manoeuvring became the prelude to most matches. Keeping that in mind, if we are to understand the origins of Helen and Edward's courtship, we should look at earlier Fanshawe marriages.

The official reference book always to be consulted is 'The History of the Fanshawe Family' by H.C. Fanshawe where in 535 pages details of the marriages made over four centuries are shown. The links uniting families can be seen in vast, extensive family trees[1] - but unfortunately that history was published in 1927, at a time when stories such as Helen's were almost contemporary. The author was discrete, and as a result only included basic biographical details for

---

[1] Prepared by Beaujolais Mabel Ridout - John Gaspard's eldest daughter.

later generations. In any event, more information might then have had limited interest, as today's 'persons of interest' were then the parents and grandparents of living family members with stories too familiar. Now we are interested, sources are scattered and many 'positive' facts have become elusive.

Despite that our interest in the family relates to the ways earlier Fanshawe parents approached marriage for their daughters and what 'constants' if any may have applied. One 'constant' is found rooted in the experiences of Thomas Fanshawe, 2nd Remembrancer in the Tudor court for he was strongly opposed to forcing a daughter to marry against her wishes. Outraged when a marriage was pressed upon a younger cousin he brought her stepfather to court. He lost the case but the experience ensured he protected his own daughters by the terms of his Will and for many generations that wise counsel influenced his heirs. Unlike many families of their status, few Fanshawe marriages have been between close cousins or step-relatives - the exceptions were mainly in the Civil War when assets and orphaned girls were protected.

The position of Remembrancer of the Exchequer held by several generations of Fanshawe men effectively restricted their membership of London's great Livery Companies, but those rich city magnates were often their closest associates. Marriages between liverymen and Fanshawe daughters were not infrequent as they not only consolidated family interests but also secured status for a daughter in her husband's family. Similarly, later Fanshawe men who were administrators and lawyers, safeguarded a girl's dowry or marriage settlement and through these many marriages can be traced the family names carried down succeeding Fanshawe generations - Evelyn, Gascoyne, Gaspard, Dalrymple, Faithful and more.

Such marriages applied until almost the 19th century, then partners started to come from families not so obviously connected by society or commercial interest. Those changes reflect wider society, as with greater access to travel and transport, entertainment moved into the public space. A 'leisure industry' burgeoned and with this new mobility, society began to gather for 'seasons' in London and fashionable spa towns. Naturally opportunities then followed for accompanied young ladies to be introduced at public assemblies.

Courtship and Marriage for Helen's Grandmother and Aunt

In the generations just before Helen, we can look at the courtships of her grandmother, Mary Fanshawe (née Parkinson) and her daughter, Mary Annetta.

Immediately noticeable is the fact that Mary Parkinson was an unusual choice of bride for a Parsloes man as her family was not from London or the Home Counties but well-established in Lancashire. Even more surprising was her place of birth in 1747, for it is recorded to have taken place on her father's plantation near Kingston, Jamaica. Except for time at school in York, little is known of Mary's young life.

'The History of the Fanshawe Family' offers no conclusions regarding how Mary Parkinson was introduced to John Gascoyne Fanshawe, except to note the close proximity of the Parkinson estate at Prescott near Liverpool to Childwell Hall – where the owner was the wife of Bamber Gascoyne, a politician, born in Barking and an uncle of John Gascoyne Fanshawe.

Mrs Ann Gascoyne Fanshawe died six years before her son's marriage in 1772, but her brother might simply have arranged for his nephew's introduction to Mary Parkinson, if he visited 'en route' to the Fanshawe 'Northern' estate at Wyersdale in Lancashire.

Some years after marriage, Mary welcomed her sister Sarah into the Fanshawe family at Dagenham. She was the widow of an Irish doctor, John Bonynge, resident in Jamaica when she married in 1778. Returning to England after his death in 1784, she came to Parsloes to help her sister raise her children – Helen's father, Thomas Lewis Fanshawe was the youngest. Spending the rest of her life at Parsloes, she had a great influence on her nephews and niece and generously channelled her considerable assets towards their advancement.

In June 1803, Mary's daughter Mary Annetta Fanshawe, married at the age of twenty. Later the same year John Gascoyne Fanshawe died after many years of ill health – so perhaps it should be assumed Mary Annetta's marriage was arranged by her mother Mary and Aunt Sarah

Mary Annetta's husband was Henry Charles Boisragon, a newly qualified doctor from Edinburgh University who arrived in London during 1799. Although raised in Ireland, he was from a Huguenot family and a grandson of the émigré Louis Chevalleau de Boisragon.

Was this couple introduced through connections of Aunt Sarah? She was the widow of a medical man with Irish heritage and we know she helped her nephews establish their careers through her connections…

After marriage, Mary Annetta and Henry moved to Bath to set up his medical practice. Then when Cheltenham became more fashionable, they moved to that spa town and the cultured and elegant Henry Boisragon soon became Cheltenham's most popular and eminent physician. With that success he moved his practice to Royal Crescent and by 1814 he was gazetted as Physician Extraordinaire to HRH George, Prince of Wales.

Mary Annetta and her husband were the parents of three sons, each more than ten years older than Helen and her brothers, but they were the only 'Fanshawe' first cousins.

Marriage through friendship

If chance played a part in the events leading to those earlier marriages, it certainly did not apply to the courtship of Helen's parents. The choice of wife for Thomas Lewis Fanshawe was Catherine, close sister of his school friend, Denis Le Marchant who had shared his room at Eton.

The couple had known of, or knew each other, long before their marriage and possibly met in their early 'teens'. In letters written during 1811 by Major General John Gaspard Le Marchant to Catherine his eldest daughter at boarding school in Marlowe, he mentions visits made to her by Denis from Eton. Unfortunately, Thomas Fanshawe could not have accompanied Denis that time, as he was already at Oxford - but the two boys might easily have made earlier visits together.

After her father's death the next year, Catherine immediately went home to Guernsey - she joined her younger brothers and sisters but left Denis to remain at Eton until later, in the tradition of his family, he went to Trinity College, Cambridge.

By that time, Thomas Fanshawe had completed his BA at Oxford, being ordained in 1816 then inducted into Dagenham Church – where the Patron of the Living was his aunt Sarah Bonynge.

Obviously the school friends kept in touch and after Cambridge Denis came to Lincoln's Inn. He was soon ambitious for a political career and when his sister Catherine visited perhaps she partnered him at social events or may even have visited Parsloes? Unfortunately, the details of how those three young adult lives were kept together is not known and while we imagine and speculate, official records for 1821 positively confirm the marriage of Catherine Le Marchant to Thomas Lewis Fanshawe on the Isle of Guernsey.

Catherine brought to Thomas her extended family of young in-laws which seems to have delighted him. He had brothers of his own but they were so many years older and even his sister Mary Annetta, the closest to him in age, was nine years his senior. His early childhood must have been very lonely, and at the age of eight he was sent to preparatory school in Twickenham. Eton followed where he remained for an unusually long period of seven years. Late in those institutionalised years he found friendship with his younger Eton roommate, Denis Le Marchant who must have had many tales of younger brothers and sisters at home.

Probably Thomas visited Guernsey and the Le Marchant family long before his marriage and was familiar with the family. After they were married, Thomas and Catherine soon began to welcome their family to enjoy the hospitality of Dagenham Vicarage and Parsloes – and many came, bringing ever growing numbers of partners and children.

The collections of letters belonging to Mrs Fanshawe span the years 1844 to 1877, and the affinity between the Fanshawe and Le Marchant families continuously shapes the narrative. While they blended together and fostered each other's interests, Dagenham's village people were growing used to seeing Channel Island visitors and the parish registers officially confirm several 'Le Marchant' marriages and christenings were celebrated at Dagenham.

The two school friends left their legacy in the other's family through inter-familial marriages in succeeding generations and the family names they carry down are their witness.

Edward Hanson Denison

In common with many families of all classes we have seen that by the 1840's the Fanshawe family at Parsloes were accustomed to welcoming and adapting to partners from outside their own circle. Whilst more unusual links enrich ancestry stories, they often puzzle descendants and researchers trying to establish how couples might have met - and Helen and Edward Hanson Denson are just such a couple.

Assuming Helen & Edward were formally introduced, it was initially hoped that a search for Edward's details in the Fanshawe Collection at Valence House would reveal his origins, but no more than the few basic facts in 'The History' was available. This presented a problem to be solved as Helen's letters could not be shared without some details of Edward's life, especially as the letters show he had a strong personality that needs a shape …

Details of Edward's birth in 1814 were soon found which immediately confirmed he was the only son of a gentleman - Joseph Denison of Rusholme Park, Manchester, and had inherited considerable advantages.

His mother Sarah Hanson, ten years older than his father, was born in 1774 and on her marriage, she was the widow of Joseph Kershaw and the mother of his son named William.

Edward's half-brother died in 1832, leaving a widow, Jemima St John Kershaw and two children, Jemima and William (Willie) who were close to Edward and his father and are mentioned by Helen in her letters.

Edward always coupled the name Hanson with his surname Denison to give importance to his mother's family. The most probable reason for this was as a memorial to Joseph Hanson (1774 –

1811) his maternal uncle. His name was well known in Manchester and had earned the title 'The Weaver's Friend' through his early campaign for the rights of workers and improved conditions in the factories and mills.

The Hanson family had grown wealthy from the manufacture of checks and cotton goods but when Joseph Hanson inherited the family business he sold it. Too young to retire to the pleasures of Strangeways Hall his country estate, he became involved in local politics and supported Manchester's cloth workers. By speaking at large gatherings he urged improved conditions and was unafraid to take the side of Luddites. Those social politics were dangerous and Hanson was soon labelled a 'Radical' and brought to trial in the High Court. His punishment was a prison sentence, made extra harsh as he had crossed the line of class and status. To the workers, he became a hero and when he was released, a great crowd gathered outside the prison to lead him home. Sadly, his health was badly damaged and his survival was not long.

The Denison family also had northern origins and first grew to prominence in Leeds as bankers and merchants. By Edward's time several branches of his family were involved in national politics – his distant cousin was John Denison, Speaker to the House of Commons (1857 - 1872). However, Edward's father Joseph Denison was born in Liverpool and according to 'Burke's Genealogical and Heraldic History of the Commoners of Great Britain and Ireland' (1833), was *'of Rusholme Park near Manchester'*, a property purchased in 1824.

Joseph Denison was a solicitor and notary in Manchester who during court evidence in 1838, confirmed had been…*'in practice about 28 years'*. Contemporary notices in 'The Manchester Guardian' and other newspapers reveal his office premises as in Princess Street under the partnership name of Duckworth & Denison - specialising in land and property transactions, both in and around Manchester.

Manchester was by that time, reputedly the world's greatest industrial centre. It had expanded so quickly due to industry, it still had yet to be granted city status and the town was grossly overcrowded. Out of that environment came men of imagination with plans for new business ventures and Joseph Denison was among them. He devised a scheme to promote the use of his personal property and land for profit and after convincing associates, the group then persuaded others to speculate.

The scheme was to use Rusholme Park with adjoining purchased land to create space and to build villas for Manchester's new 'middle classes'. It was a highly attractive plan which encouraged movement away from the overcrowded centre to spacious living conditions in the leafy outskirts. Approval was granted, the first plots were built and Joseph Denison's vision of suburbia 'Victoria Park' was set to become reality. Driving the plan forward, the company was registered with Joseph as the appointed legal expert and shares in the company were then offered at one hundred pounds.

Of course, integral to 'Victoria Park' was Joseph Denison's estate at Rusholme Park so the scheme became his personal reality in 1838 when he moved his family to Stock Grove near Leighton Buzzard. Auction notices in Manchester newspapers confirm that at the time of the move the opportunity was taken to sell many home furnishings …*'well-made and handsome household furniture'*…plus *china, cut-glass, carriages harnesses and cattle* … *'over three days beginning Monday 12th February 1838 at Rusholme…the effects of Joseph Denison Esquire who is leaving the neighbourhood'*.

Announcements were also made for a further sale on Friday 16th February, at the same Manchester auction room …*'the select but valuable miscellaneous library of Joseph Denison, Esquire'* – and first editions were among the books listed. A notice of sale was also appended to the advertisement relating to shares in private pews in two local churches.

Although this move was a major upheaval it must have been viewed by the Denison family as a new beginning which is why it is sad to see the death of Edward's mother, Sarah Denison recorded on 13th August the following year.

The 'Victoria Park' scheme began to unravel about that time too. The events that ensued are legal and complicated but require no explanation here as they are fully recorded through the court case 'Foss v Harbottle 1843'[1] and are well known. The case refers to a claim brought by a disgruntled minor shareholder of the Victoria Park Company. It must have been recognised as having the potential to be important from the outset as it was referred to the Court of Chancery. There the judge ruled in favour of the company; setting a legal precedent that since has been fundamental in corporate law and widely studied.

This has interest to us as possibly a flurry of intense activity before the case, occurred when Edward was preparing for bar examinations. Did he join forces with his father to gain practical experience? Both probably lobbied the best in the legal profession; some perhaps were already in Edward's London based network of Eton and Trinity men or among his new contacts at Lincoln's Inn?

Joseph Denison with decades of professional and social experience was clearly an excellent 'networker'. His confidence would have

---

[1] Extensive information available via an internet search: 'Foss v Harbottle 1843'.

coached Edward into the manners of society and similarly, as Helen writes home to her family we see her growing in worldly assurance. Perhaps a subtle benefit of the extended bridal tour, was that time abroad meeting new and different people allowed a young woman's confidence to grow?

In her letters to Mrs Fanshawe, Helen refers to family visits previously taken in France, particularly Boulogne as she admits to being familiar with sea crossings, although a poor sailor. Edward also confirms the depth of his earlier travel in Europe as he tells his mother-in-law *'I have previously seen the Danube – the Elbe, Moselle, Main and the Guadalquivir'* and also *'I never felt anything hotter, even at Athens'*.

Helen explains that Edward had a direct and practical method for learning languages – was this the way he handled their travel arrangements and tour itinerary? With Murray's travel guides, he regularly amended their routes and where 'business' is mentioned, most probably it refers to when he called on bankers to exchange currency for their next border crossing. Accompanied by his manservant, Edward sought out the most comfortable and modern transport for each stage of their journey, always looking to adapt their travel to take advantage of newly opened sections of the burgeoning European railway networks.

To learn when Edward became a seasoned traveller, the clues are in the gaps between the years of his education. He took his degree at Trinity College, Cambridge in 1838, then five years later took the bar at Lincoln's Inn. So having established that he left Eton in July 1829 it would have been several years before he registered for university and could have travelled until about 1835. He may have been abroad again in 1841 for he has not been traced in England's census that year - and he wrote from Frankfurt in 1844 …*'I am happy to see a difference even within a year or two…'*

By 1843, Edward's London home was Thurloe Park, Brompton – confirmed when gazetted Justice of the Peace for Middlesex. This property may have been shared initially with his father but later it became Helen and Edward's first home while Joseph Denison was active in business – acquiring and managing tenanted commercial properties in the most central streets of Manchester.

The Introduction

Whilst a picture of Edward's single life emerged, no progress was made on how he came to know Helen. So it became necessary to change concentration and look at when, how and where their families might link through wider society.

With time in mind, Helen's eighteenth birthday on 13th February 1844 seemed significant as the difference of twelve years between Helen and Edward would probably imply their courtship would not have begun before her 17th birthday in 1843.

We also know that in 1843 Edward began to establish his career – the moment when many 19th century gentlemen seriously considered marriage for the first time. There are many examples of this pattern in Helen's family, not only among her uncles but also her brothers. John Gaspard married at twenty-nine when he gained a secure post at the Board of Trade, and Thomas 'Basil' at thirty-four, when he was able to purchase his commission as major in the 33rd Regiment.

Assuming Edward had prospects of financial independence from his father, or may have received a legacy from his mother's Hanson estate, the year 1843 would have been appropriate for him. In any event, Joseph Denison and his only son were so close that finding a wife for Edward would probably have been their joint enterprise. Chance would not be their approach - they would use all their connections and contacts so if we assume neither Edward nor

Joseph could have met Helen and her parents without an introduction, then a trusted person with mutual connections had to have been involved.

Although the Fanshawe family at Parsloes had few close relatives they had a wide circle of friends. They were mostly from families of local Essex gentlemen or the Anglican clergy in surrounding parishes and after carefully exploring those possibilities nothing was revealed to connect them to Edward before his marriage.

Attention naturally fell back to the family of Helen's mother as the Le Marchant family were numerous. The closest was Helen's father's old friend, 'Uncle Denis' Le Marchant and theoretically, he would have the most interest and possibilities to help. The entry for Helen's marriage in the Dagenham Parish Register shows that Denis Le Marchant was the first of six witnesses but this may merely signify his presence as head of his family especially as the next to sign was Edward's niece, Jemima Kershaw representing the Denison family. An Eton friend of Edward then followed before two family friends, until almost last John Gaspard, the bride's brother. This document gives the impression of a truly happy occasion when the two official family witnesses spaced out their signatures and then others followed on to celebrate. How could the Vicar object when he was the bride's father!

Interconnecting Circles

Looking at Denis Le Marchant, we know he married at the age of forty in 1835 and his wife Sarah 'Eliza' Smith was thirteen years younger. She was a distant cousin of Henry Shaw Lefevre, an already widowed brother-in-law of Denis. This young Aunt 'Eliza' was popular with both Helen and Mrs Fanshawe as both enjoyed her young family, especially the small boy they affectionately called 'Powder Puff'.

Having become aware of those two linked families, the possibility was open to discover how social introductions were being achieved in their circles. Historically, the country house weekend is well known for social introductions during the 19th century, and we know that these large families with many siblings were part of that world.

Further investigation revealed that the families were already related by the marriage of Le Marchant Thomas to Margaret Vaughan. She was the daughter of the Rt. Hon. Sir John Vaughan, Justice of the Court of Common Pleas, but more important in this context was her mother, the Hon Augusta St. John - a first cousin of Emma Laura Whitbread - the wife of Charles Shaw Lefevre who was the elder brother of Henry Shaw Lefevre.

Henry Shaw Lefevre added further to this complication when he married for a second time in 1835 - as his new wife was Elizabeth Emma Foster, a niece of Augusta St John.

With such relationships, so difficult to unravel even on paper, many in these families were related to the same person at several levels. Just imagine the conversations that may have followed an introduction at these country houses…but they lived in that world of leisure when time was at their disposal while they enjoyed the comforts of those beautiful houses.

They gathered on some occasions at Billingbear, an old Tudor manor in a Berkshire country estate owned by John Thomas and his son Le Marchant Thomas Le Marchant. Helen's letters tell us that in the summer of 1844, John Gaspard and his cousin Anna Maria Tupper were among the house guests…*'you seem to have met some very agreeable people at Billingbear…'*

John Thomas, married to Anne Le Marchant[1], was a wealthy merchant who exported to America and Russia from the ports of London, Guernsey and Liverpool. He traded in cotton cloth manufactured in Lancashire yet unfortunately nothing could be found to link him to Joseph Denison or even Joseph Hanson.

Nevertheless, Helen's family were clearly familiar with Billingbear's *'agreeable people'* and mutual friends were among the male guests. Many were involved in politics or were merchants and bankers, but in common was their education at Eton, Oxford and Cambridge. Through these friends and their families most had found wives, and among the other lady guests were their own sisters, cousins and nieces.

The Le Merchant Thomas family had a London residence in Harley Street, but in summer months they could be found at Seaview near Ryde, Isle of Wight. This comfortable lifestyle made possible through trade, was perhaps augmented by a Whitbread family inheritance received through the family of the deceased Augusta Vaughan[2], as her grandmother and great uncle were the only surviving children of Samuel Whitbread, London's wealthy brewing magnate.

When at Seaview, other families in the Le Marchant Thomas' circle often decamped and occupied rented houses nearby, when presumably they joined together for entertainment. For Helen's parents, Seaview was a favourite resort and their visit in 1844 was confirmed in the letters, as well as her own the previous year - *'I must first congratulate you on taking up your quarters at Sea View. I often think how much you must be enjoying yourselves & fancy I know the house*

---

[1] Anne Le Marchant was a first cousin of Mrs Catherine Fanshawe.
[2] Augusta died 1813 and in 1823 Sir John Vaughan married the widow of Augusta's uncle, the 14th Baron St. John of Bletso and consequently Margaret Vaughan's stepbrother was the 15th Baron St. John of Bletso.

in which you are staying for I recollect observing some nice ones when I passed Sea View last year with Helen & Uncle Lefevre, on our way to Ryde'.

Another country house mentioned and familiar to Helen was Heckfield Place in Hampshire whose owner was the eldest brother of Henry Shaw Lefevre, her uncle. Charles Shaw Lefevre[1] was a Whig politician and his second wife Emma was another 'Whitbread' lady, a daughter of the great brewer's only son.

Such tangled relationships only became apparent when exploring sources to connections to Edward, and in an attempt to remain focused, a vast family tree was gradually written up. That effort suddenly became validated when the name of one family emerged as also included on the very margin of Edward's pedigree. For it meant that if confirmed, Edward would not be related to Le Marchant Thomas but would be 'connected' to Billingbear – a place where he and Helen could so easily be introduced through those *'agreeable people'…*

Tracing the ancestry of the hostess at Billingbear, was relatively simple for Mrs Margaret Le Marchant Thomas, as a daughter of the Hon. Augusta St John, descended from a member of the peerage and Margaret's grandfather was found to have been 13th Baron St John of Bletso.

All that was necessary then was to link Jemima St. John, the wife of Edward's half-brother William Kershaw to the same family and Jemima's grandfather was found to be The Very Revd Hon. St. Andrew St John, Dean of Worcester - a younger brother of Margaret's great-grandfather, 12th Baron St John.

---

[1] 1st Viscount Eversley - Speaker of the House of Commons (1839 – 1857).

As a consequence it was then clear that Jemima St John and Mrs Margaret Le Marchant Thomas were second cousins once removed.

Jemima St. John had been born and grew up on the Isle of Man where her father was a clergyman and it was there that she married Captain William Kershaw of the 43rd (Monmouthshire) Regiment of Foot. The date of her death is not known, so it is possible she predeceased Captain Kershaw for after his death in 1832 his step-father, Joseph Denison was the guardian of the two children.

Without doubt, Joseph Denison would have taken responsibility for maintaining the children's noble connections and naturally, this social connection allowed Edward access to the Le Marchant circle at Billingbear. From what may be interpreted of their characters, the enterprising 'Uncle' Tom' and his son Le Marchant Thomas probably greatly enjoyed the company of Joseph Denison.

The complexity of those linked relationships suggests other marriages were nurtured in the atmosphere of that extended family. Such a well-travelled path provides a very plausible explanation for how Helen found a suitable husband to appeal to her and also please her parents. They had every reason to have confidence in Edward Hanson Denison as their families were part of that blended circle and yet quite remarkably, Edward and Helen were genetically unrelated.

Helen's uncle, Denis le Marchant had also purchased a country estate called Chobham Place in 1840 - but as it was not mentioned in Helen's letters we must assume it was not linked to her courtship with Edward. In letters from her brother, Basil during the 1850's we learn that the shooting parties at Chobham were very popular with his Uncle's parliamentary political colleagues and merchant friends from the City. Helen's father enjoyed those sporting events and reciprocated with his own similar gatherings on the Dagenham

Marshes for field sports were a passion with all the Fanshawe men including Edward – whose father's estate at Stock Grove was well stocked with game. Edward indulges that mutual interest in the letters with his comments to his brother-in-law John - *'send me word of what shooting you have had with all other accounts of your doings and larks – that is a good fellow!*

Common interests and family brought the Fanshawe and Denison families so quickly together that Edward and his father were soon assimilated into the Parsloes family. Whilst Edward was absent in Europe, Joseph Denison happily entertained his son's new relatives *'Edward heard from his father this morning, he encountered Uncle Denis and Uncle Tom having dined & passed one night at Stock Grove & seemed to have enjoyed their visit much'*…

As a worldly older man, Joseph Denison clearly enjoyed the confidence of Helen's parents and was soon acquainted with their concerns for the education of their younger sons Basil and Richard. Perhaps places were unavailable at Eton or they wished their boys to have a different education, but the idea of Shrewsbury School could only have come from Mr Denison.

Shrewsbury is one of the original top seven public schools listed with Eton; and has Sir Philip Sidney and Charles Darwin among the alumni, but even with those credentials it was an unexpected choice for the Fanshawe family. But we should not ignore the school's accessibility to Manchester or the fact that Willie Kershaw, Mr Denison's step-grandson, registered at Shrewsbury the previous year.

Helen indicated her father-in-law's interest when she wrote on 30th May… *'I hope they will like Shrewsbury and do they go down with Papa and Mr Denison as you once talked of?'* and then on the 8th September - *'the accounts you have had of Basil and Richard seem most satisfactory and*

Papa and Mamma must be much pleased they have taken such good places and I hope they will continue to like Willie and that they have a nice companion' - perhaps finding two places together had been the problem?

That confidence in Edward's widowed father seems to confirm that father and son were well known to the wider family. Even if the connection to Le Marchant Thomas was ignored; at Westminster Denis Le Marchant would have known Joseph Denison's political cousins. Had Joseph lobbied for advice in connection with 'Foss v Harbottle 1843', an invaluable contact would have been Denis Le Marchant – an earlier Clerk of the Crown in Chancery[1], subsequent Secretary to the Board of Trade, then Joint Secretary to the Treasury - his legal experience was vast.

This was a busy period in Denis Le Marchant's public life and jostling alongside came his late family life. When his second son Francis was christened in London during December 1843, it might have been an occasion when professional and private guests mingled.

Denis Le Marchant's character is interesting for after maturing from the 'careless' schoolboy hinted at in his late father's letters, he became reliable 'Uncle Denis' to all his family. A published historian who by writing his father's biography in 1841, preserved the Major General's achievements for the nation. Successful as a barrister he turned Whig politician, elected for Worcester in 1846 - anticipated earlier by Helen as she wrote *'I suppose just now you are in a state of great excitement hoping Uncle Denis may come in now'*...and after several ministerial posts, Denis Le Marchant was appointed in 1851 as Clerk to the House of Commons where serving for twenty one years he left a very distinguished record.

---

[1] 1834/36.

Conclusion

The aim of so many facts and impressions is to provide 'flesh' to the characters in Helen's letters. In this way the letters may be read as close as possible to the way Helen intended for the communication of news about family and friends linked Helen to all in her familiar world.

It was intimated when the letters were donated to Valence House that for many years they had not been read, but that never implied later generations of Helen's family were not curious to learn the content. Reading Helen's letters is difficult even after electronic scanning and the pages of her tiny handwriting are daunting.

In 1844, regular international mail services were just being established and savings on postage and paper were essential. Common to many correspondents of the time, Helen used a system called 'cross-writing' or 'cross hatching' where each sheet is written across vertically and also horizontally. Such letters were and are very difficult to read and it is possible that Helen's loving family could never fully read her letters.

Fortunately, with the help of a computer, most of Helen's words and ideas emerge and each newly 'transcribed' sentence revives enthusiasm. As Helen's story took shape I realised I had begun a friendship with responsibilities and the research notes have been included to help understand Helen's thoughts and how they were coloured. Once you begin to know Helen and follow her journey, inevitably curiosity about her life before marriage and what came after, will follow just as in the case with any friend.

After many months of reading obscure family publications and exploring the histories of many of the families encircling Helen's family, I am confident that in those early Victorian years, when introductions were discrete, a country house was the calm and perfect setting for Helen and Edward's introduction. If it was not at Billingbear or even Seaview, almost certainly their match evolved through those circles, and later they were brought together by polite conversation.

That part of Helen and Edward's story remains hidden but as partners were then often first matched for suitability and compatibility before their love grew, perhaps we should defer to the wisdom of Jane Austen ... *'It is a truth universally acknowledged, that a single man in possession of a good fortune, must be in want of a wife'*

Deirdre Marculescu
Valence House Museum
2022

Transcribers Notes

The original letters were written on light, thin paper and posted without envelopes. The letters were folded and the addressee's details were written in the centre of the reverse of the last complete sheet of notepaper. After folding, invariably the spaces above, below and to the side of the address 'box' were filled with Helen's post scripts and afterthoughts. Only when all the spaces were filled were the letters sealed and posted.

Helen Fanshawe Denison's handwriting was legible and fluid although extremely small. It is hard to imagine that her family could read the letters without some form of strong magnification. To add to the problems of visibility, she made economies of paper and postage and wrote first across each page in the normal way and then after turning the sheet into the 'landscape' position, wrote across it again just as if she was using a new sheet of paper.

Sometimes these 'portrait and landscape' texts pages immediately followed each other – but at other times she wrote several pages as portrait and then turned back to write over all those pages in landscape. This causes the most problem to the reader, as the correct sequence of continuation is often difficult to find.

During the Victorian period this habit of 'cross writing' personal letters was not unusual. It must have made letters difficult to read for the recipients but perhaps they were aided by being familiar with the writer's style. Probably also the topics would naturally have been known to them or were in response to matters raised in their own letters.

Undoubtedly these letters gave Helen's family at Parsloes many hours of challenging reading but perhaps unravelling ever word increased their pleasure.

With the use of modern lighting, scanners and computers the challenge still remains!

Helen's efforts to tell all within a limited number of pages meant she chose to leave out a considerable amount of punctuation and paragraphs. Consequently, when it came to transcribing I took an early decision to insert punctuation and paragraphs for the ease of modern readers.

Helen's voice can be heard through her letters even after nearly two hundred years and you can clearly discern the personality of the women she would later become. No 'improvements' were necessary to her letters as her education allowed her to express all thoughts and emotions and even when she wrote in haste, her letters were almost without error.

The symbols below are used in the context as described:

HFD	abbreviation for Helen Fanshawe Denison
[ ]	transcribers addition or amendment.
[xxx]	Indecipherable word or part of word with x relating to approximate number of letters
( )	indicates bracketed comments made by HFD in original letters.
Underline	words underlined are as per the original

1844. Marriage solemnized in the Parish Church in the Parish of Dagenham in the County of Essex

No.	When Married.	Name and Surname.	Age.	Condition.	Rank or Profession.	Residence at the Time of Marriage.	Father's Name and Surname.	Rank or Profession of Father.
164	May 7th	Edward Hanson Trueton & Helen Fauntleroy	full age under age	Bachelor Spinster	Barrister at Law	Southend Buckinghamshire Dagenham	Joseph Trueton Thomas Leigh Fauntleroy	Gentleman Clerk

Married in the Parish Church according to the Rites and Ceremonies of the Established Church by Licence by me, T. Knollys

This Marriage was solemnized between us, { Edward Hanson Trueton Helen Leigh Fauntleroy } in the Presence of us, { Denis Le Marchant Frances Elizabeth Fauntleroy Joseph Surtees Hilton Wyliff John Gaspar Fauntleroy Robert Sutton }

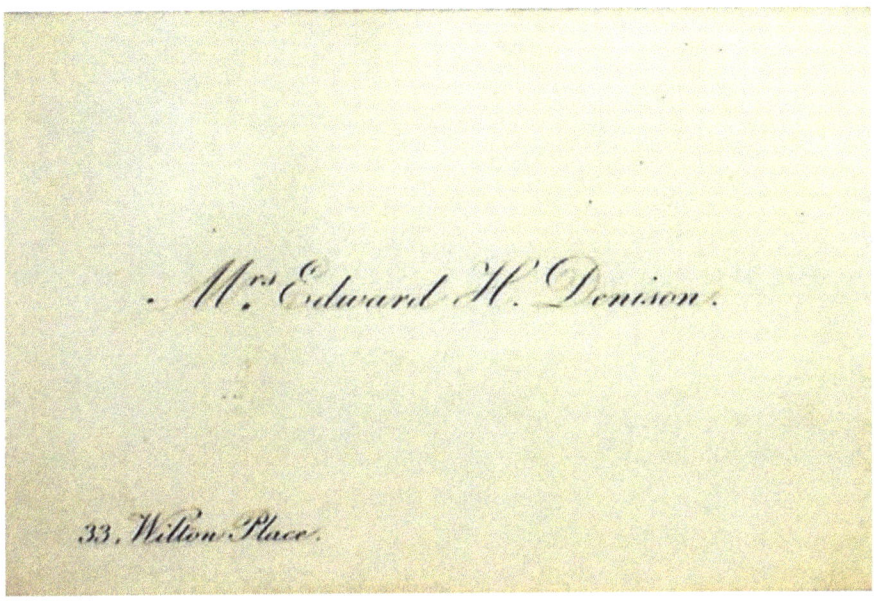

'...it is this multitude of adventures which happen, not to the traveller, but to his mind; in a word, it is everything and it is nothing: it is the diary of a thought even more than a journey.
As the body moves, thanks to the railway, stagecoach or steamboat, the imagination also moves. The whim of thought crosses seas without ships, rivers without bridges and mountains without roads. The spirit of every dreamer puts on the boots of seven leagues. These two journeys mixed together, that is what these* letters contain.

Le Rhin* (1842)
Victor Hugo

Letter from Helen Denison to her brother John Gaspard Fanshawe

Hotel de Belle Vue[1]
Brussels
May 20th (1844)

My dearest John

Your most kind and welcome letter arrived here Sunday morning, much to my delight for it is such a pleasure for me to get news from home whilst I am so far away.

Though we came here late on Friday evening, I have not been able to find time to write before this morning and I expect each minute Edward will come in and interrupt me. So I will make the most of my time and begin by thanking you dearest John, for the adorable lock of your hair and dear Papa's. It was very good of you to sit and write me such a nice long letter and give me so many interesting particulars.

In my last, I gave you a full account of our passage and our proceedings as far as Bruges. We left that town on Thursday morning and went to Ghent which is certainly a very fine old town,

---

[1] Hotel Bel Vue was the grandest hotel in Brussels having Napoleon, Wellington and royal princes included among the famous guests. The hotel building is now a museum dedicated to Belgium's history, democracy and culture but a modern Hotel Belvue stands on another site. In 1849, John Murray's travel guide listed the charges to be expected at the Bel Vue: one franc for a wax candle, one franc and fifty cents for breakfast or tea, 3 francs table d'hôte, 3 francs and fifty cents for a bottle of ordinary wine, 4 or 5 francs for dinner in private and 2 francs for lodging – the daily total was assessed to not exceed 12 francs.

some of gable-end houses are very handsome and much older and more ornamented than those houses at Bruges.

The first evening we went to the Beguinage[1], a convent containing 700 nuns and we saw them all at chapel and the effect of so many dressed alike in black stiff apparel and knelt in pray, covered with a white cloth - looked like a big table napkin - so that their faces were certainly hidden; was most curious.

We went to the Cathedral[2] whilst mass was being performed and heard some very fine music. You would enjoy the singing above everything. There are some very handsome monuments and fine pictures but the principal one is by Van Eyck of The Adoration of the Lamb. I only wish you could be here to see some of the beautiful paintings we have seen since we have been abroad.

The Town Hall and the Palais de Justice[3] are very handsome buildings. This Grand Place is a very nice promenade, a famous exchange for the young men who are the most disquieting looking race of beings I ever beheld. Their faces are completely covered with hair, in fact you can distinguish nothing but a pair of black eyes and a thin pinched nose – the rest is whisker, moustache and beard and their dress most rustic.

By the way, I am becoming a fast <u>French scholar</u> and get on capitally!!! But I cannot manage the Flemish. The people look so good humoured and so nice. There is not a great deal to see at Ghent beyond the pictures and one or two churches.

---

[1] Flemish béguinages were groups of houses, gardens and churches surrounded by walls with open gates. The 'Beguines' were unmarried or widowed ladies who lived and worked together in Christian communities but were not bound by holy vows.
[2] The gothic cathedral of St. Bavo of Ghent.
[3] Palais de Justice 'in the renaissance style' was not complete. Work began in 1836 and was finished in 1846.

Now, here comes Edward to tell me I must get ready to start immediately for Antwerp by ten. So goodbye 'til the evening!

We got to Brussels on Friday night and went to the same hotel as the King of Saxony[1] who we saw arrive next day.

We went all about the town looking into the shop windows and I have seen such numbers of pretty <u>chic dresses</u> but it is dreadful work going into any of the shops. They do talk you over and try to press on you to buy so many pretty things that I assure you it required us to make several degrees of resolution to withstand all their temptation.

The boulevards are very pretty and generally crowded with the most fashionable people, but we have been unfortunate in our weather. It was so cold and such frequent showers that most people stayed at home.

On Saturday evening we went to the vaudeville theatre[2] where I was very much delighted, especially being the first time in my life of going. The actresses were uncommonly pretty and they acted Les Bohemians des Paris[3] capitally. It is a most absurd thing and you would have laughed most heartily at one or two of the characters. Edward said they were first rate. I wish I had time to give you a few particulars but I cannot. The theatre is very small.

The cathedral is beautiful but not to be compared with the one at Antwerp, which we have been to see this evening. On Sunday we went to the Chapel Royal which has high and capital services but their prayers and readings is in such a drawl that it was next to impossible to keep ones attention.

---

[1] King Frederick Augustus II.
[2] Théâtre Royal du Parc. Rue de la Loi - opened in 1782.
[3] 'Les Bohemians de Paris'(1843) by French dramatist Adolphe D'Ennery (1811–1899).

Robert Southey - Collected Letters

'I wish you had been with me at Ghent, where the Beguines have their principal establishment. The Beguinage is a remarkable place, at one end of the city, and entirely enclosed. You enter through a gateway, where there is a statue of S. Elizabeth of Hungary, the patroness of the establishment.

The space enclosed is, I should think, not less than the area of the whole town of Keswick or of Christ Church; and the Beguinage itself, unlike almshouse, college, village, or town: a collection of contiguous houses of different sizes, each with a small garden in front, and a high brick wall enclosing them all; over every door the name of some saint under whose protection the house is placed, but no opening through which anything can be seen.

There are several streets thus built, with houses on both sides. There is a large church within the enclosure, a burying-ground, without any gravestones; and a branch from one of the innumerable rivers with which Ghent is intersected, in which the washing of the community is performed from a large boat; and a large piece of ground, planted with trees, where the clothes are dried. ...there are about 6000 Beguines in Brabant and Flanders, to which countries they are confined; 620 were residents in the Beguinage.' - October 1815

'The first evening we went to the Beguinage, a convent containing 700 nuns and we saw them all at chapel and the effect of so many dressed alike in black stiff apparel and knelt in pray, covered with a white cloth - looked like a big table napkin - so that their faces were certainly hidden, was most curious.'

The Adoration of the Mystic Lamb – Hubert & Jan Van Eyck – 1432

Completed in 1432 by Hubert & Jan van Eyck this altarpiece is considered one of the world's greatest art treasures. Comprised of many panels, several have been sold, removed and even stolen during the centuries since.

Helen & Edward could not have seen the complete altarpiece as in 1844 several panels were owned and kept by the King of Prussia and not returned to Ghent until the end of World War I.

Today, the altarpiece is again incomplete as the panel entitled 'The Just Judges' was stolen during 1934.

'…then we travelled towards Ghent, again through three villages, and I paid 4 stivers for the journey, and 4 stivers for expenses; and on my arrival at Ghent, there came to me the dean of the painters and brought with him the first masters in painting; they showed me great honour, received me most courteously, and commended to me their good-will and service, and supped with me. On Wednesday early they took me to the tower of St. John's, whence I looked all over the great and wonderful town, where I had just been treated as a great person. Afterwards I saw the Jan picture, which is a very splendid, deeply studied painting, and especially the "Eve," the "Mary," and "God the Father" were extremely good.'

Albrecht Durer
Memoirs of Journeys to Venice and the Low Countries,
Part II 'Diary of a Journey to the Netherlands' (July 1520 – July 1521)

Pieter-Frans De Noter (1779 – 1842) 'An impression of Durer's visit'
Rijksmuseum (Wikicommons)

The Chapel Royal, Brussels
Built in 1760 in the style of the chapels of the Palace of Versailles and the Château of Lunéville in Lorraine.
In 1804 Napoleon granted use of the chapel to Protestant religions and it became a meeting place for English travellers who were frequently among the congregation at the chapel's Sunday services.

During 1842, the novelist sisters Charlotte and Emily Bronte were employed at a school in the Rue Isabelle.
The Chapel Royal was close by and throughout their stay, both sisters were in regular attendance at the services.

Rue d'Isabelle (1894) - J. Carabain

Autumn 1842, the Bronte sisters returned to Haworth Parsonage their Yorkshire home, but Charlotte returned alone to Brussels the following year and remained until early 1844.
Whilst at Brussels, both sisters were greatly influenced by Professor Heger, the husband of the school proprietor. He encouraged them in their writing and Charlotte who was particularly attracted to his strong personality, drew upon her personal and teaching experiences in Brussels when later she wrote the novels 'The Professor' and 'Villette'.

I must tell you that I have been buying some lace which is really beautiful, tell Mamma it is made in the same way as Honiton[1] lace, and sequins on to the net, but the work is so fine and delicate, and the designs most elegant. Edward has proposed me a very handsome [length] of it and some lace to match for any purpose I like. I also bought a piece of Mechlin[2] and [filigree] as I have never found this before (xxx)…

Yesterday evening we went to the opera where we had all the kind of opera that you used to discuss so much - from Dr Faust[3] and Il Barbiere di Siviglia[4]. I never enjoyed anything more in my life – the music was <u>very good</u> and the singing also and in fact the whole thing. You would have been enchanted - when we came to the aria that you and Mamma so frequently played together as a duet, it brought back many recollections of home to my mind and I wished I could then be amongst you again.

I do so long to meet you all - although I am enjoying myself as much as possible - I turn my thoughts very often here to the many, many happy days I have spent at dear old Parsloes and I long for them to come again. You have no idea how difficult it is to find time to write. Every minute here is something to be done or something to be seen. I am remarkably well and getting quite fat.

We came to Antwerp today and went to the post first thing, but no letters had arrived yet, I hope however we shall hear tomorrow. We leave this town Thursday and go to Brussels for one night, then go

---

[1] Bobbin lace made at Honiton in Devonshire, traditionally incorporating designs of natural flowers and leaves with scrollwork.
[2] Mechlin lace or 'Point de Malines' - old Flemish bobbin lace that was so transparent and fine that it was most often worn over another colour or used to dress the hair.
[3] 'Scenes from Goethe's Faust'– an oratorio by Robert Schumann written 1844.
[4] 'The Barber of Seville' by Rossini written 1816.

on to Namur taking Waterloo on our way. Then go to Liege, which is rather out of our line, but the country is so pretty from Assesse along the Meuse[1] that it is quite worth seeing. We shall then proceed to Aix la Chapelle[2] where we remain over Sunday. Monday we go on leisurely till we reach Frankfurt, which we expect to be about the middle or end of the week.

Martin and Pierre are excellent servants. I find Martin a great comfort to me; she sees to everything and is very careful. I think from what she told me the other day, there is no doubt she once had a husband for she told me that now her poor child had only herself to look after and then her eyes filled with tears. Which I concluded to signify that her husband was dead.

Before I forget it, I must tell you that Edward is much obliged but he has leased his horse out at Stockgrove[3] and therefore will not send it into the 'marshes'[4] but is equally obliged for the trouble you have taken.

Many thanks for telling us about Everett[5], I never thought of that man. It was quite an oversight leaving him out, so pray give him a sovereign for us and make some excuse, we will settle with you [when] we come back.

I don't think I told [you] that we found out my pony was only showing himself, then next time I rode him the same thing

---

[1] Arising in France, the River Meuse is 575 mile long and passes through Belgium and the Netherlands before reaching the North Sea.
[2] Aix le Chapelle the city close to the Belgium/German border that has the German name of Aachen.
[3] Stockgrove Park, Buckinghamshire - home of Edward's father, Joseph Denison.
[4] Dagenham Marshes on the north bank of the Thames – partly within land owned by Revd Thomas Lewis Fanshawe of Parsloes.
[5] Possibly John Everett a master carpenter living at Rainham, a village very close to Dagenham.

happened again. So then Edward rode him to Arundel (he was always quite docile after he got into the stables) and it helped perfectly well. Has Papa sold his yet?

Tell me if any changes have taken place since I left and how you are all getting on – and how Aunt Caroline[1] is? Any little scrap of news will be most thankfully received.

Only fancy Fred Tyler[2] married off Arabella[3]! Oh John, see men can be fickle as well as women!!! What in the world has set you much against matrimony and have you seen some proofs lately of its making men so very miserable?

I hope you have enjoyed all your visits; when do you and Annie[4] go to Billingbear[5], is she still as much smitten with Capt. Bob[6] and is Aunt Mary[7] still staying at Parsloes? Ask Mamma to give Helen Lefevre[8] my utmost congratulations on her unexpected good

---

[1] Mrs Caroline (Le Marchant) Somerville (born 1804), sister of Mrs Fanshawe married Capt. John Somerville at Dagenham parish church 1838.
[2] Probably Frederic Tyler (1826-1857) of Beam Lane Farm, Dagenham.
[3] Probably Arabella Freeman granddaughter of Sarah Tuck owner of Marshfoot Farm, New Road, Dagenham (b.1825), still unmarried at Census 1851.
[4] Anna Maria Tupper (1826 - 1846) eldest daughter of Anna Maria (Le Marchant) & Daniel Tupper of Guernsey - first cousin and frequent guest at Parsloes.
[5] Billingbear Park, Waltham St. Lawrence, Berkshire - a Tudor mansion and home to Guernsey connected relatives, John Thomas & his wife Anne Le Marchant. Their eldest son, who was given the first name of Le Marchant, changed his surname in 1865 by Royal Warrant to Thomas Le Marchant - this resulted from a matter of inheritance but his new full name 'Le Marchant Thomas Le Marchant' leads to confusion.
[6] Robert Algernon Smith-Dorrien (1814-1879), brother of Frances Smith, who in 1846 married Mrs Fanshawe's youngest brother, Col. Thomas Le Marchant, (1811-1873).
[7] Mary (Le Marchant) Gostling, a sister of Mrs Fanshawe and wife of Lt Col. Charles Gostling 9th Batt. Royal Artillery.
[8] Helen Shaw Lefevre (1828 – 1893), eldest daughter of Henry Shaw Lefevre and Helena Le Marchant (Mrs Fanshawe's deceased sister). After their mother's death in 1833, Helen and her two younger sisters lived much of their time at a small

fortune, I was delighted to hear she was getting on so well and I am sure she deserves such a reward for her patience.

Whatever your visits, [I] have been infinitely pleased with my account of Mr Howgreaves house - we shall never live there.

It is raining fast this evening and I hope it is doing the same with you as I suppose it's expected. The last few days have been especially cold. Edward has been very busy arranging about the carriage which has been having another box and several strings added, and he has business letters to write. But he sends his very best love to you and hopes of writing in a few days, and tell Annie I will do the answers by then.

Remember me to the servants, I shall write again as soon as I hear from Mamma – and with most affectionate love to her and the rest of the party, Papa, Annie etc., etc., and a large portion for yourself, believe me, ever dearest John, ever your own most attached sister,

Helen Denison

P.S. I was quite satisfied with the servants (if mail).

---

boarding school. Holidays were spent with various relatives, particularly at Heckfield Place, home of their father's elder brother, Charles Shaw Lefevre, Viscount Eversley, Speaker of the House of Commons.

Letter addressed to Mrs Catherine Fanshawe – mother

Hotel de Flandres[1]
May 22nd 1844

My Dearest Mamma,

I take advantage of this unexpected opportunity of writing you as long account as anytime might permit of our proceedings since we left Worthing. We left at seven on the morning and got to Brighton whence I was very sorry not to find a letter from John but I knew he would have written had he been able, so I am looking forward to every packet from home at Brussels with the greatest pleasure. I hope it will contain as good news of you all dearest mother, as your last did.

We have had accidents and a few little mishaps at Brighton. We reached here by train to Folkestone & passed through a most beautiful country, it really is about a week going by that line, for the reason Edward and I wanted to see the house and sent Pierre & Martin on to Dover.

You will be delighted to hear the house will not do in the least, it is very out of the way, very exposed cold situation & the countryside no means pretty, so we had a fourteen mile, not very agreeable ride for nothing. We then went on by the train to Dover passing under the Shakespeare Cliff and saw the sea wall. Tell Papa it is most wonderfully piece of workmanship and beautifully done[2]. I think it is the nicest and most comfortable line we have been upon.

---

[1] 'Near railway station, excellent, moderate charges, table d'hote – the fish dinners on Fridays are renowned' - A Handbook for Travellers on the Continent' published by John Murray 1849.
[2] South Eastern Railway extension from Folkestone to Dover - opened 1844.

We took up our quarters for the night at the Ship Hotel[1] which brought back old times to my mind. It was most fortunate we had not fixed on that day for our passage, for the sea was so high and it blew a tremendous gale that several accidents happened. One gentleman called John Bridgeman was washed overboard and had he not been a most excellent swimmer he must inevitably have drowned. He was in the water twenty minutes - the sea remaining terribly high. He was very ill, leaning over the side of the ship when a wave washed him over. When he was taken in he soon came round and the waiter at The Ship told us he was enjoying his [dinner].

The Ostend boat also, which started on Saturday from London, got within eight miles of Ostend and was then obliged to sail back to Margate and they expected any moment she would go down. I had some unfortunate passengers come across with us yesterday. We had to get together a little before five and were all under way by seven o'clock. We had a very fair passage, though the sea was still rather strong from the late storm. I was very ill and very soon had to descend for some time. I tried going to the side of the vessel but the effect of any starting up as soon as I had stopped myself at best measure, but thought I had risen above from the deck.

We had a quantity of Frenchmen near about and I could not help thinking of you dearest Mother, when you were so ill crossing from Boulogne and had as your companion a very dirty man who kept spitting. One gentlemen went so far as to make his appearance in a very dainty pair of half boots and high shoes, but his feet were au natural, not a particle of stocking and Edward tells me this is a very usual French practice. He was very uncomfortably ill <u>I believe</u> but unfortunately I was too ill myself to laugh at him in his misfortune.

---

[1] Ship Hotel, Custom House Quay, Dover.

Charlotte Bronte's life experiences fuelled her imagination and writing, so it is very possible to speculate that something of the Fanshawe family's history may have been known to her and her sisters.

Living at Haworth on the Yorkshire Moors, the Bronte sisters are known to have travelled to surrounding towns where tales of an ancient family at Fanshawe Gate could have been related in tones of gothic mystery.

By the 1840's, the Fanshawe family living at the old Hall were not of the senior branch, but though less sophisticated than their London cousins, over centuries they had lived, worked and supported their community in positions of authority and the family name carried distinction.

By the 18th and 19th centuries, Fanshawe men occupied senior ranks in several regiments so if the fictional father of 'Ginevra' was a younger son, the situation as described for his daughters could have been reality.

Clearly, Charlotte Bronte recognised Fanshawe as a regional name with status, but is there a more fanciful alternative to imagine?

Charlotte Bronte and Helen Fanshawe, both daughters of clergymen might have been introduced at the Chapel Royal - or perhaps, news of Helen's visit came via a letter from a member of the chapel's congregation?

'Now, Miss Ginerva Fanshawe (such was this young person's name)...'But I know what it is to be poor. They are poor enough at home – papa and mamma and all of them.

Papa is called Captain Fanshawe. He is an officer on half-pay, but well descended, and some of our connections are great enough; but my uncle and god-papa Dr Bassompierre who lives in France, is the only one that helps us. He educates us girls. I have five sisters and three brothers. By and by we are to marry, rather elderly gentlemen, I suppose, with cash...'

Charlotte Bronte
'Villette' (1853)

On 7th February 1844 the first passengers travelled on the new South Eastern Railway double-track extension from Folkestone to Dover. This section was the final link required to make direct rail travel possible from London to the port of Dover and on to the Continent. Blasting through the white cliffs, the civil engineer Joseph Cubitt, oversaw the boring of three tunnels - the Martello, Abbotscliff, and the Shakespeare. After the Shakespeare Tunnel the track passed over trestles at the foot of the cliffs to traverse the beach.

'...passing under the Shakespeare Cliff and saw the sea wall. Tell Papa it is most wonderfully piece of workmanship and beautifully done. I think it is the nicest and most comfortable line we have been upon. We took up our quarters for the night at the Ship Hotel.'

We went straight to the hotel at Ostend and had our lunch and as there is nothing to see in the town, we went on direct by train[1] to Bruges where the reaches are very similar to our own marshes, there was one part we passed reminded me very much of Ripple Side road towards Marshside[2].

Just after we arrived here yesterday afternoon, there was a very violent thunder storm and the lightning struck a house a few doors above us. We were most fortunate to escape – there was no danger for us but I was trembling as I expected to see lives lost.

I was amazed to see the fine women and little children walking about the town in those wooden shoes. They wore such neat caps 'cele' caps and little shawls and cloak on their heads and some of the girls were very pretty.

The town I like very much with some houses very fine but it has given off a great deal. This hotel we are now in, the last months probably has been in the toughest times and yet we have splendid rooms and really very handsomely furnished. They are very light and have not at any lack of conveniences as in some hotels. Their chimneys are also very good [*last three lines of writing indecipherable*].

I have spent a most delightful day - last night I was dreadfully tired and had a most splitting headache but today I feel wonderfully well and have recovered. Hence decided to go on to Ghent as we intended to give us a little more rest, and this is the pleasantest town (to my view).

---

[1] The Ostend to Bruges line had opened in 1838 but the station at Bruges was only built in 1844.
[2] Rippleside – approximately a mile from Dagenham village was reached by an ancient tree-lined track bordering the marsh between the rivers Roding and Thames.

The country between Ostend and Bruges is at first very flat but there are some beautiful crops and the land is near to the coast and uncommonly pretty. Many of the roofs gables are built in a sort of steps as…

…and some   of the most ancient architecture outside. The effect looking down the street is very pretty. The market place[1] is a very handsome square and at one corner there is such old specimens of gothic architecture.

This morning we went to L'Hopital of St. Jan[2] where I do wish you could have been with us - you would have so much enjoyed seeing the fine pictures we did, by Hans Memling. I was perfectly delighted with them, the colouring is most beautiful and they are in excellent preservation, they were painted in 1479 and look as fresh as possible.

The subject of the principal picture was the Virgin and Child with St. Catherine[3]. The expression of the faces is so sweet and yet there is something so subtle that you cannot help admiring them. The figures are stiff but still there is so much to make amends for this fault that one almost overlooks it. I cannot tell you how much I have been wishing all day you could have been with us to enjoy the different sights. There is also in the same church a wooden coffer

---

[1] Site of a weekly market since 985.
[2] The oldest surviving hospital building in Europe - now the Memling Museum displaying the works by Hans Memling.
[3] The St John Altarpiece - triptych altarpiece completed 1479 and commissioned for the Old St. John's Hospital when the new apse was built - where it still remains. Made of five paintings on a central inner panel with two double-sided wings. When closed, the wings show the hospital donors and their patron saints. When open, the interior central panel depicts the enthroned Virgin with Child flanked by saints, and on the left wing is the life of John the Baptist, and the Apocalypse is on the right.

Hans Memling
St Jan's Altarpiece

Painted in Bruges during 1479 - the triptych interior paintings depict the Virgin and Child, the life of St John the Baptist and the apocalypse as told by St John the Evangelist.

Founded in the 12th century, St. Jan's Hospital later expanded into a monastery giving aid to travellers and remained in continued use as a hospital until 1977.

The building now houses the Memling Museum with the paintings.

Wards of Hospital St. Jan (1778)
Jan Beerblock (1739 – 1806)

SAINT URSULA SHRINE
1489
BY
HANS MEMLING

THE LEGEND OF ST URSULA

There are many versions of this ancient legend from the 4th century but it is popularly said that Ursula was the virtuous and beautiful daughter of the Christian King Dionotus of Brittany whom the pagan King of Anglia, wanted as a bride for his son Etherius.

Ursula only accepted after prayer having received divine guidance that first she must make a three year pilgrimage to Rome in the company of eleven thousand virgins from the English kingdom and all would be carried in eleven ships.

The epic journey brought them safely to Rome but travelling homeward along the River Rhine they reach the city of Cologne just as it was besieged by Huns. A tragic massacre took place - all the virgins were beheaded and for Ursula, her death came from an arrow shot by the leader of the Huns.

The relics of St. Ursula are contained in this gilded northern gothic 'church shaped' box. On the exterior Jan Memling told the legend of St Ursula through six bow-arched panels.

'there is another church called St Ursula's, in which lyeth the bones of 1100 virgins in places locked up, and Saint Ursula in a fair tombe by them, which came all thither with her for their devotion'...*William Crowne (1637)*

A true relation of all the remarkable places and passages observed in the travels of the Rt. Hon. Thomas Lord Howard, Earl Of Arundel & Surrey, Earl Marshall of England – Ambassador Extraordinary to the Emperor of Germany 1636

containing the bones of St. Ursula[1] and in the centre there is a painting of her massacre after the legend[2] of the 11000 virgins at Cologne - also by Memling. All his paintings undergo the most minute inspection they are so beautifully finished. I cannot tell you how much I have been delighted by them.

The monuments inside the Onze-Lieve (Notre Dame) Cathedral are splendid but we could not see the edifices near the tombs of Charles the Bold[3] & his daughter Mary[4] which are very well worth seeing; as the sexton was not to be found. So we are going again tomorrow morning before starting for Ghent.

This evening we went into the Cathedral and were just in time to see high mass performed, it was a grand day with then being the Feast of St Maria. The altar was decked out with the most beautiful flowers but the most shocking part was to see such a number of poor unfortunate people praying to the image of the Virgin & Child which was decked out with the most tawdry finery, it was a great doll draped with the most gaudy satin you could imagine and holding in its arms, another little tiny doll equally gaudily apparelled.

---

[1] Hans Memling's wooden shrine containing the relics of St. Ursula can still be seen today in St John's Hospital.
[2] Ursula is believed to have been a Roman/Briton living between 300 – 600AD. She travelled to Central Europe to join her intended husband accompanied by a reputed 11000 maidens. They were all captured by invading Huns when they arrived at the city of Cologne, and were cruelly massacred when they refused to surrender their virginity.
[3] (1467 – 1477) - last Duke of Burgundy descending from the House of Valois.
[4] Mary of Burgundy whose marriage to Archduke Maximilian of Austria began the centuries long wars of succession that ending in the War of the Spanish Succession 1701-1714.

At the end of the service the priest went around[1] with a silver phial containing some relic[2] of St Maria which all the people kissed. The ceremony we saw at Boulogne was nothing to this. I wish I had time to give you many more particulars but I find I cannot now, for besides getting very late, my papers warm with the heat – it will soon be time to close.

This is a very selfish production for it is all relating to myself but I thought you would like to hear what has been occupying my attention and what I would sincerely wish you could all have also enjoyed. I am sure dearest Mother you will believe me when I tell you that all are very, very often in my thoughts and it is a very <u>great pleasure</u> to think of all who are so dear to me at Parsloes and how much I should like to see you again.

We shall be at Brussels Friday evening when I shall be most anxious to get your much wished for letter and I think for the future I shall begin a letter and write a little every day, making a sort of journal.

I often think how much we have to be thankful for, when I think how fortunate we have been to be here when we have.

I really must say good bye and with most affectionate love to yourself, Papa, John and boys – in which Edward unites. God bless you dearest Mother and believe me I am your most affectionate daughter,

Helen Denison

---

[1] The Procession of the Holy Blood takes place on Ascension Day – occurring on 16th May in 1844.
[2] The Relic of the Holy Blood - a venerated phial said to contain a cloth with the blood of Jesus Christ, brought to Bruges by Thierry of Alsace in the 12th century, following the 2nd Crusade.

Note:

Sections of the following letter proved unreadable as 'thin' ink on thin paper created shadow images from the reverse which doubled the 'cross-hatching'. Because of this some. lines which connect pages could not be discovered.

Letter to Mrs Catherine Fanshawe - mother

Antwerp
May 30th 1844

My Dearest Mamma

Your very long letter arrived yesterday & I was able to take comfort from it immediately but I was afraid I was unwell and was obliged to keep to my bed after a very congestive cold and a bad head. But by taking it in time I am quite well again and feel as fresh as ever.

I cannot tell you how much I enjoyed seeing the various churches and pictures. I only wish you could have been together with us. I can tell you that you would have been exhausted with how many is be seen but it is enticing to know that there is constant appreciation of the beautiful. We are remaining here a day longer than we intended that I may have another look at Rubens' beautiful picture of the annunciation[1]

I had no idea I should enjoy seeing all the paintings as much as I do but I find constant practice at styles I shall soon be able to tell the difference myself. I think I gave John a full account of the proceeding as far as Brussels, so I will not repeat it. I hope the letter I wrote from Bruges will have reached you because I believe the letter I received from you in Bruges…

---

[1] Annunciation painted in 1609 by Peter Paul Rubens was commissioned by the College of Jesuits in Antwerp where presumably it was seen by Helen – the painting is now in the Kunsthistorisches Museum in Vienna. However, Ruben's painted a second Annunciation in 1610 which is now displayed in Antwerp at the Rubenhuis – but it was not acquired until 1954.

We have been very fortunate as all through the long May days ….

I like Martin very much she is most thoroughly good natured. I have not heard her utter a single complaint, not even of the dust, which she might have done with reason and that I think, is saying a great deal.

I am very sorry to hear Papa has had a cold but [I] hope it is quite over now. A great number of people are laid up in this hotel with this illness and different aches proceeding from colds. Tell him I wish him every success in feasting with his friends and hope he will find as nice ones to fill their place.

I would write to him but cannot send an enclosure and as you said in one of yours that man and wife were the same, this is also written for his present.

I suppose Hewett[1] is now married; does he still intend spending his honeymoon in Sark?[2] It is rather late but you might have recommended Worthing to his mother as there he would have had horses to ride to make the place perfect.

I am sorry you give so graphic account of Aunt Mary she does not seem to have recovered from the effects of the last illness, but give her my best love and tell her I hope that the air of either Brighton or [Worthing] will be equally efficacious. Her speech appears the same, I really think nothing more will cause through.

Annie, I suppose went yesterday to Billingbear. I am going to try to write to her this evening. I have no doubt she will enjoy her visit much but I should think at times she will have a great difficulty in

---

[1] Revd. Hewett Carey (b.1812), a first cousin of Mrs Fanshawe - married Harriet Miller at Radway, Warwickshire on 25th June 1844. His parents were Lt Col. Peter Carey and Julia Hewett.
[2] Pierre Carey Le Pelley, then 'Seigneur' of Sark was another Carey relation.

restraining her fits of laughter, especially if she remains there some time. The scenes between her and Uncle Tom[1] must have been most amusing. I am most obliged to you for letting Uncle Tom know somehow, because we admired his taste as displayed in his brooch. I think it very handsome and find it exceeding[ly] useful; give him our best love when you see him.

How is poor Miss Farquharson[2], have you seen or heard anything of her lately? I have been wanting to write to her but really it is so difficult to find the time as one stays in a place a night or two and is occupied nearly the whole day in sightseeing - and in the evening, Edward likes to walk abroad and look over Murrays[3] travel book. That subject takes up and alone occupies most of our time as it covers our journeys. Edward is just now writing a long letter to Mr Bayliff[4] to which I am to add a few lines to Mrs Bayliff. How obliging the man is but as bad as <u>Papa</u> about writing, for we have not heard once from him since we have been abroad.

I am delighted to hear Basil is better, I suppose he will be at home another fortnight – give them both my warmest love. I should very much like to have seen them on their holidays. I hope they will like

---

[1] John Thomas died 1849, a draper and cotton/cloth merchant traded with America in 1790 and later Russia from Manchester, London and Guernsey – he lived in Upper Harley St, London and Billingbear. His wife was Anne Le Marchant, a cousin of Mrs Fanshawe.
[2] Harriett Farquharson born in Gibraltar 1810 - governess to the children of Francis Glenny at his 90 acre farm in Chadwell Heath (Census 1851). Glenny was involved with local charity and parish matters, doubtlessly bringing him and his household into contact with Helen's family.
[3] Murray's Handbooks for Travellers - guides published by John Murray of London from 1836.
[4] Revd T L Bayliff (1805 – 1889), Vicar of Albury, Herts, formerly a Curate at Little Ilford Essex. He with his family became lifelong friends of the Fanshawes and during the Crimean War, Richard Lane Bayliff served in the 33rd Duke of Wellington's Regiment with Helen's brother Basil.

Shrewsbury[1] and do they go down with Papa and Mr Denison[2] as you once talked of?

I am glad you have made my garter[3] of use and sent it down to the Hewetts - give them my love when you write.

By the way, will you direct after Frankfurt, your mail to Baden-Baden and Zurich?

Has Fred Tyler got settled whether it is to be Harriett Biggs[4] or Arabella? Her letters seems to have gone rather furtive than was prudent; remember me to her and her grandmother. I should fear from what you say, from Mr Thompson that at his age there is very little chance of him recovering from such a serious illness. I hope for your sakes Mr Baugh[5] will not leave Ilford. He will be a great loss to you for he was almost your only neighbour and was always very cheerful. Remember me to him when you see him.

When you write to Guernsey will you give them all my best love and also thank Eliza[6]. Tell her I will write to her as soon as I possibly

---

[1] Shrewsbury School – public school attended by Thomas 'Basil' and Richard Fanshawe as boarders.
[2] Edward Hanson Denison's father - Joseph Denison formerly of Rusholme Park, Lancashire & of Stock Grove, Buckinghamshire.
[3] Helen's traditional bridal garter was probably passed on as 'something borrowed or something blue'.
[4] Probably Charlotte Biggs (b.1826) eldest of several daughters at Manor Farm (possibly known as Harriett as her mother was also named Charlotte). In 1849 Charlotte married John Pickering Peacock, the eldest son at Longbridge Farm. These young people were from families that owned many acres of land employing local families. 'Youthful' Fred Tyler, was no doubt considering his options from this circle, but no local records have been found confirming he married.
[5] Revd. Foillett Baugh (b.1820), incumbent Vicar of Ilford left the parish in 1845 after a major disagreement with parishioners as he attempted to modify divine services.
[6] Eliza Tupper (born 1828) – daughter of Helen's aunt Anna Maria Le Marchant and Daniel Tupper of Guernsey. In 1850 she married Revd Robert Le Marchant, Rector of Little Rissington.

possibly can. In the meantime, will you furnish her with every particular that she would like to know.

Edward continues [figures] next to manage …

…I shall try to get xxxxx as near xxxxx xxxxxxxx style as possible but if you would like me to get any other sort as bunches or vases of flowers or figures, just let me know and I will do just as you like.

I hope I shall hear from you at Frankfurt, I cannot tell you, dearest Mother how much I prize the letter from home and how frequently I read it over again.

We go to Waterloo on Saturday and then to Namur where we remain over Sunday. I shall give you full particulars of the plains of Waterloo as I am sure considering your military turn that will interest you much. I am discovering quite as fast as French and shall speak it most <u>fluently</u> on my return.

How glad I shall be to see you all again!

…Essex & though it is very well cultivated and the soil appears extremely rich, there are so few fields, they are all quite young. The avenues of hawthorns are very pretty for the foliage is very rich and the xxxxx xxxxx are perfectly iridescent. There are quantities of xxxxxx trained against the houses ….

…the park and the boulevards are pretty and great xxxxxxxx but these are disappointing as the weather was very showery. The tower of the Cathedral is handsome but nothing will sufficiently answer etc, to be confused with the Antwerp Cathedral, the spire is perfect, so elegant and so handsome - in fact it is so beautiful that one could look at it for xxxxxx and not be tired, only find fresh beauties to admire.

Tell Miss Farquharson if with you, that I paid special attention to the large paintings of Rubens. After told, I saw the 'Descent from the Cross'[1] and was in fact struck with it. Unfortunately it has suffered a good deal from time, it is not in a really good advantage as…….

…ideas I'd so greatly wish dearest Mamma you could also see them and enjoy the sightseeing. This evening in the cathedral which is quite old and is most beautiful, the groups of figures are very well arranged and they display as much expression in the faces (which are very small) as in a painting. Edward says he never saw as good a specimen of carving.

The interior of the cathedral is not so fine as the church of Jacques, which is splendid. All the decorations of marble and stone are some very fine monuments but the principal one is the family one belonging to Rubens and family, and over it is a picture painted by himself in 17 days - of the Holy Family[2] and very beautiful.

There is no doubt that the church pews[3] being very ugly things in church, and it certainly has a much finer effect to see a full open space before you with nothing to intercept the view. But I do not think the chairs look pretty and thought it was very usual in Norman Catholic counties. I do not think you should like to see people sitting about the church during services and another very serious objection is that very frequently a person comes and places himself quite close to you, who has just been making himself alone, and that completely disturbs everything.

---

[1] Descent from the Cross - central panel of a triptych by Peter Paul Rubens painted 1612–1614 remains in the Cathedral of Our Lady, Antwerp.
[2] Our Lady with the Saints' Church of St Jacques, Antwerp.
[3] High church pews were still in place at Dagenham Church. They were removed and replaced by 'low deal benches' during restorations in 1877-78. (*A History of Dagenham*).

…dearest Mother I really must conclude this night – Affectionate love to yourself, dear papa and John and the children which Edward unites. I hope that you are getting up your old looks – believe me as ever your most devoted loving daughter

Helen

Letter to Mrs Catherine Fanshawe - mother

Cologne
June 5th (1844)

My dearest Mamma,

Since I last wrote to you from Antwerp, we have seen much to interest us, and have had lovely weather generally to enjoy the beautiful scenery. We left Antwerp on Friday and travelled to Bruges where we remained the night.

In the morning we went to see the lace manufactory which is quite wonderful. We only saw a few at work as we went late. It is the most tedious work you can imagine and fifty eight reels of the finest thread are required to be all in use at the same time to make one tiny leaf of a flower. The pattern is all pricked out first. The mistress told us that only those who had learnt from their infancy could be employed in the lace factory and only the successful workers could make the flowers. These are transferred on and some of which we also saw in the manufacturing.

There are some very old women sitting at work at the flowers and it is very curious that though they are so short sighted they cannot see the garden close before them, yet they are able to continue working apparently without any difficulty. Their rooms are fresh and airy and they seemed very happy but some of the poor unfortunate girls looked wretchedly ill and some of the long veils they were making for the Royal family when they marry, were extremely elegant.

This Saturday we bid adieu to Brussels and posted on to Namur taking Waterloo in on our way. How you would have enjoyed being with us there, even I who cannot boast of professing to much military ardour, was perfectly delighted. The first thing you are shown on entering the village is the church containing monuments within, to the memory of many hundreds of poor Englishmen who shed their blood on the plains of Waterloo. We also paid our respects to the Marquis of Anglesey's[1] leg and foot which is shown in a public house close by. We then proceeded to the field of the battle and were driven as far as the Mound and Hougoumont – at the top of the Mound is erected a monument with a colossal lion to commemorate the spot and it commands a very extensive view of the country around. I enclose you a little plan showing the two enemies and their generals. There was a valley between them but the place is altered since the battle, as there would have been new earth to form the mound, most certainly crops of corn now cover the land and peace only remains there – the mound and two monuments to mark the spot.

The Chateau of Hougoumont is an interesting old place, from its having withstood the attacks of the French so gallantly. Three times they took and retook the redoubt but never could enter within the walls of the castle; if they had, the English would have lost the day. Nothing remains of these old places but a large church of old walls and a farm house.

Friday June 7th - We were on the move all yesterday so I could not go on with my letter. From Waterloo we went to Namur where there is very little or nothing to see. It has however a very delightful promenade along the banks of the Meuse and some public pavilions where the elite assemble in the afternoon to drink <u>beer</u> whilst the band plays. You never saw such a sight and some, indeed most of the ladies are, I should think even Annie in her state dress would be a joke to many and a sight. I have not seen a pretty woman since we left England, except one at Brussels, rather so.

---

[1] Field Marshal Henry William Paget, 1st Marques of Anglesey, KG, GCB, GCH, PC (1768 – 1854), British Army officer and politician.

We posted from Namur to Liege and there took the 6 o'clock train[1] and arrived at Aix la Chapelle at 10 in the evening. The first and last part of the drive along the river road, very pretty but not to be compared to scenery between Liege and Verviers. That really was beautiful, such pleasing variety - hills well-wooded and the different trees in the richest foliage, then cliffs and plains and broad winding through villages and valleys and making the scene quite perfect. I enjoyed it immensely.

Tell Papa we have seen quantities of rose trees trained up long poles looking remarkably pretty, it is quite the fashion in this country. I have not observed any new flowers but the small trees grow more luxuriantly and make very pretty hedges. We passed some vineyards, of course quite young yet.

The Cathedral[2] is a curious old place, parts of it is handsome but there is such a mixture of good and bad that it is spoilt in a great measure. The inside was being repaired. It is very interesting as having the burial place of Charlemagne[3]. There is a plain slab with Carlos Emperor inscribed on it and the chair of state in which he sat. Within the crown was the fleshless head of Charlemagne and clothed in his imperial robes before his body was removed - this however we could not see.

In the evening we went by train to Cologne and when we had chosen our rooms in the Hotel we found that Queen Adelaide[4] and

---

[1] The Rhenish Railway Company extended the line from Cologne to Aachen into Belgium in 1843 - creating the first cross-border international railway line.
[2] Aachen Cathedral.
[3] Charlemagne, King of the Franks & Lombards, Emperor of the Romans (748 – 814).
[4] Princess Adelaide of Saxe-Meiningen (1792 – 1849), Queen of the United Kingdom and Hanover, consort of King William IV – this was her last visit to her homeland.

'We also paid our respects to the Marquis of Anglesey's[1] leg and foot'

Less than thirty years after the Battle of Waterloo the site had become well-trodden by tourists.
The Church of St Joseph with many memorials to the fallen, and the 141ft high Lion Mound quickly became focal points of a visit but there was a special 'side-show' rarely missed by Princes and commoners alike - Lord Anglesey's leg.
In the heat of battle, the noble lord received his wound whilst riding at the head of the cavalry of 13,000 men and 44 guns. Reputedly, he is said to have cried out, 'I've got it at last!' and from close by, Wellington replied, 'No? Have you, by God?'

Amputation soon followed and the stoic Anglesey is claimed to have made only one comment… 'The knives appear somewhat blunt'.
Lord Anglesey survived his ordeal and perhaps unsurprising in view of his mastery of understatement, became a politician. He died in 1854 but his dismembered leg had a separate life - it was purloined by the landlord of his HQ and displayed as a macabre reminder of the experiences of war whilst producing a lucrative income as a curiosity that tourists for many years felt strangely compelled to pay to see.

'This King, who showed himself so great in extending his empire and subduing foreign nations, and was constantly occupied with plans to that end, undertook also very many works calculated to adorn and benefit his kingdom, and brought several of them to completion. Among these, the most deserving of mention are the basilica of the Holy Mother of God at Aix-la-Chapelle.'
Einhard (775 -840).
The Life of Charlemagne

Aachen / Aix-la-Chapelle - 'Cathedral is a curious old place, parts of it is handsome but there is such a mixture of good and bad that it is spoilt in a great measure. The inside was being repaired. It is very interesting as having the burial place of Charlemagne...'

her sister[1] were expected - which piece of information by no means pleased us, for we had to suffer before at Brussels for being at the same hotel as royalty. The rooms proposed for her here were beautifully finished and very grand preparations were being made for her reception.

We could get no waiter to come and aid us till after half an hour after we rang: our furniture was taken out of our rooms at Brussels, but this time Her Majesty went off with the Imperial[2] to our carriage so we had to despatch Peter to try and recover the lost property. He returned the next day, to our no small delight having discovered it amongst the Queen's luggage. We saw her very plainly; one of her ladies in waiting was an enormous woman, immensely tall but not really stout.

The Cathedral at Cologne is a most splendid specimen of Gothic architecture, it has a tower and pillars; it is not completed. The morning after was one of those joie de fete, 'Fronleichnam'[3] of Cologne. There was a grand procession round the town; the girls dressed in white and the priests in the more costliest robes. The town itself is very dirty and I should think it came from horse farms inside. Stores of Eau de Cologne could not purify it of all the horrid scents!

We came to Bonn on Thursday where we are still staying. We are in a capital hotel and the views from the garden are perfect. That exciting and abounding river the Rhine flows at the bottom of the path and we are nearly opposite the Seven Mountains. The last of

---

[1] Princess Ida Caroline of Saxe-Meiningen (1794 – 1852) wife of Prince Carl Bernhard of Saxe-Weimar-Eisenach (1792 – 1862).
[2] Case for luggage on the top of a coach.
[3] Religious feast of Corpus Christi falls on the Thursday exactly 60 days after Easter Sunday, which in 1844 was 6th June.

them, the Drachenfel we can see very clearly with the telescope, but are going there tomorrow by steamer.

We have been taking a walk in the town this morning and met a number of the German students belonging to the university. They are the most extraordinary looking objects[1] you ever beheld. To begin with they are filthy dirty, and their dress is a pair of large trousers, generally green or some fancy colour, a velveteen jacket with a taffeta embroidered cap (sometimes a large felt hat like Papa's only a much broader brim) stuck on the top of their heads, displaying a quantity of long hair flowing over their shoulders and to complete all, a long pipe dangling from their mouths. A more ungentlemanly set I should trust would be difficult to find.

June 9th - Just returned from church after a blistering walk. The heat has been intense the last day or two but we are now going to have a thunder storm which I hope will cool the air. This is the second one we have had since we have been at Cologne. Here is a very nice little chapel and the clergyman read the prayers remarkably well that we took a part in service. We concluded with the offertory on the altar. There was a crucifix and a pair of candlesticks with candles that had eventually been lighted. I must not forget to tell you that I have observed that at the cathedrals and churches we have been in lately

---

[1] Queen Victoria's husband Prince Albert was a student at Bonn during 1837/8. The following extract is from *'Prince Albert his Country and Kindred'* published in 1840: 'The German student is a character per se; he is one of those novelties which people go 'up the Rhine' to see – he is a curiosity. His dress is curious; and so are the songs he is always singing; he is curious in meerschaums (pipes) which are seldom out of his mouth; and he is a connoisseur of beer. He is subject to curious laws…and has a curious way of addressing his fellows…curious in metaphysics but more particularly so in the science of aesthetics which the looker-on cannot help wishing he would apply to his personal appearance, for his hair and beard seem sadly in want of a comb, and certainly in the last necessity for the scissors. In short the German student stands on high relief from the general picture of mankind…But he has better traits than eccentricity – he is really a student.'

there have always been free open seats the same as at Barking Church[1] in the nave and the effect is much better than the chairs. I think you would agree if you were to see them. How do you get on with your subscriptions for the old organ?[2]

We travelled yesterday as we intended, to Konigswinter by steamer. The extreme had dimmed and the great heat was over, so we went up the Drachenfel, Edward walking and I on a donkey. It would be impossible for me to describe to you the lovely view, I never saw anything so beautiful. You would have indeed enjoyed yourself - I wish above all things you could have been with us!

The ruins of the old castle are on the top. One side you look down upon the Rhine which winds very prettily as is much fabled. Standing on the plains by the banks of the river are numerous picturesque little villages and in the centre of the Rhine there are two small islands. The Convent of Nonnenwerth[3] stands in one which tradition says Hildegarde[4] retired when she heard her lover was killed in battle. There are several interesting old legends connected with the Castle of Drachenfels and Roland's Tower[5] at the opposite which we read before we visited the spot. The sides of the Seven Mountains[6] are very well wooded and between them are the

---

[1] Church of St Margaret of Antioch - 13th century parish church of Barking within the grounds of Barking Abbey, where Helen's Fanshawe ancestors were buried.
[2] Dagenham Church: 'in 1844 an organ was placed in the church by voluntary contributions. It was put on the gallery, or 'singing-loft' where the village orchestra had formerly been' - *A History of Dagenham by J P Shawcross (1904)*.
[3] Remains of a 12th century Benedictine monastery on the island originally called Ruleicheswerd (Rolandswerth).
[4] The Benedictine Abbess Hildegard of Bingen - 12th century writer, composer and philosopher considered a founder of scientific natural history whose work relating to the properties and uses of herbs and plants is still widely published.
[5] Drachenfels (Dragon's Rock) and Roland's Tower are steeped in myth and legend – the most popular being Siegfried, hero of the Nibelungenlied.
[6] Siebengebirge – seven volcanic-formed hills including the Drachensfel.

most beautiful valleys you can imagine. The effect of looking down from a great height on the fields covered with all the varieties of grain was very curious. Edward has been making one or two sketches of the views.

We are going to Koblenz[1] tomorrow, most probably by steamer as the roads are so very dusty. I do not think we shall reach Frankfurt before another week or fortnight so will you send me another letter please, and another direct to Baden-Baden[2]?

Pray give me a very long account of yourselves and all that you have been doing. I think of you very often and should much like to see you again, it seems such an age since we parted. Tell John, I hope he had much enjoyment at Montem[3], I've read an account of it in the papers, of the accident that happen there to some poor unfortunate boy[4].

How gay the Queen is pictured with all her royal visitors? The papers here say that O'Connell[5] [penalised] is very unjust. I suppose suppose most of the people in England are delighted.

---

[1] On the banks of the Rhine at the confluence with the Moselle - known as 'German Corner'.
[2] Spa town, fashionable from early 1800's as a summer resort of Europe's elite.
[3] Triannual festival at Eton College which took place on 31st May 1844. Prince Albert was among the many guests that year but the old traditional event was unpopular with Eton's Headmaster who ensured it was discontinued by 1847.
[4] According to *The Atlas – 1st June 1844* 'The only accident which occurred happened to a young gentleman named Fox who, while fencing with another boy, received the point of the dress sword in his eye' In other reports it was confirmed that the 17 year old was rushed by the Surgeon at Windsor to the eminent surgeon Mr Tyrrell at the Royal London Ophthalmic Hospital. Sight in the right eye was completely destroyed and the left was also in danger.
[5] Daniel O'Connell – Irish politician who fought for Catholic emancipation and his seat in Parliament.

'...so we went up the Drachenfels - Edward walking and I on a donkey.
It would be impossible for me to describe to you the lovely view...'

The castled crag of Drachenfels
Frowns o'er the wide and winding Rhine.
Whose breast of waters broadly swells
Between the banks which bear the vine,
And hills all rich with blossomed trees,
And fields which promise corn and wine,
And scattered cities crowning these,
Whose far white walls along them shine,
Have strewed a scene, which I should see
With double joy wert thou with me!

Drachenfels - The Dragon's Rock steeped in the mythical legend of Siegfried, the hero of the Nibelungenlied who slayed Fafnir the dragon of the cave then in an attempt to become invulnerable, bathed in its blood.
This powerful and dramatic story was the inspiration for Richard Wagner's opera 'Der Ring des Nibelungen' (1876)

'Childe Harold's Pilgrimage' (1818)
Lord Byron,

'The Night Watch on the Drachenfels'
Heinrich Heine (1797 – 1856)
'... sang of Germany's renown in fight.
Her health we drank from Rhine wine beakers bright,
The castle-spirit on the summit tower'd,
Dark forms of armèd knights around us lower'd,
And women's misty shapes appear'd in sight.
And from the ruins there arose low moans,
Owls hooted, rattling sounds were heard and groans;
A furious north wind bluster'd fitfully.
Such was the night, my friend, that I did pass
On the high Drachenfels...'

Tell John, I hope he had much enjoyment at Montem...

The Eton Montem of 1844 was the last. Crowds, brought by the arrival of the railway at Eton and Slough became a problem and added to the growing concern of the headmaster who was against Eton's boys 'demanding' money from travellers and townspeople.

Despite this the traditional procession dating from Tudor times took place one last time. The boys were dressed in their costumes and as was customary, members of the royal family attended. Prince Albert - stopped on Windsor Bridge happily complied with the request for 'salt' and gave £100.

John Gaspard Fanshawe must have enjoyed the day and arriving back in Dagenham would have shared colourful tales with his father – who in 1805 & 1808 was with his friend Denis Le Marchant a 'Poleman' at Montem.

Illustrated London News - June 1844
"This celebrated ceremony, of which the origin is lost in obscurity, and which now occurs triennially, is the tenure by which Eton College holds some of its domains; the waving of a flag by one of the scholars on a mount near the village of Salt-Hill, and to which, without doubt, it gives the name; since on this day every visitor to Eton and every traveller in its vicinity, from the monarch to the peasant, are stopped on the road by youthful brigands in picturesque costumes, and summoned to contribute 'salt' in the shape of coin of the realm to the purse collecting for the Captain of Eton, the senior scholar on the Foundation who is about to retire to King's College, Cambridge"

Is Annie staying at Billingbear? When do the boy's holidays begin and has Basil quite got over his accident? Give them all my dearest love.

Mind and send me very particular accounts of Aunt Caroline – I suppose she is getting rather nervous! I am very glad Aunt Tupper[1] and her baby are getting on so well, give them my love when you write not forgetting Aunt Mourant[2] and Aunt Eliza[3]. I shall try and write to them at Frankfurt but the constant moving about now from place to place, takes up so much time it is impossible to write, much as I wish it.

Where are the Carey's - have they paid you their visit yet? I shall write to Minnie as soon as possible.

Mind dearest Mamma, to give me a long account of yourself, Papa and all the rest of the party. I hope again, one and all are quite well and enjoying this lovely weather.

When you direct to me at Geneva be sure and write underneath 'SUISSE' in large letters or it will be sent to Genoa.

Once more, much love to all and large portion for yourself - and Edward included. Believe me ever dearest Mother, your most affectionate attached daughter,

Helen Denison

---

[1] HFD's aunt Anna Maria Le Marchant wife of Daniel Tupper of Melrose, Guernsey and her son Francis Gerard St. George Tupper born 17th April 1844.

[2] Sophia Carey, aunt of HFD's mother and the widow of Peter Mourant of Candie House, Guernsey – had no children of her own but in 1812 when Major General Le Merchant's children were orphaned, she became their guardian. 'Aunt Mourant' died in 1862 and Candie House is now home to Guernsey's Priaulx Library.

[3] Sarah Le Marchant - Sarah 'Eliza' Smith, wife of HFD's uncle, Sir Denis Le Marchant of Chobham Place, gave birth to her third child Francis shortly before Helen left England. The Smith family home was Suttons at Stapleford Tawney, a few miles from Dagenham.

PS

How is Miss Farquharson?
Remember me to the servants. Did John get my letter about Geneva? When does he return from Billingbear and when do you leave home? Has Mr Baugh returned from Oxford – remember me to him!

Letter to Mrs Catherine Fanshawe - mother

Coblenz
June 19th 1844

My dearest Mamma,

We returned to Coblenz yesterday evening and fortunately [found your letters from] many journeys – kindly kept by the hotel staff. Thanks for them both - you have no idea at what a treat it is to me to get a letter and I am delighted to hear such good accounts of you all. I hope Papa's cold has finally left him now - we are remarkably well and enjoy the beautiful scenery excessively.

Since I last wrote we have been so busy on the move and I shall try to tell you of our proceedings as I have much to say. We went from Bonn and by the steamer to Coblenz last Monday week.

Directly we got on board Edward recognised an old gentleman and his wife but could not recollect who they were. The recognition turned out to be mutual for they kept on looking at us and as soon as they finished their dinner the old gentleman came by and spoke but the most extraordinary part of this story is that when they told each other their names they both said they had never heard of them before and could not recollect where they had meet before. Still we were none the wiser when we parted. I did not speak to the wife for she was an elderly person and old and very little in size, and I was told very proud, but while she was speaking the old gentleman came and talked to us and he made himself very agreeable.

Coblenz is very prettily situated and exactly opposite to us were the ruins of the noble fortress of Ehrenbreitstein[1]. You would be delighted with the view from this lovely suite. I think it is even

---

[1] Fortresses stood on this site for centuries but HFD refers to the construction built by the Prussians between 1817 and 1828 - the previous building was destroyed by the French in 1801.

unsurpassed in beauty by the view from Fort Alexander[1] on the Rhine - which is where we get a beautiful view of the Rhine Stolzenfel Castle[2] then the King of the Palatine palaces and the castles of Lahneck,[3] which belongs to the Duke of Nassau[4].

Edward has taken Advocat Articles[5] and I have a great wish to learn as soon as we settle a living place. I shall certainly have a master.

We went to Ems[6] last Thursday for the day, the drive to it is lovely but the town is situated quite in a hole and fatiguing hot. It is extremely gay, there is a very handsome gambling room and very pretty gardens. We dined at the table d'hote where we met two London people who crossed over with us from Dover but they certainly were a disgrace to our nation for I could not have believe any persons having any pretensions to being ladies or gentlemen could have behaved the way they did. They interrupted the attention of all present, foreigners and all.

---

[1] 'A defensive wall and embankment was built along the Rhine, including a battery at the "German Corner". Frederick William III decreed Koblenz was to be flanked and surveyed by other new fortresses with extensive outworks and with the Holy Alliance in mind, they were named after members of Russian and Austrian dynasties. Fort Alexander named for the Tsar was built 1818-22, as a quadrangle with sides 500 metres long, facing west up the valley of the Mosel - the traditional approach of the French.' *The Castles of the Rhine: Recreating the Middle Ages in Modern Germany - Robert R. Taylor.*
[2] The ruins of Stolzenfel Castle were given to the Crown Prince, later King Frederick William IV of Prussia in 1823. Extensive restoration to the building and gardens were completed by 1842, when it became his summer residence.
[3] Lahneck Castle is sited on a steep slope opposite Stolzenfel Castle.
[4] Grand Duke Adolphe of Luxembourg.
[5] Edward Hanson Denison was called to the Bar as a member of Lincoln's Inn in November 1843. Any interest that Helen may have had to study law could only have been academic - ladies were not admitted to the Bar in England until 1922.
[6] Bad Ems - east of Koblenz, a popular bathing resort much visited by royalty and celebrities in the 19th century.

On Friday we went by the steamer up the Moselle and have been well repaid, for it much excels the Rhine as far as we have yet seen in the beauty of its scenery. The windings of the river are most extraordinary and of course give it a very elegant appearance. The hills are very high on each side and generally covered with hayricks and woods. It is very rare indeed, one sees a piece of ground lying fallow and wonderful to say that also has been worked - the crops look particular fine and the hay very good and in most parts it has been gleaned and carted.

I supposed you are not so far forward and I hope you have had rain since. We have had some last night and this morning, but it does not seem likely to last long.

The first days of our excursion up the Moselle we went as far as Trarbach[1] half way to Trier, but from it being a very slow and altogether a bad boat, we did not get up till 4 partly having left Coblenz at 8 o'clock in the morning. When we reached the most beautiful spot where the river takes a tremendous [turn] we got out of the boat and we walked to the top of the hill where there lies old ruins[2] and a charming view. The woman who lives in the ruins of Grevenburg is a famous shot and she has a corner of the garden containing a numbers of birds, falcons, ospreys that she has killed.

The town of Trarbach was a pokey little hole and more of a hamlet, but everything was very clean and we were fortunate to find some really good accommodation. The villages are dispersed very prettily along each side of themselves and especially some of those under the ruins of the old castle that are overhanging which adds much of picturesque appearance. We left Traben about [xxx] of the afternoon

---

[1] Trarbach on the right bank of the Moselle facing Traben became a major wine centre by the end of the 19th century.
[2] 14th century Castle Grevenburg was destroyed in 1734 by the French.

and in the evening we got [xxxx] and in taking time as is meet by an easier road and got back home to our old quarters at night then the next afternoon we put ourselves on the steamer and went to Coblenz - it really seemed like returning home. Do tell us if you should not more have enjoyed our excursion to Schloss Eltz[1] - I wish you could have been with us dearest Mamma?

Edward has just come in to tell me it is time to start for St Goar!

Just fancy we met on the steamer an Englishman, the son of a Colonel Baldwin and this was his dress - a short sky blue silken dressing gown covered with pretty flowers first, a velvet cap, vermillion coloured trousers and green slippers worked with gold. Surely he must have been returning from a masquerade or he would never have made such a goose of himself.

Bingen - Since I last took up my pen, we have been at St Goar for a day and took a visit to Bingen where we arrived yesterday afternoon, but as Edward is going to write and thank you for your kind amusing letter, I shall leave him to describe the beauties of these two places and I shall avail myself for this opportunity for entering more fully into family details.

I cannot thank you sufficiently dearest Mother for all the particulars you gave me in your kind and most interesting letter and I am much impatiently awaiting the arrival of Tuesday or Wednesday when we go to Frankfurt and I hope again to hear further news of you all - and I suppose just now you are in a state of great excitement hoping Uncle Denis[2] may come in now that there is a chance of Sir Robert

---

[1] From 1965 to 1990, '500 Deutsche Mark' banknotes included a sketch of Schloss Eltz.
[2] Denis Le Marchant – oldest surviving brother of Mrs Fanshawe was a politician whose career was advancing at this time. In 1846 he was elected M.P. for Worcester when the 'Whigs' returned to power with Lord John Russell as Prime Minister.

Peel[1] resigning? Indeed, we heard that he had but I believe that was only a post. I sincerely hope Uncle Denis may have success.

We also believe there has been a great deal of rain in England. The last I hope may also be true, I can only say we had none to speak of here and that is natural - the thermometer is constantly up - in the shade and during the night at 75° or 76°. I often picture you to myself, seated at the bow window in the drawing [room] enjoying the cool air, and Papa, hard at work in his garden. Tell him there are such beautiful flowers here that grow so luxuriantly. In many of the walks they are planted between the trees and some are so full of flowers that they are a perfect mass of pink and white. I wish I could send him some over!

John seems to have been enjoying himself greatly, I suppose both he and Annie are still at Le Marchant Thomas'? How did Annie get on with Uncle Tom's impressions for effect? Give them my love and ask them to write when they have time.

I am very sorry you still have such a bad opinion of Aunt Mary, she has indeed many afflictions which must affect her health and spirits but I hope Gravesend[2] air, disagreeable place as it is, will have the desired effect. When do you expect to pay your visit to her?

I fear you have a very small chance of escaping some of odoriferous scents[3] you mention especially this hot weather. When they are at

---

[1] Sir Robert Peel Conservative Prime Minister (1834-35 & 1841-46), previously Home Secretary and founder of the Metropolitan Police Force.

[2] An old port on the south bank of the Thames, close to the A2 road between London and Dover. Early in 19th century the well-off from London visited Gravesend taking summer air, but their visits grew less after 'steamers' brought the town within easy reach of London and day-tripper tourism.

[3] Along the eastern reaches of the Thames, problems were already occurring during summer months that eventually culminating into London's 'Great Stink 1858'. After the Metropolitan Buildings Act 1844, soap factories opened at Stratford and Silvertown that released effluence and unpleasant smells into the River Lea which

their climax, if you <u>are</u> able to think, just imagine my sufferings at Cologne.

Has Uncle Tom got quite strong again, give him our best love and when you write, tell me how Aunt Eliza and the little ones are?

I am expecting every letter will bring some news of Aunt Caroline, I do hope all will go on right and that his young cadet will afford both herself and Uncle Somerville much happiness.

You seem dearest Mother, to be still going on the same as usual, I should much like to know when your gaiety begins and I wish this plan Mrs Tuck[1] was so much afraid of were true, and trust you would all come and join us at Frankfurt or Baden Baden. Would it not be delightful?

How is Aunt Margaret,[2] I hope she has quite recovered from her last illness?

I certainly was much astonished with the village news and cannot understand Harriet Biggs being engaged to Fred Tyler, do they intend to marry soon and how do they intend to manage? Remember me very kindly to them and particularly to Mrs Tuck and Arabella and Mrs Winmill[3]. I am very sorry to hear such a bad account of Miss Thompson and hope she is not so ill as people think. How do the Milners[4] get on and was it before from what John told me, that poor Helen would have been released from her daily visits

---

flowed out into the Thames close to Barking. Helen's comparison surely relates to the manufacture of 4711 soap and perfume – a famous product of Cologne since 1799.

[1] Mrs Tuck (owner) & Arabella Winmill, Marshfoot Farm, Dagenham (1851 Census)
[2] Lady Margaret (Taylor) Le Marchant, wife of HFD's uncle, Lt. General Sir John Gaspard Le Marchant, who in 1847 was appointed Lt. Governor of Newfoundland.
[3] Local farming family - notably George Winmill active in local charitable bodies.
[4] John Milner and family at Heath House, opposite The Three Mills, Chadwell Heath.

to Mrs Rosenberg by this time. She must indeed poor girl, be anxious for the arrival of the young gentleman or lady. When I first read your letter I thought you were alluding to the Queen's confinement[1]. Give Helen and Uncle Henry very best love.

You do not mention Basil in your letter, so I conclude he is quite over his accident. I imagine them both very happy at home! I should like above all things to take a peep at all the inmates of Parsloes again - though absent my thoughts are <u>very constantly</u> with them and we never omit, on Sundays more especially, drinking the health of all dear friends in England in a bumper[2], those at Parsloes of course, coming first. How often I wish I could pass my Sundays at Dagenham, I should much like to have partaken of the Sacrament with you on Whit Sunday but I suppose I shall not be able to partake of that sacred institution again till I return to England – it will indeed be a pleasure to receive it again in Dagenham Church.

We generally find a Protestant church in the places in which we stay, but when we don't we read prayers at home.

I almost forgot to mention that the first thing that greeted me in our rooms when we arrived at our hotel at Bingen was a sofa worked by Mrs Hornby's beautiful pattern. Miss Sterry gave her our black ground and pattern to match for the back and two very pretty pillows. The effect is admirable and I cannot help wishing each time as I look at it, that I think if you would like the same sort of thing for your library.

In the [-] way, as the Honiton lace [-] Edward gave me the best of it to lace match for sleeves. Besides by which I think [*this whole section*

---

[1] Queen Victoria's 2nd son Prince Alfred, Duke of Edinburgh, born 6th August 1844.
[2] A toast.

is not possible to read but appears to concern the lace that has been purchased and also feathers for Mrs Fanshawe.]

We have bought several of Alexander Dumas and Victor Hugo works which are very amusing. They are 'Sur les Bords du Rhine'[1] and there is one that we have not yet begun, 'Michel Ange'[2].

I wish I could join you in your reading, you must have found 'The Reign of Elizabeth' extremely interesting. I am really ashamed to say that in answer to your question about the *[corner of paper missing]* I am obliged to confess it has never been begun.

I fear you will have great difficulty in deciphering this letter and my paper has come to a close before I have told you one half that I want to - but I shall write again when I get to Frankfurt, either to you or to John or perhaps both. We go to Wiesbaden probably on Sunday - I have [also hopes of] Baden Baden…I think I told you to direct your letters to [-] Suisse.

Thanking you a thousand times for your very kind letters and your affectionate wishes and [our] happiness goes to demonstrate. A large portion of love to all, with a great deal for yourself in which Edward unites.

Believe me ever dearest Mamma, your most affectionate attached daughter,

Helen Denison

Please remember me to the servants and Sarah [Sterry]

---

[1] 'Excursions on the shores of the Rhine'- Alexandre Dumas (Paris) 1842.
[2] Michel-Ange suivi de Titien Vecelli – Alexandre Dumas (Bruxelles) 1844.

Victor Hugo 1802 - 1885

'Notre-Dame de Paris, (1832) was probably already a favourite book at the Vicarage but still to come was Victor Hugo's masterpiece, 'Les Miserables' (1862).

'Le Rhin' or 'Sur les Bords du Rhine', is a compilation of letters from Hugo who was prolific in both poetry and prose - written during three Rhineland journeys made between 1839 and 1841.

Victor Hugo never shied from issues of social injustice and conflict and eventually having fallen from favour with Napoleon III, he left France for a period of exile in 1851.

He settled in Guernsey, staying fifteen years at Hauteville House, St. Peter Port. On such a small island, with an exclusive elite society, almost certainly Victor Hugo the 'celebrity author' became acquainted with some of Helen's many Guernsey cousins.

'We have bought several of Alexander Dumas and Victor Hugo works which are very amusing. They are 'Sur les Bords du Rhine' and there is one that we have not yet begun, Michel Auge.'

Another of the great writers of France, Alexandre Dumas had an enormous appetite for life, adventure and romance. He was just getting into his

Alexandre Dumas 1802 - 1870

stride in 1844 - The Count of Monte Cristo, The Three Musketeers, The Corsican Brothers, La Reine Margot - an endless list that were published in rapid succession. All would delight the Fanshawe family and it is not difficult to imagine candles burning late at old Parsloes!

Letter from
Edward Hansen Denison to his mother-in-law Mrs Catherine Fanshawe

Frankfurt
June 30th 1844

My dear Mrs Fanshawe,

Thank you for your very kind & amusing letter which I will now try to do my best to do justice to. I am sure it will give you as much pleasure as to hear, as it does me to tell you that we are getting on most prosperously. Helen is a most excellent traveller – the climate, the manner of living and even the fatigue of travelling agree with her wonderfully – and from the past, I have every hope for the future.

I am afraid Helen has left me very little to tell you about our travels & so I must confine myself to a few general remarks, with the exception of our last few days on the Rhine which she tells me she has missed.

These last few days were spent at St. Goar[1] & Bingen that is within the very thick of its beauties & traditions for things seem to be together and concentrated within Cologne & Mainz, a distance of 100 miles about, in a course of some 6 or 7 hundred miles from the glacier in Switzerland where it springs, to the north of Holland where it comes out and away. Those waves may perhaps be washing the banks of the Thames the next time you walk down onto the Marshes. It would be poetical but neither a <u>safe</u> or <u>speedy</u> way to commit a letter to the care of the Rhine at Mainz – directed Parsloes. I shall prepare the postman, a <u>German one</u> –.

---

[1] St Goar - below the ruins of Burg Rheinfels, opposite Schloss Katz and Schloss Maus and downstream from the Lorelei Rock – one of the most scenic stretches of the Rhine.

I consider that we have now <u>done</u> the Rhine - we have steamed upon him, sailed upon him, driven along his banks – looked down upon him (in admiration I mean & not in contempt), drank him in tea, & (I) have swam in him – so now I think we have a right to <u>write</u> about him.

I have previously seen the Danube – the Elbe, Moselle, Main and the Guadalquivir[1] – and I maintain that old Father Rhine, if surpassed by the firs, is far superior to the others.

But stop - there is this against him – he is easily got at, you may book yourself in Leadenhall St.[2] to go almost to his source. How then can anything so common, so 'everydayish' (if I may use such a word) be worth looking at? The Rhine may have been worth seeing 25 years ago, before the discovery of steam navigation but <u>now</u>, to hear people talk one must go for the scenery to the last – to the desert in fact - and your true traveller 'at the worship's mess'[3] - you know the quotation… I am not alluding to the form worship like the Exeter Hall[4] missionary mayors think every place short of <u>Central Africa</u> beneath his notice. The steam boats that bring Cockneys bring civilization also – to them we owe the comforts that await at the foot of the Drachenfels & at… everywhere in short.

While at St. Goar we went to see the ruins of a fine old castle, some two of three miles off, Helen on donkey-back & I on foot. We were

---

[1] Spain's second longest river which passes through Seville & Cordoba.
[2] Street in City of London associated with East India Co., shipping and insurance.
[3] 'Now your traveller, he and his toothpick at my worship's mess…' a quote from Philip the Bastard, brother of Robert Falconbridge in William Shakespeare's play 'The Life and Death of King John' (Act 1 Scene 1).
[4] Built on the north side of the Strand (site of the former residence of the Earls of Exeter) - Exeter Hall opened in 1831 and included two large meeting halls, the larger being able to accommodate 4,000 people hosted religious and bible society meetings. The halls also became the venue for Anti-Slavery Society meetings and the phrase 'Exeter Hall' a metaphor for the Anti- Slavery cause.

especially pleased as we saw there what they did not show us at Schloss Eltz (the castle on the Moselle that Helen told you about) – that is every nook & cranny about the place, in both under & above ground. The thickness of the walls of these old strongholds is extraordinary – which you may imagine from the fact that this one has stone vaulted roofs supported by massive stone pillars even on the <u>third</u> storey – <u>and well might their walls be thick for their deeds were evil!</u> It was a sort of a <u>Rebecca Riots</u>[1] in the thirteenth century which turned (lawless) <u>robber's nests</u> - as the Germans used to call them for good reason, into ruins. The <u>turnpikes on the Rhine</u> had become so frequent and out of all reason in their demands so the people rose as in Wales, and pulled the turnpike houses down. The traveller is perhaps greatly pleased at the present day but in a more agreeable manner the Knight most likely only gave kicks for your halfpence while modern robber at all events gives beefsteaks.

On our way from St Goar to Bingen we stopped for a few hours at a little town called Bacharach[2] serving excellent wine, sent our domestics on. Bacharach was celebrated within time of the Romans for its excellent wine (hence its name Bacchi as on the altar of Bacchus) – as it is now, but all the same for that, what we got was <u>awfully sour</u> so that Bacchus was either a very bad presser of wine or refused to patronise what was so unworthy of him.

---

[1] An 1844 act of parliament amending the law relating to Turnpikes in Wales resulted from 5 years of protests called the Rebecca Riots when farmers and agricultural labourers, dressed as women to avoid violence against them, took action against the toll gates which they viewed as unfair taxation.

[2] Bacharach an important centre for the wine trade since the Middle Ages grew from the Rhine not being navigable by large ships through nearby 'Bingen Lock'. Wine brought to that point had to be transported through the natural lock in small vessels and then off-loaded into bigger ships at the harbour. Through the trading a town naturally grew with a name evolving from Bacchus, Roman god of wine.

This curious little place is perhaps the most perfect specimen existing of a town, or village perhaps one ought to call it, of the Middle Ages. Surrounded with walls & towers of the earliest style of fortification – streets narrow with overhanging houses & these same houses of every possible varieties of fantastic, quaint & old fashioned forms – black, green & dirty. Besides these attractions, and believe me they are attractions (excepting the dirt but without that they cannot be natural, for I take it that however <u>good</u> the old times may have been they were most amazingly dirty). I find the same pleasure in looking at these mournful old places that I should in seeing the embalmed remains of Alexander the Great or Caesar if such existed.

Above the town stands the ruin of one of the most elegant & beautiful gothic churches[1] in existence. After taking an early dinner at the hotel below, we mounted the hill under a scorching sun, with the intention of climbing quite the higher to the ruins of an old castle[2] to get a much better view but it was so intensely hot (I never felt anything hotter, even at Athens) that we gladly took refuge under the friendly shelter of a walnut tree and positively thanked the platform on which the church stood. Here we stayed for a good hour alternately looking up at the beautiful view & down across the Rhine. Perhaps the very colour of the journey is between Bacharach & Bingen and for my part I much prefer the latter. It is there that the noble river expands himself to his greatest width – a good half a mile at the very least & tho' the banks lose their grandeur – they gain in beauty.

The few days we were at Bingen the weather continued unnaturally hot. Last Monday for instance the thermometer showed 82° with shade, but thank goodness it has since been much cooler, never

---

[1] Wernerkapelle was built in 1428 and has been a ruin since 1689.
[2] 12th century Burg Stahleck is 520ft above sea level.

exceeding 70° and I hope we shall get on to Switzerland without much more scorching and when once there, we are all right.

We are resting and enjoying ourselves here very much - to me it is my <u>foreign home</u> but my acquaintances are reduced to one: the <u>Doctor.</u> Without any exception it is the dearest & most comfortable town on the Continent. Things tho' <u>dear,</u> are <u>good</u>.

From this we post to Heidelberg; look at the great ton[1] that holds 300,000 bottles and then proceed per <u>railway</u>[2] to Baden (for it is a flat uninteresting journey), stay there a few days & then proceed to Strasburg, look at the Cathedral[3] and eat foie gras patty[4] and away by another rail for the land of mountains.

You see by my account how very much travelling is now facilitated & I hope it will tempt you and Mr F to visit these foreign parts. I by no means despair of hearing the Vicar discourse in rapture of Bingen & St. Goar!!

---

[1] 'Everybody has heard of the great Heidelberg Tun and most people have seen it, no doubt. It is a wine-cask as big as a cottage, and some traditions say it holds eighteen thousand bottles, and other traditions say it holds eighteen hundred million barrels. I think it likely that one of these statements is a mistake, and the other is a lie. However, the mere matter of capacity is a thing of no sort of consequence, since the cask is empty, and indeed has always been empty, history says. An empty cask the size of a cathedral could excite but little emotion in me.' — *Mark Twain, 'A Tramp Abroad', 1880.*

[2] The Mannheim - Basel line was still under construction and the section of line linking Heidelberg to Baden Baden only opened 6th May 1844.

[3] Standing at 466 feet, the Cathédrale Notre-Dame de Strasbourg, (13th century) was considered the tallest building in the world - "*Sublimely towering, wide-spreading tree of God*" (Goethe).

[4] Strasbourg was a major producer of the speciality 'pate' called Foie Gras (fat liver) made from the liver of duck or goose. Referring to 'Patty', Edward was not incorrectly spelling the French word 'pate'; only anticipating 'Strasbourg Pie', a pastry containing the pate. The writer William Makepiece Thackeray refers to this delicacy and how it is popular with the diplomatic classes.

As to our manner of living, it differs as much as the places we are in – one morning we are climbing up hills by 6 o'clock (N.B. this <u>does not happen every day</u>!). Sometimes we dine at 1pm another at 9 pm – in short we are <u>regular</u> only in <u>irregularity,</u> but we must be, to adapt ourselves to the circumstances. But for the most part we are early to bed – early <u>to rise</u>, which we find to produce the <u>first</u> effect maintained by the proverb[1], but I do not discover that the 2nd is brought about by it, and as for the last – <u>why it is not for us to say!</u>

We have begun to dine at the table d' hote occasionally when we are likely to meet decent people, and we find it saves us trouble as well as money and affords us amusement into the bargain.

If I had space I should much like to give you the results of my observations of the German character. I must confess that one has about as much right to judge of it <u>on</u> the <u>Rhine</u> as a foreigner would have to judge of the English character by the <u>Ship Hotel</u> at Dover, but as I have seen a little more of it in this time so I think I may sport.

The Germans are certainly an honest, steady, orderly & good natured people, but there are two flaws in the national character which truth, stern truth compels me to add, namely – a total <u>disregard for warm plates</u> and a <u>severe contempt for salt spoons</u>. That great civilizer the steamer is gradually introducing the latter – I am happy to see a difference even within a year or two - & I should say that in the course of 2 centuries & a half they will be in pretty general use.

As you know I dare say, one distinguishing mark or as some might call it, failing of the Germans is their adherence to the things that lie in their aversion for anything like change - and therefore one may

---

[1] 'Early to bed, early to rise – makes a man healthy wealthy and wise'.

reasonably conclude that so fearful an innovation will be, until every German, conservative! If they had elections, I should expect to see other flags of the Liberal Conservative vanish etc., <u>Liberty</u> & <u>Salt spoons.</u>

I would add a few political observations on the state of this country but if this letter is not opened here, it will be in England – the <u>land of Liberty</u>! – if Sir J Graham[1] thinks fit. Such a state of things is a disgrace to a country, pretending to call itself <u>free.</u>

Helen is getting on famously with German, altho' she will not quite follow my system, which is <u>never</u> to use <u>grammar</u> or <u>dictionary</u>, which I maintain to be the only true & philosophical way of learning a language – those two aids were given for the express purpose of increasing the difficulties & of making a master necessary to explain them – I speak chiefly of the grammar.

I am afraid you will be quite tired of deciphering what will so ill repay you for the trouble – therefore conclude with my fondest regards to yourself, Mr Fanshawe & John and remain your affectionate son-in-law

E H Denison

I cannot give you any return for your excellent description of the exhibition (salon) as the only pictures I have seen lately were Nature's which to my taste are far superior, and much more difficult

---

[1] Sir James Graham (1792-1861) Home Secretary in Sir Robert Peel's government, ordered the opening of letters that passed through the London Post Office between a foreign refugee in England and Guiseppi Mazzini, a freedom fighter planning insurrection in Calabria. This information was exposed in parliament by Thomas Duncombe a colourful and radical Whig politician, who like the public, was shocked that information gleaned in that way could be passed to the Italian court, and directly result in the death of the rebels.

to describe. I am very glad to hear Landseer[1] has come out with old force again. I suppose he is now undoubtedly our best painter.

I quite forgot, Basil & Richard will be at home – pray give them my love and tell them I hope their first half year at Shrewsbury will prove a very happy one.

EHD

---

[1] Edwin Landseer (1802 – 1873) exhibited 'Shoeing' in 1844 – now in the Tate Britain.

Letter addressed to: Mrs T L Fanshawe, Parsloes, Dagenham, Essex - crossed through & redirect to: 'Sea View, Ryde, Isle of Wight, Hants

Frankfurt
June 30th (1844)

My dearest Mamma,

A thousand thanks for your delightful letter which I found immediately on my arrival at Frankfurt. We came here on Thursday - you will perhaps wonder? I did hasten to answer it sooner but the fact is I have been waiting, hoping each day I should get a line from one of you to tell me about Aunt Somerville. I do hope she will not keep you long in suspense. I am very anxious to know how she got through her troubles, & I also wanted to hear about the worsted paillasse[1] for the library chairs which I intended buying here – but that is of no importance for I think I know your taste pretty well.

I will thank you now for the letter you have directed to Baden Baden though I have not yet read it. I am sure dearest Mother, like all your others, it will be most interesting & I am so glad to hear that you & Papa and all the rest are so well. I should dearly like to see you again – you have never told me if you are <u>growing fat</u> – do not forget that in your next.

Edward has met here an old friend of his, a Mr Potts[2] who has come abroad with his wife whom he married in February, he is not quite

---

[1] Usually a straw mattress – perhaps here HFD is referring to seat cushions.
[2] Almost certainly Henry Potts (1810 – 1884) and his wife Cecilia married at Dover on 15th February 1844. Potts came from a Welsh landowning family, left Shrewsbury School in 1826 and took an MA at Magdalen College, Cambridge. Later he became a J.P and Lord High Sheriff of Flintshire. Both he and Edward were reported as attendees at 'The Fancy Ball' in Manchester in September 1836. Edward undoubtedly found Potts interesting as he was a sportsman, recorded as an early gentleman cricketer playing for Cambridge in 1831 and also the rider of the winning horse in the 1837 Liverpool Steeplechase - officially recognised as the first 'Grand National'.

so late from the scene of action as we are. She is a very good natured ladylike sort of person so I find her rather an agreeable companion. They have been so constantly with us during the whole day that with a little walking, my time has been fully occupied in playing the agreeable.

Edward has just told me he is going to write to you so I shall leave him to describe the scenery about Bingen – he will do it far more descriptive & I shall dwell more into home pastures.

The first day we arrived at Frankfurt, Mr & Mrs Potts drank tea with us, the next day we drank tea with them. Mr Potts has bought a horse & gig as he talks of spending the summer here, so Edward found one & we took a very pleasant drive in the evening to Offenbach[1]. The view would have been perfect had there not been a thick mist over the hills.

This is a great place for the Jews[2] & the oldest brother of the Rothchild's[3] lives here like a prince. He has a magnificent palace outside the town, is visited by the grandees & gives splendid feasts to kings & princes more lavishness even than they give themselves. He presides at the head of the table with his wife, but they neither of them say a thing themselves.

Yesterday we drove to Homberg[4] which appears a flourishing place & is quite taking the place of Wiesbaden – but is it not shocking to

---

[1] Offenbach, now part of the large urban area of Frankfurt was more cosmopolitan than its larger neighbour in 1844. Goethe and Mozart were among the many famous personalities who had visited.
[2] The Jewish ghetto in the 'Judengasse' Frankfurt (1462 – 1811) was home to the largest Jewish community in Germany.
[3] The Jewish family that established their banking business in Frankfurt in the 1760's when the founder, Mayer Amschel Rothschild (1744–1812), was a court factor to the German Landgraves of Hesse-Kassel.
[4] Bad Homberg.

think that the gambling tables are the source of all their riches? We went into the rooms which are very historical, there was one gentleman playing, a Belgian who had lost cards for an enormous sum at Wiesbaden. He was staking very light but seemed to be winning whilst we were there. We have seen several ladies playing, regular gamblers they are at the tables we heard, nearly the whole day. I think it is a bad as bad can be in men, but in women it is too terribly wrong in appearance.

We returned from Homberg in the afternoon, delighted with our beautiful drive & just in time to go to the opera in the evening. It was a very local German opera, very pretty & the music very good, there was only one female singer, Miss Calipaci & she executed her part very well. She has a very fine & at the same time sweet voice. The men were not quite so good but we enjoyed our evening very much & the whole thing was over in two hours – starting at 7 & well over by 9 o'clock.

Frankfurt, it is a very handsome town & the street we are in is remarkably <u>clean</u>, a great recommendation, but almost as noisy as London for the Hotel Russie where we are is near the port & the traffic of carriages & steamships is immense. There are extremely nice gardens all around the town which are the fashionable promenades.

What a pleasure it will be when we meet again to tell you of all our travels & enter into particulars more fully than one can do by post and many thanks dearest Mamma for all your kind wishes that this little tour may also afford us by & by as much enjoyment - I am sure it will.

Travelling is made so easy & the hotels are so comfortable that I have been thinking it is by no imagination practicable for you to make up a little party & come & enjoy some of the continental

'...it was so intensely hot... and positively thanked the platform on which the church stood. Here we stayed for a good hour alternately looking up at the beautiful view & down across the Rhine.'

'...to Bacharach a town where we landed, it is seated on the right side of the Rhine, having a castle on a high rock within the walls, and under that a church, which is from the plain ground 100 steps before one can come into it, here the poor people are found dead with grass in their mouths; from hence by a village on the same side, in which none but lepers are.'

'A true relation of all the remarkable places and passages observed in the travels of the Rt. Hon. Thomas Lord Howard, Earl Of Arundel & Surrey, Earl Marshall of England – Ambassador Extraordinary to the Emperor of Germany 1636'

'This is one of the oldest, the prettiest and the most unknown towns in the world...this old fairy town, in which romance and legend abound, is peopled by inhabitants who – old and young, from the urchin to the grandfather, from the young girl to the old dame – have, in their cast of features and in their walk, something of the thirteenth century... At Bacharach a stranger is looked upon as a phenomenon. The traveller is followed with eyes of expressive bewilderment'

Victor Hugo
'The Rhine' (c1840)

> 'Yesterday we drove to Homberg which appears a flourishing place & is quite taking the place of Wiesbaden.'

With the discovery of the 'Elisabethen' spring in 1834, the small town of Homburg was able to develop into a spa resort with all the attractions so enjoyed by 19th century fashionable society.

In 1842, the French entrepreneur brothers, Francois and Louis Blanc built and opened the first spa building and casino at Homburg. They also recognised further potential to increase their business and financed the building of the railway line in 1860 connecting Homberg to Frankfurt. Those very successful capital investments led them to later purchase the Casino at Monte Carlo.

The author, Fyodor Dostoyevsky was among the many Russians who visited Homburg casino, and used his experiences in his novella 'The Gambler' -
'I can't stand this lackeyishness in the gossip columns of the whole world, and mainly in our Russian newspapers ... first, the extraordinary magnificence and splendour of the gaming rooms in the roulette towns on the Rhine, and second, the heaps of gold that supposedly lie on the tables ... there is no magnificence in these trashy rooms, and as for the gold, not only are there no heaps on the tables, but there's scarcely even the slightest trace...It was crowded. ...I confess my heart was pounding, and I was not coolheaded; I knew for certain and long resolved that I would not leave Roulettenburg just so; something radical and definitive was bound to happen in my fate.' (1866)

scenery. It only costs £50 each for travelling expenses & the rest you may get very cheap.

I am delighted to hear Uncle Henry Lefevre has made such a generous proposal & shall be more glad to hear that his plan is put into force, change of air is just the thing you all so much wanted and your mind will be quiet at ease if you have this opportunity for the boys – give them both my most affectionate love. I am extremely glad to hear they are both quite well & Basil has recovered [from] his accident.

You are, to be indeed fully occupied with visitors. I am very sorry to have missed the Careys[1] but one cannot be in two places at once. They must indeed be delighted to have Frank[2] with them again. He does not appear to have achieved much during his long absence, from as far as I can recollect, he was handsome likeness of Caroline before he went to Van Dieman's Land[3]. Did you think Maria had improved much by her married status? Henry, I suppose is married by this time. I wish him much happiness and if you should be amongst those he intends honouring with & visits, pray tell him to write very soon.

John seems to have been attended with his usual good success with winning gloves[4] from his friends. I am glad he and Annie enjoyed

---

[1] Lt. General Peter Carey, brother of Mary Carey, Helen's maternal grandmother - married Julia Hewitt daughter of his superior officer General Sir George Hewitt, Commander of the Forces in Ireland (Army list 1804). The Carey family lived at Harlow Common, Essex (Census 1841).
[2] Francis Carey (1820-1887) younger son of Peter Carey, was a Captain in 1844 and later, Lt General of the 26th Regiment of Foot 'The Cameronians'.
[3] Tasmania.
[4] As a prize for a wager between friends, gloves would have been very acceptable - see *The Handbook of Fashion (1839)* 'among trivial matters, nothing, perhaps, more often distinguishes a gentleman from a plebeian, than the wearing of gloves. A gentleman has worn them so constantly from his earliest years that he feels

their visit to Billingbear – what is John doing now? I suppose he's waiting with you, if Uncle Henry Lefevre's plans[1] come to anything and I most sincerely hope it will not fall to the ground. We read in the paper that the Romford bank[2] had failed and I was very sorry to see the fact confirmed in your letter. I hope Papa is no difference by it, how will he manage about the money for the fishing[3] club? Poor Mrs Grant[4] and Julia[5] and Mrs Moss[6], I am very sorry they are among the losers[7]. How does the little Miss Grant get on, is she in a meagre flourishing condition? She certainly looked very miserable when last I saw her.

When does Aunt Eliza go to you, and how are all her little ones? Pray give her my best love - and Uncle Denis – I am glad Uncle Tom[8] is quite well again, is he still staying in town?

---

uncomfortably without them in the street, and he never suffers his hands to be bare for a moment'.

[1] Henry Lefevre opened his bank shortly after this time where John Gaspard Fanshawe was employed.

[2] Romford Bank – Johnson & Company, failed 6th June 1844.

[3] Probably the Angling Club, in existence in various forms from the early 18th century at Dagenham Breach (called also Dagenham Lake or Gulf). *Victoria County History - Essex Vol 5.*

[4] Mrs Ann (Tassell) Grant of Soberton, Hampshire, mother of the Vicar of Romford.

[5] First cousin of Mrs Catherine Fanshawe - eldest daughter of Lt. Gen. Peter Carey & granddaughter of the Rt. Hon. Gen. Sir George Hewett, Bart., GCB. - Julia Carey who married in 1838 Rev. Anthony Grant, Vicar of Romford (young brother of the inventor Sir Thomas Tassell Grant KCB FRS).

[6] Wife of the owner of the Three Mills at Chadwell Heath.

[7] 'The liabilities are not expected to exceed £55,000, as the business of the Bank was not extensive and was chiefly confined to the agricultural class in the immediate neighbourhood of Romford and cattle dealers; many cases of extreme hardship are said to exist for the circumstance of those classes being ill able to bear the loss they will sustain'. *The Bankers Magazine & Journal of the Money Market (October 1842 – April 1845).*

[8] Possibly either Thomas Le Marchant - brother of Helen's mother or more probably elderly John Thomas of Billingbear.

I wrote to Aunt Mourant at Bingen and said I should very much like to hear from her and asked her if she had time to write to me at Geneva. I hope I was right?

We saw by the papers that there [had] been very stormy weather again which lasted from Thursday to Monday and that a large steamer had been lost between Edinburgh and Hull with all the passengers and crew, besides several other mortals. What a fearful thing it is to be cast aground.

[lines linking the following sections have not been found]

…and indeed [xxxx] that are not very pleasant at all but is certain not herself of it. I believe facing every day that we should hear she and Peter have deals and quarrels for she complained to me that Peter never could walk out with her and as not at all attentive. She also said that when he chose the room, as he always took care to leave in a very nice state for himself with a stable sofa and armchair and very comfortable, he then gave her a small room. So I told her for the future to choose her own room, and not to make herself unhappy because Peter would not walk with her for I had no doubt she would be much happier without him. She contented herself with saying he was always thoughtful. And since the storm has passed over and I have heard nothing further of Peter's ungallantry. He is very civil and obliging to us.

…I am very sorry to hear that Gaspard has failed in his examination. It will be a sad disappointment for himself poor boy, as well as his parents. How much longer will it detain him in his Academy?

…Guernsey does indeed seem to be in a [xxxxxx] state. I should be very curious to know how the affair [xxxxx]. Is not the [xxx] [M Dan Tupper/Duppee] the brother of Mrs Teesdale/Inesdale? Surely it is very odd?

…We are very much concerned with the man. He is a Pole, and as is the custom with the Russians that pick [their services], but years in the navy he said the King of Prussia was very much disliked that they told him in the last meeting that they did not believe almost all he said and when his health was proposed they would not drink it. He also said that as soon as Prince Philippe[1] died there would be a revolution in the Rhienish Provinces. He went on a great deal more about the King of Prussia[2] & Edward said he had never heard a foreigner speak so boldly.

I do hope dearest Mamma you are not over working yourself with the school, I shall be very glad to find you have not over taken yourself. I never thought Mrs Bright would remain with you long.

I have bought a little book with all the different views on the Rhine, there is one of the Drachenfels. I wish you could have been with us to enjoy its beauties.

I long to be with you to tell you all I have seen, there are some incredible legends & traditions belonging to almost every place, which adds to the interest but they are too long to write, so I must wait to till I get home.

How is Miss Farquarharson, where is she now & has she been staying with you lately? Give her my love when you write to her.

Yesterday when we went to church there was a great fuss being made with some old woman, the service did not begin till she came, so afterward Edward asked Sir A [Ducxxxx] the doctor here, who

---

[1] Louis Philippe I (1773 –1850) was King of the French from 1830 until 1848 when he abdicated and became an exile in England.
[2] Frederick III (1831-1888) husband of Victoria, Princess-Royal of Gt Britain.

she was and we discovered it was the Duchess of Kent[1] I always fancied she was very handsome but whether her remains were unbecoming or what it was I can't say, she certainly looked nothing but as a very good natured plain old woman.

Have you heard any news of Aunt Mary since she has been at Gravesend, I hope the air is doing her much good? I want to know if you have left off your mourning yet? If you still have the same wish to be in dark colours, think how drawn you would look seated on one of the red damask sofas in the drawing room in a sombre black velvet dress.

Edward is teaching me German and I am getting on capitally. I am reading the New Testament, so you see I am not quite idle. Tell Papa, with my best love that having [heard] so constantly we now think the only possible way for sure for him have [xxxxx] would have been to have carried them back with us in the carriage, or as Peter is such a clever man, I might have made him to change places with Edward.

I have been practicing on an old pianoforte in the room & when I get to Italy then I shall certainly have a music master.

I will finish now very much [xxxxxx] with my disjointed letter. I have been called away unexpectedly.

Goodbye dearest Mother, & special affectionate love for yourself, dear Papa, John, Basil, Richard etc.

Believe me, your ever devoted attached daughter,

Helen Denison

---

[1] Princess Victoria of Saxe-Coburg-Saalfeld (1786 –1861), German princess and mother of Queen Victoria of the United Kingdom. Her 2nd husband was Prince Edward, Duke of Kent (4th son of George III).

Letter to John Gaspard Fanshawe - brother

Baden Baden
July 9th (1844)

My dearest John,

We only arrived here last night at 9 o'clock, so I am reading your most truly welcome and interesting letters this morning for which I thank you many thousand thanks. I hope you have not been waiting long for an answer. Pray thank Mamma again for one from her, which I shall try and answer tomorrow, it is very good of her to write so often and such nice long letters. I did not expect you, dearest John would be able; I know how difficult it is to find time when one is moving about.

I am delighted to hear you have been enjoying yourself so much, I should indeed be delighted if I could see you all again and have a long chat. I have so much to hear and ask, and so much to say that it is useless to attempt getting it all in a letter.

I could not help laughing at the description you gave of poor Mrs Croft[1], it certainly was not flattering. I can just fancy you making such a speech – it is to [be] hoped Miss [Blunt/Blavett] will not repeat it.

I think my next John, will be to give you an account now of my travels and then move more fully into the various topics of your letters.

We enjoyed the week we remained at Frankfurt now; from any we have yet spent since we have been abroad, for besides being a very clean nice town with very pretty walks and drives all about, we met

---

[1] Charlotte Croft - 23 year old wife of Revd Richard Croft, Vicar of North Ockendon a parish about 5 miles from Dagenham. She was a daughter of close friends of HFD's parents - the Bramfill family of Upminster Hall and Stubbers.

there some English people, Mr & Mrs Potts a newly married couple. Edward has known him for the last fifteen years, he is excessively educated and so is she, and they were both very agreeable. They were always with us, or we with them. You have no idea what a peculiar charm anything English has… I often think of you all at dear old Parsloes and have many a longing to be with you all, it does seem such an immeasurable time since we parted.

To continue - we of course went to see the Statue of the Ariadne[1], it is perfectly beautiful - for <u>one</u> to attempt to describe it would be impossible. I was delighted with it and Edward has bought two prints of it.

There is a part of the town at Frankfurt which is the residence of the Jews and a more dirty detestable hole I never wish to be in. The mother of the Jewish family of the Rothchilds[2], a very old woman lives there in a dismal old wooden house, preferring to spend the remainder of her days where she has passed her life - to finishing her time in the splendid palace belonging to her son. I admire her feeling but I cannot approve of her taste, though I suppose she is blind to all the defects of her present dirty habitation.

We drove one afternoon to the Cemetery[3], it is beautifully kept and all the graves are very prettily adorned with wreathes and planted with flowers and very pleasing to see as it shows that the departed one is still fresh in the memory. It is a law in foreign countries that everybody should be removed from the town within four and twenty hours after death so there are rooms in the burial ground to place it, just large enough to contain the coffin and the[re]

---

[1] "Ariadne on the Panther" by Johann Heinrich von Dannecker (1758 – 1841).
[2] Frau Gutle (Schnapper) Rothchild (1753 – 1849).
[3] The historic St. Peter's Cemetery was closed in 1828 and replaced by the Frankfurt Main Cemetery adjacent to the two Jewish cemeteries.

suspended from the ceiling are five (bell) things like thimbles[1] in which they place the fingers. These communicate with a little bell so if there is the slightest breath in the body it causes the little bell to ring and so prevents a person being buried alive which might possibly happen where they are interned so soon.

We went to the Opera three times whilst we were at Frankfurt. The first pleased us much, the music and singing were good, but the two others were a regular <u>take on</u>. This is not the season for operas, from what the Potts [say] the best was at Wiesbaden[2], which we could not go to for we were only there a day and in the evening there was a Gala at the Kursaal[3] which we went to see. The dancing was very good and the music first rate. I longed to get up and have a waltz round and so did Edward but unfortunately I was not in dancing costume. If you had been with us you would have been dancing in a minute, the music was so good you could scarcely help getting up. There was nothing but waltzing, galloping (or galloppes) and the Polka[4] - which by the way, I want to know if you have learnt? Mamma tells me you have been at balls, so I conclude you have - the Polka seems now by the papers, to be quite a necessary accomplishment.

We left Frankfurt on Thursday afternoon and posted to Damstadt. It poured the whole way but we were delighted to see it and we were hoping all the time that you were also enjoying it[5]. The rain left off

---

[1] This macabre curiosity and many others seem to interest English tourists as the stories can be found in John Murray's guide books - as used by EHD.
[2] Since 829 AD, Wiesbaden 'the bathing place in the meadows' with thermal springs has attracted tourism and the city has become a celebrated spa resort.
[3] A public hall or building for the use of visitors at health resorts or spas - a casino.
[4] The Polka, originally a Bohemian folk dance was adapted and brought into the ballrooms at Prague about 1835. Its popularity then spread to Vienna and across all Europe – to arrive in London around 1840.
[5] In 1844, it is on record to have been unusually dry in UK and most of Europe during the months of May and June.

'...it is perfectly beautiful; for one to attempt to describe it would be impossible.'

Ariadne on the Panther

Johann Heinrich von Dannecker
(1758 – 1841)

Created between 1810 and 1814, Von Dennecker's marble masterpiece is one of the most important sculptures of the 19th century.

Frankfurt banker, Simon Moritz von Bethmann commissioned this marble version after seeing the model in terracotta. From 1816 it was shown to the public in a small museum in the banker's garden which became known as the Bethmann Museum and was the first purpose-built museum building in Frankfurt.

Visitors arrived from all parts of Europe, attracted as were Helen & Edward to 'The Ariadne'. In 1853 the building and park were sold to the city of Frankfurt but three years later Herr von Bethmann reopened his personal collection sited in a new annex to his family house. It was called the 'Ariadneum' and the Bethmann family donated that museum and collection to the city of Frankfurt in 1941.

In 1943 the 'Ariadne' suffered severe fire damage and restoration was not carried out until 1978 and today, Ariadne on the Panther' is in Frankfurt's 'Liebieghaus Sculpture Collection'

'I was delighted with it and Edward has bought two prints of it.'

'...the residence of the Princess Elizabeth, daughter of our James 1st and afterwards Queen of Bohemia and of Palatine; full of interest to us.'

'The Winter Queen'

'Hortis Palatinus', the baroque garden and 'Elizabeth Gate' ... gifts to delight a princess.

Frederick V had met Inigo Jones and the French engineer Salomen de Caus in England when planning such a garden with Henry, Prince of Wales. Those plans were abandoned when the young well-loved Prince died suddenly in 1612 but perhaps these lovely gifts from a new young husband to his wife, helped ease a loving sister's grief.

Princess Elizabeth Stuart, eldest daughter of King James I, married in 1613 - Frederick V, Elector of Palatine.
It was a political marriage but both were sixteen years old and mutually attracted.
Unfortunately their lives together were beset with difficulties caught up in the political and religious conflicts of central Europe.
Princess Elizabeth became a widow at thirty-six but had ten children… her youngest daughter Sophie, Electress of Hanover provides the Royal House of Windsor with their vital link to the lineage of the monarchs of the Stuart and Tudor dynasties.

'The mother of the Jewish family of the Rothchilds, a very old woman lives there...'

'Rothchild' were reputed to be the world's richest family in 1844. Their banking house was established during the 1760's in Frankfurt by Mayer Amschel Rothschild. Later he despatched his sons to London, Paris, Naples & Vienna where each developed his own business - well placed to take advantage of the political and economic 'stresses' and gains of their nation and city's events so that this family's wealth, astutely distributed over many generations has power and influence even today.

Gutle Rothchild had raised 10 children in the Judenstrasse and at the age of 91 was disinclined to move to the palatial home of her eldest son on Bockenheimerland Strasse. But mother and son had to meet and the spectacle of the elegant wife of Baron Amshel Rothchild in her carriage conveying the old lady back and forth was regular entertainment for her poor neighbours in the ghetto – whilst also attracting many tourists.

"Rothschild is the lord and master of the money markets of the world and virtually lord and master of everything else."
Benjamin Disraeli

"I paint as if I were Rothschild." Paul Cezanne

As Helen and Edward were travelling down the Rhine, the dance sensation from the East was moving swiftly through the ballrooms of Europe. It was only thirty years before that the waltz had revolutionised the way a respectable couple could hold and move together in dance but by 1844 young people were ready for the whirling and flying feet of the Polka!

'I expect to find you a most accomplished Polka dancer and shall certainly get you to teach me on my return. We could not muster up courage to take lessons...'

With origins in the folk dances of Bohemia, the Polka caused a sensation in Paris in 1840, when first performed as part of a stage production at the Odeon Theatre. After, 'Polka Mania' swept through the society ballrooms and by early 1844 it arrived in England - even young Queen Victoria was greatly taken up with learning all the steps. The detailed instructions for the turns and moves were quickly printed in magazines, as well as often humorous cautions concerning the 'footwork etiquette' to be heeded when 'polkaing' on a crowded dance floor.

In addition to dancing in the Kurhaus' of European spa cities, there was also gambling to beguile the unwary tourist...

'Wiesbaden during the bathing season, from June to the end of September' comprised of visitors 'of all ranks of the wealthier classes from every part of Europe'. In the principal saloon of the Kursaal are two roulette tables (unless on ball nights) and in the adjoining rooms, an equal number of Rouge et Noir tables. From 11 o'clock in the morning till 1 o'clock - during the entire evening, these centres of temptation, are encircled by an eager crowd of various classes, both sexes, all mute with attention to the chances and changes of the game; the silence broken only by the monotonous and oft recurring cry of *'faites votre jeu Messieurs'* or *'rouge gagne et la couleur perd'* uttered by the dealers... and the clink of the gold and silver coin'. *(Irish author)*

'...but is it not shocking to think that the gambling tables are the source of all their riches?'

by a little before eight o'clock so we walked about the town till it was dark - there was nothing particular to see…

In the morning it was raining again incessantly so we agreed to wait a little. About twelve o'clock it cleared up and we set off again, along the most beautiful road in the whole of Germany. We had incessant showers and at two o'clock it set in again, a regular heavy steady rain for which we were rather sorry as it somewhat destroyed the beauty of the scenery.

We reached Heidelberg in good time, it is the prettiest little town you can imagine, beautifully situated along the sides of the Neckar over which is built a very picturesque old bridge[1] and on the heights above the town are the remains of the old castle which was twice besieged by the French and at last was burnt. It was the residence of the Princess Elizabeth, daughter of our James 1st and afterwards Queen of Bohemia and of Palatine; full of interest to us.[2] It is still a very imposing building, you may imagine its strength, the walls are sixteen feet thick and the part which is in the best state of preservation consists of a strong [Palladian] façade with Grecian pilasters. The grounds are very nicely kept and command most lovely views. The entrance is through a very pretty archway built by Elizabeth's husband overnight to please her - and as a bookseller told us, a very pretty piece of gallantry on the part of her husband.

Heidelberg like Bonn is filled with students, on the whole they appear to be rakes[3], but still a very superior set of beings, they clearly are outlandish looking. They are forever fighting duals, a

---

[1] 'Alte Brűcke' - Old Bridge built in 1786 by Prince Elector Carl Theodor.
[2] Although it is probable that HFD's interest was general it is possible she knew her own family history in detail – and knew her direct ancestor Sir Henry Fanshawe (1576-1616) had been close to Henry, Prince of Wales, the much loved brother of Princess Elizabeth, who died so tragically in 1612, only weeks before her wedding.
[3] An immoral or dissolute person.

recent day paper has written they never generally turn out and only fight till they cut each other and bring blood. Almost every student we saw either had a tremendous gashed nose and wound or a cut lip or face[1]. They are some [strange] description of beings and most independent countenances, and stare you out insisting to see who comes worse off. Their great appetite of wine is drunk off, the one who downs in one draught and finishes this, receives a most beautiful pipe from the five or so other students who have lost, the same keeps with him. It was Peter's great amusement to come and tell us some extraordinary story about these men which had been told twice by the waiters at the different tables.

I am sure, my dearest John, I have taken up enough of my letter about myself, so I shall leave the rest of my travels for Mamma – which will be almost the same things, as you read her letters.

And now I shall ask you about yourself - I hope you have not suffered at all from your dissipation and have had no more nose bleeding and have got rid of your cough and cold. I do so often wish you could be with us, the climate is delightful. There is no damp and you may sit out till what hour you like - still it is quite dry. I have never had the slightest cold and am in excellent health – so is Edward.

I am very curious to know if you like <u>Miss Pele[2] as much as ever</u>. How long do you think Annie will remain there and do you know if she received the letters I wrote her from Antwerp, directed to Mrs Le M[archant] Thomas? Tell her when you write, I did not forget it

---

[1] The 'mensur' was a duelling scar seen as a badge of honour in upper class German and Austrian society from the early 19th century and it continued until WWI.
[2] Miss Pele was probably Miss Eliza Pell (1822 -1888) daughter of Sir Albert Pell and Hon. Margaret St. John, sister of their hostess at Billingbear. The young lady married Alexander Pym in 1847 and among their descendants are politicians who served recently in Conservative governments.

was her birthday on Sunday, we drank her health and wished her much happiness - and also all dear friends at Parsloes.

I shall try and write to you so that the letter may reach you on the 20th which will contain my congratulations on your having reached your twentieth birthday. I should dearly like to be with you and say all I wish and feel in person. You seem to have met some very agreeable people at Billingbear. Mr Vaughan[1] was always a favourite of yours. It was very curious your meeting Mrs P Duncombe[2] in the way you did. Jemima[3] tells us in her letter, she [Mrs Duncombe] is going with her husband to stay at Mr Foulis[4].

---

[1] 'Mr Vaughan' probably Margaret Vaughan's uncle, Sir Charles Richard Vaughan, GCH, PC, (1774 – 1849) a diplomat who travelled widely through Europe, the Middle East, Russia and America. He reported directly to the King regarding Washington and America. Palmerston considered him 'a steady sensible man, though not very showy'… He was unmarried, lived in Mayfair and on his death left detailed notes of his itineraries and remains a discreetly intriguing gentleman, fascinating at any time.

[2] Sophia Frances wife of Sir Philip Duncombe Pauncefort-Duncombe (1818 – 1890), who married during the summer of 1844 or maybe the lady was her mother-in law? The curiosity of the meeting lies in the fact that the Duncombe estate was at Brickhill, Buckingham – in the same neighbourhood as Edward's father at Stock Grove.

[3] Jemima Elizabeth Kershaw – daughter of EHD's elder half-brother William Kershaw. She was the same age as Helen and an official witness at her Uncle's marriage to HFD. Her own marriage to William Francis Oswell was during September 1849 at St Helen's Church, Bembridge, Isle of Wight.

[4] 'British History Online' relating to the estate of Brompton Hospital provides information of Henry Foulis connecting him to other guests at Billingbear: 'The problem was resolved in 1849 when a new benefactor appeared in the person of the Reverend Sir Henry Foulis, ninth baronet, of Ingleby Manor, Yorkshire, Prebendary of Lincoln and rector of Great Brickhill, Buckinghamshire. Foulis, who does not appear to have had any previous connexion with the hospital, offered to pay for a chapel to be built as a memorial to his recently deceased sister, Sophia Frances Pauncefort-Duncombe *(see ref. 2 above)*.

How fortunate you were to see the Races[1] this year where there were so many grandees. I should like to have seen the Emperor of Russia, he is not a sort of person one meets with every day. What did you think of him all the papers say he is a fine man?

I was very sorry to hear of poor Gassy's[2] disappointment, how much he must have been annoyed, as well as his parents – remember me to both when you see him as I suppose he will not return to England for several years. He is fortunate to going to a place with so good a climate.

I am all anxiety to get my next letter, I expect it will be full of news and good - I hope I shall hear of the sea side plan, Aunt <u>Caroline</u> and the <u>Queen</u>.

I thought of you all a good deal in Montem week. I knew it would be a very happy one to you as Oddy[3] was going! Does he like his private tutor[4] better? And how is Isabel[5] going on? Whenever you write give me as much home news as you possibly can however trivial it may appear to you, it will have the greatest interest to me.

---

[1] Royal Ascot.
[2] Gaspard Le Marchant Tupper (born 1826) first cousin to HFD - son of Anna Maria Le Marchant & Daniel Tupper - then a young Cadet in the Royal Horse Artillery, he was to be stationed in Bermuda. He had a long army career and retired as Lt. Commander.
[3] JGF's friend at Eton - Oswald A Smith, eldest son of Oswald Smith (1794 – 1863) of Blendon Hall, banker and politician whose third daughter Frances married Claude Bowes Lyons, 13th Earl Strathmore in 1853. Consequently, Oddy's niece was Lady Elizabeth Bowes Lyons, wife of Prince Albert, Duke of York - King George VI.
[4] Oddy admitted to Trinity College Cambridge in 1843 was presumably preparing for his matriculation success at Easter 1845.
[5] Isabella Smith - Oddy's eldest sister, married Cadogon Hodgson Cadogon in 1847.

I suppose you have met Grace De Lancy[1] and will soon be expecting Uncle Denis. I wrote to Aunt Eliza the other day and asked her to write if she will, then entirely forgot to tell her where to direct her letter. Will you, dearest John be kind enough to do so for me - Poste Restante, Geneva En Suisse – where we shall be, in about three weeks.

The name of the tailor is Binney & Richardson, Old Bond Street[2], on the left hand side going from Piccadilly.

How do you find the boys? I suppose they are delighted with the thoughts of Shrewsbury – give them my warmest love.

Have you heard anything of Mr Denison? He certainly is not fond of his pen for we have never had a line from him since we have been aboard and both Edward and I have written to him. Edward has not forgotten his long promised letter to you, he says he will write when he has a little more leisure in hand. Meantime we will be delighted to hear from you.

How I wish I were going to Parsloes instead of this letter, but I must conclude now with most affectionate love and many thanks for your kind letter - pray send me another soon, distribute plenty of love from myself and Edward to dearest Mamma & Papa, Basil & Richard.

God bless you dearest John, and believe me ever your most attached sister

Helen Denison

---

[1] Distant family member from Guernsey – possibly the wife of John De Lancy (born 1801) mentioned as a child in the letters of HFD's deceased grandfather, Major General John Gaspard Le Marchant.
[2] Binnie & Richardson, Tailor at 31 Old Bond Street, London.

Letter to Revd Thomas Lewis Fanshawe - father

Lucerne
July 19th (1844)

My Dearest Papa,

I found Mamma's most interesting & delightful letter at Zurich & should have written then to her, only she told me your quarters were to be begin at the end of the month. So I thought I would like to write to you before you left and as she told me once before, husband & wife were the same thing, it is all right.

Since I wrote from Coblenz, I have bought a fresh bottle of ink, so I hope you will not have such difficulty deciphering my letter. The fact was, the ink was very thick & I just used more water than I intended.

I must first congratulate you on taking up your quarters at Sea View[1]. I often think how much you must be enjoying yourselves & fancy I know the house in which you are staying for I recollect observing some nice ones when I passed Sea View last year with Helen & Uncle Lefevre, on our way to Ryde. Having the Bayliff's there at the same time must make the party very complete.

I was delighted to hear that Aunt Caroline[2] is quite safe, still it must be a great disappointment to her, the first child not living. I assure you I was quite in a fidget until I read Mamma's letter, less there should be any bad news.

---

[1] Sea View – a small quiet coastal town to the east of Ryde, Isle of Wight fashionable in early Victorian years – it has extensive views across the sea and the River Solent.
[2] Mrs Caroline (Le Marchant) Somerville was forty years old in 1844 and comments in these letters confirm her stillborn baby was her first child. Unfortunately, she no later children and on her death in 1876, her estate passed to her eldest sister, Helen's mother.

But now for ourselves, from Monday to Thursday we did nothing but sit in the carriage from the first thing after breakfast till the evening, waiting two hours in the middle of the day to rest the horses. There is no posting in Switzerland so we were obliged to hire a vetturino[1] at Basle and his four horses, which went from thirty to forty miles a day and went three or four an hour. Had the scenery not been extraordinarily beautiful I think we shall have been reduced to Martin and Peter's place of <u>quarrelling.</u> I do not think they can bare the sight of each other though it is only Martin that shows her dislike. At present she has made no certain complaint so I take no notice.

On Monday we went to Schaffhausen. It happened to be a most lovely evening and when we arrived the sun was setting and there was a most beautiful pink and sentry red, high over the tops and reached the distant Alps. I cannot describe to you my feelings of delight on first seeing these mountains. They did look so very grand and majestic [showing] their many heights one after another and losing themselves at last in the clouds. They are so sublime one can scarcely imagine them belonging to earth as at first sight they have the appearance of a border of flossy clouds floating along the horizon. I shall certainly conclude my first visit to the Alps as one of <u>the best epochs in my life.</u> I wish you could see them, you would be so ecstatic of delight – all the beauties of the Rhine dwindle down into nothing after being in Switzerland!

---

[1] 'the Voiturier of France, as well as the 'Vetturino' of Italy and the Lohnkutscher of Germany, is one who has a vehicle for hire, which he will drive in any direction, at any time, for any period, and at the best bargain that he can make, without the strict surveillance to which the post-system is subjected. The carriages usually appropriated to this purpose in France are a kind of cabriolet of a heavy and jolting construction. The charge for the hire is about eight or nine francs per day, exclusive of a small fee to the driver' - *'The Penny Magazine for the Society for the Diffusion of Useful Knowledge (1844) – Chas. Knight & Co. London.*

Then on again, what a splendid view we just had at Schaffhausen, for the hotel is situated on a hill and from our windows we looked over to the waterfalls and immediately behind in the distance was the beginning of the Alps. The falls are very fast from the volume of water, but the height is not great - they make a tremendous roar! We crossed the river to get near to them and then, went on to a sort of stage which has been hewed out within a few feet of the falls. It looks very awful when one gets so close - for indeed I did get a good soaking notwithstanding I was covered with a great mackintosh cloak and hood made on purpose. Directly Edward saw a great sheet of water coming he entered into the cover and I had to suffer for my play!

This was even before breakfast and then during the remainder of the day we sat in the carriage 'til we reached Zurich. There is nothing particularly worthy of notice in the town. What stirred my fancy most was seeing a man and woman parading through the streets, the woman dressed exactly like her companion (in man's clothes), a hat, a sort of loose brown frock-coat drawn in at the waist, trousers and wellingtons. I believe this is not the national costume.

Nothing can exceed the beauty of the lake on a fine evening at sunset, the banks and neighbouring hills are joined with a most lovely radiance and thickly dotted over with houses. The lake is a beautiful deep blue and the water so clear and [natural] that I could not help my thinking, if I must drown I would sooner be drowned in such a beautiful piece of water than any other.

We have been staying at Lucerne for two days but the weather is so bad and in view of that we have not been able to attempt going up the Rigi-Kulm[1]. It is now covered in the clouds and what little can be

---

[1] Rigi, known as 'Queen of Mountains' between Lakes Lucerne, Zug & Lauerz and at the high point gives a panoramic view of Lake Lucerne and the Alps.

seen of it looks very black and [forbidding] - perhaps it will be fine tomorrow.

I think we shall go on to Zurich - Edward, myself and Peter up over the mountains and leaving Martin to follow by the diligence with the luggage and then we must ascend the Rigi when we return to Lucerne at the end of our Swiss tour. The lake of Lucerne is considered the most beautiful but as yet we have only been able to see a small part.

We heard from Mr & Mrs Bayliff at Zurich, they do not give us any news, except they are much pleased at having you such near neighbours and how Basil & Richard are learning to swim. I have no doubt they are in the height of their enjoyment - tell Basil I wish him joy on having gained the prize, it must be a great satisfaction to him & I hope he will gain many more.

I was most interested in Mamma's account of Hewett's wedding, I quite agree with her, I think the arrangements would have been much more agreeable for the friends, than for the bride and bridegroom.

I hope Aunt Mary[1] is getting on better at Woolwich, she does not appear to have been free from cold since she has been in England. I should be very glad to hear that the fine bracing air of the countryside had done her good.

John, I suppose is now at Blendon[2] consoling Oddy on the loss of his brother[1].

---

[1] Mary (Le Marchant) Gostling, wife of Lt Col. Thomas Gostling 9th Batt. Royal Artillery apparently remained at Woolwich until at least 1851 (Census). During the Crimean War, Colonel Gostling was stationed in Malta with 'Aunt Mary' who provided a place for convalescence for Helen's brother Basil following his illness at Sebastopol.

[2] Blendon Hall, Bexley, Kent.

I have just been calculating and find that this letter will scarcely reach you before you leave Sea View so I shall direct it to Parsloes.

Edward heard from his father this morning, he encountered Uncle Denis[2] and Uncle Tom[3] having dined & passed one night at Stockgrove and seemed to have enjoyed their visit much. He is quite well & very busy commencing some writing respecting the murder of a keeper at Brickhill[4].

Mamma tells me the roses there have been beautiful. I should so like to have seen them for though those we have seen abroad have been nice heady ones & they certainly do grow most luxuriantly - still anything at dear old Parsloes had a most peculiar charm for me. I often look forward with the sincerest pleasure of returning to my old home and meeting all my dearest friends again. Christmas will certainly see me in England again.

I enclose you a list*[5] of all the places we will be going to see in Switzerland - they are all in order. The only expedition which I think shall very probably not be accomplished is the one to Neuchatel[6].

There are such handsome little cows here, some of them very like Alderney[7] has and I wish I could send you over one: I think you

---

[1] Hugh Smith, a younger brother of Oswald Smith - died at the age of two.
[2] Sir Denis Le Marchant - then Under-Secretary of State for the Home Department.
[3] Lt. Col. Thomas Le Marchant. A younger uncle serving in the 7th Regiment, Dragoon Guards. Later, as Colonel, he was the Assistant Military Secretary at Nova Scotia.
[4] The murder of a gamekeeper on the Stockgrove estate in 1836.
[5] Not retained with the letters.
[6] Neuchatel – on the shores of Lake Neuchatel, close to the Jura Mountains.
[7] Alderney cows were a separate breed until 1940 when with the prospect of imminent German occupation almost the entire stock was moved to Guernsey. Unfortunately, they were then inter-bred with Guernsey's own stock and the 'Alderney' became extinct. Today they exists only in memory through poems of A. A. Milne and other literary references.

'Blendon Hall' Bexley

Oswald Augustus Smith, and John Fanshawe registered at Eton in 1841 and as friends would have been able to visit each other's family estates north and south of the River Thames using local ferry connections.

As the letters show, each knew the other's family and 'Oddy' the older brother of his family was naturally upset when a sibling died but possibly particularly when the child dying in 1844 was Hugh, born only two years before when another brother Harry had died at the age of five.

Bell's Life in London and Sporting Chronicle *8 September 1844*

The tankard for the winning team with the score book were retained by the family until 2019 when sold at Sotheby's as part of an estate collection - the portrait of 'Oddy' shown above was also in the sale.

John and Oddy were more than school friends - they shared family connections through the brothers of Mrs Fanshawe who were linked to, Oddy's father. Oswald Smith was a member of the Smith banking family (founded 1658) and a partner in Smith, Payne & Smith (later merged into RBS).

The family enjoyed an extremely comfortable lifestyle and indulged a passion for cricket with an annual match between Blendon Hall and May Place - a fixture where local, family and business society mingled.

'There are such handsome little cows here, some of them very like Alderney¹ has and I wish I could send you over one...'

...enjoying the youthful simplicity which could speak with so much exultation of Mrs. Martin's having "two parlours, two very good parlours, indeed; one of them quite as large as Mrs. Goddard's drawing-room; and of her having an upper maid who had lived five-and-twenty years with her; and of their having eight cows, two of them Alderneys...

'Emma' Jane Austin (1815)

...An old lady had an Alderney cow, which she looked upon as a daughter. You could not pay the short quarter of an hour call without being told of the wonderful milk or wonderful intelligence of this animal...

"Cranford" Elizabeth Gaskell (1851-53)

'The Kings Breakfast'
...The King asked
The Queen, and
The Queen asked
The Dairymaid:
"Could we have some butter for
The Royal slice of bread?"
The Queen asked
The Dairymaid
The Dairymaid
Said, "Certainly,
I'll go and tell
The cow
Now
Before she goes to bed."
The Dairymaid
She curtsied,
And went and told
The Alderney:
"Don't forget the butter for
The Royal slice of bread."
The Alderney
Said sleepily;
"You'd better tell
His Majesty
That many people nowadays
Like marmalade
Instead"...

A.A.Milne (1924)

The gentle and docile Alderney cow has become extinct - removed to Guernsey in 1940 during German occupation they were interbred. Only through literature can we now imagine the taste of the Alderney's sweet milk.

'Edward heard from his father this morning ...& very busy commencing some writing respecting the murder of a keeper at Brickhill.'...

Joseph Denison, the tenant at Stockgrove House, near Leighton Buzzard was intrigued by an infamous crime that took place on the estate in 1836 whilst the owner Colonel Henry Hanmer JP & MP was resident.

The morning after 19th August 1836, James Giltrow, the Colonel's gamekeeper was found bludgeoned to death. From evidence left at the scene the alleged perpetrator was quickly arrested and questioned. A coroner's inquest followed and the suspect was charged with 'Wilful Murder' and committed for trial. He confessed to have been 'night poaching' and being scared when caught by the gamekeeper who he tried unsuccessfully to convince to let him go. In the struggle that followed, he struck him with the stock of his gun and becoming out of control bludgeoned the gamekeeper until he was almost unrecognizable.

The judge offered no leniency and 23 year old, Thomas Bates was hung at Aylesbury Prison on 31st March 1837.

Persons taking or destroying Game by Night to be committed for the 1st Offence, for 3 Months, and kept to hard Labour, and to find Sureties;

During the 18th and early 19th century poachers were a major concern to landowners. The Game Reform Act of 1831 opened the possibility of annual licences for game hunting to those without land, but night poaching persisted despite the Night Poaching Act of 1828 - passed to avoid the type of circumstance as occurred at Brickhill - *'whereas the practice of going out by night for the purposes of destroying game has very much increased of late years, and has in very many instances led to the commission of murder and of other grievous offences and it is expedient to make more effective provisions than now exist by law for repressing such practice...'*

The act remains in force today; prohibiting night poaching - the taking and destroying game (hares, pheasants, partridges, grouse, heath and moor game, black game and bustards).

The original provisions of the Act included punishment up to transportation, dependent upon the number of previous offences.

2d Offence, 6 Months, and kept to hard Labour, and to find Sureties;

3d Offence, to be liable to Transportation,

'Uncle Denis'

Sir Denis Le Marchant, 1st Baronet (1795 – 1874). Barrister, civil servant, writer and Whig politician. Held the appointment of Clerk to the House of Common from 1850 to 1871.

Lord Palmerston addressing the House Of Commons during the debates on the Treaty of France in February 1860

would admire them so much. By the way, how has your new Guernsey cow[1] turned out and have you been making any alterations within the farm or garden?

The wild flowers and the list of plants you sent are almost here in reality. We have seen very fine Irideae[xxxxx] [2] and the Convolvulus[3] grows in the open air on the banks, to perfection.

We have always honey at breakfast and tea and generally it is very good, but the Swiss seem to use nothing but the ambrosia[4].

Having been to the scene of William Tell's[5] exploits, adds much to the interest - just opposite to the right is Mount Pilatus[6], it is very lofty and grand and the summit is a point in a lake, in which tradition says that Pontius Pilate ended his miserable existence by throwing himself into it.

I do hope you are having finer weather. More than we have here, it was most incapacitating for the last fortnight. It is perfectly useless attempting to see anything as long as it continues.

---

[1] Guernsey cows - a placid and docile dairy bred larger than the Alderney.
[2] Within the species Iris - due to the season those seen were possibly gladioli.
[3] The family of Convolvulaceae has 1000 species including invasive bindweed. In the Victorian era the most popular was a cultivated variety 'Morning Glory' with vivid blue trumpet-shaped flowers.
[4] Ambrosia - bee pollen or bee bread with high nutrient content is valued by herbalists. These balls of pollen gathered by field worker honeybees are introduced to the hive as the primary food source.
[5] The 'Exploits' of William Tell took place on and around Lake Lucerne but Altdorf was his home town, to the south of the lake where his statue was raised in 1895.
[6] Several peaks overlooking Lake Lucerne form the Massif Pilatus and the highest is Tomlishorn (2,128m). The legend told by Helen is one of many but the name might only relate to the word 'pileatus', meaning 'cloud-topped'.

I hope you will find everything flourishing at Lancashire[1] and your visit to Southampton will afford you much enjoyment. Pray remember us to Mr De Jersey[2] and Edward desires to be particularly remembering to Carey De Jersey – he has not forgotten his hospitality to him last summer.

What a pleasant little addition Mrs [-] has had to her [-], I trust it is not to be despised these days, I assure you, I am learning the value of money for I have only had three batz[3] (half a franc) since I left England!!!

(My dear husband Edward wants to make some slight remarks of his own and has begged me to leave a short space for him to add a few lines) - Pray tell Mama with most affectionate love that I quite agree with her that if ever there was a good woman she is one who can go faster than no man, for I have no doubt on the subject. Tell her a thousand thanks for her long and most necessary letters - she does not know how much I value them - I shall write to her in the next place where we stop.

Will you also tell Basil and Richard that though I should be delighted to hear from them, I hope they will not let it interfere in their holiday, sea wishes and any of their pleasures. They had better make the most of their time by being out of doors!

I am very glad to hear Uncle Tom is so well, give him my love and Edward's – and has Mr Baugh joined your party at Seaview? And what has become of Uncle Henry all this time – is he quite well?

---

[1] Wyersdale is the Fanshawe property in Lancashire, often referred to as 'the Northern estate'.
[2] Guernsey family related to Mrs Fanshawe through Mary Carey, her mother.
[3] Batzen - the old coinage of many Swiss Cantons was replaced in 1850 by the Swiss Franc.

Goodbye, dearest Papa and with most affectionate love to yourself, dearest Mama, John, Basil, Richard and all, in which Edward unites! Believe me, ever dearest Papa

Your most devotedly attached daughter

Helen Denison

Letter to Revd Thomas Lewis Fanshawe – from Edward Hanson Denison (written across Helen's previous letter…)

Lucerne
July 19th (1844)

My Dear Vicar

I sincerely hope that this will find you as well as it leaves us. I only wish you were with us to enjoy this prince of countries and this summer Paradise – except by the way when it <u>rains </u>as it has done for a day and a half without ceasing – but that is not much like Paradise, I will own! Switzerland in rainy weather is just like what I remember of the miserable appearance of Vauxhall[1] on a wet night. But I now take up my pen under better auspices.

Today we have had a glorious day and tomorrow we resume our wanderings in earnest. We leave our carriage here for it is as much of the same use in this country as a hide jacket to a 'toad' or knee buckles[2] to a highlander and we mean to scramble over this country (I could I am certain), and if Helen only started the riding over the hills as well as she has done the travelling hitherto, I anticipate a delightful trip.

I wish you had seen her when she first caught sight of the Alps. I thought she would have jumped out of the carriage with delight and immediately began to confess her firm determination to <u>walk over several of the highest</u> (as her Aunt Caroline did according to her words) over Mount Blanc, one fine afternoon. I have searched for some mention of the ascent among the various accounts given, but without success, so perhaps you will be kind enough to throw some light upon this for me?

---

[1] Vauxhall Pleasure Gardens, on the south bank of the Thames were by this time in decline but remained a major venue for outdoor public entertainment.
[2] Ornamental buckles were worn just below the knee to fasten knee breeches.

Of course, I shall trudge on foot with my staff and wallet like the Pilgrims of old, but shall take care to have something better than peas dry or boiled in it, and I dare say if the truth were known they had often a sly duck[1] with their green peas - like the Eton boys (and probably frizzed into the bargain, also like the Eton boys). And small blame to the Pilgrims - if they did not, they were greener than their peas, that's all I can say!

I should have wanted to have spun you a long yarn, but you will allow that is impossible – Helen having after the true female fashion, wrote this book like a casting net or a spider's web but I promise to send you one, one of these fine days or rather I ought to say these wet days, & in the meantime –

My dear Sir - wishing you all health, happiness & with my kind love to Mrs Fanshawe, Basil & my little friend Dickey,
I remain your affectionate son-in-law

E H Denison

Helen wants you to send Miss Farquaharson's address.

---

[1] Late in the 18th and early 19th century the boys at Eton are recorded as holding unauthorised Duck Hunts with the aid of local fishermen.

Letter to Mrs Catherine Fanshawe - mother

Vevey
August 13th 1844

[opens without formal greeting]

I have just despatched a letter to John, but still I cannot delay a day dearest mother to thank you for the four most delightfully interesting letters we received last night on Capt. Thompson's return from Geneva. It really is uncommonly good of you writing me such long letters when you are away from home, but if you only knew the value I set on them I think you would say your time was not thrown away.

How I shall enjoy thinking over of you in Helen's[1] circle and hearing of all that has happened since I left.

I fear I shall not be as good hand at telling stories but still, it will be a great pleasure to relate all that has interested us. I shall be able to furnish you with plenty of employment in arranging our proposed album and it will be doubly pleasant if you assist me dearest mother. We intend making a large addition to our collection when we go to Geneva.

I am so very glad you enjoyed the Sea View excursion. Altogether it seemed to have turned out most agreeable and having the Lefevres and Bayliffs with you must have rendered the party most complete. I only wish we could have been amongst the numbers but I hope when we return we shall often share in such other enjoyments.

I hope you have found your wedding ring. I can quite listen into your feelings of not liking to have another, but should you not be so fortunate as to find it I trust you will pass as many happy years with Papa in your new ring as you have in your old one.

---

[1] HFD's first cousin - Helen Shaw Lefevre.

Many thanks for all your very affectionate wishes, at present I have been as happy as any human mortal I think can ever be!

We are now detained at Vevey[1] by the weather; it is so unsettled, rain every day and 'till it changes it is useless our attempting to go to Champéry[2]. The tops of the mountains are lost in the clouds and the lake is such perturbed one might really fancy it was the styx[3]. It is in my opinion far the most beautiful of the lakes we have yet seen, there is such an expanse of water and such a lovely colour.

We all went the other afternoon to see the Castle of Chillon[4]; it has nothing in itself worthy of attention, except from the interest of Lord Byron's lines excites. You will perhaps think I am growing sentimental but the first time I read his 'Prisoner of Chillon'[5] I could have sat down and cried, I thought the feelings so very beautifully described. Lord Byron is now my constant companion and now one can even better appreciate the beauties of Childe Harold[6], having a true image before one.

Vevey is a very pretty place and the hotel is one of the best we have stayed in since we left England. We have not yet been on the lake, for from the frequent storms which come on very quickly it is rather dangerous in a small boat. I am very anxious to go to Geneva that

---

[1] Vevey - on the northern shore of Lake Geneva, close to Lausanne.
[2] Champéry a picturesque village with old traditional Swiss chalets popular with early tourists, situated at the foot of the Dents du Midi.
[3] Ancient Greek legend of the River of the Styx, the boundary between earth and the underworld.
[4] On the Island of Chillon, Lake Geneva.
[5] Lord Byron's celebrated poem, written whilst staying at Ouchy, close to Lausanne during 1816.
[6] 'Childe Harold's Pilgrimage' - Byron's semi-autobiographical poem in four parts published 1812 -1818.

we may have a view of Mont Blanc[1] – when I have seen that I shall be really satisfied! How I wish you could see some of the magnificent scenery in Switzerland. If you were delighted with Black Gang Chine[2], I am sure you would be enchanted with some of the fine and elegant waterfalls which abound in this country.

Although the scenery is lovely and there is so much that clarity and honesty creates amid recreation, still I cannot tell you how happy I shall be to return to old England and meet all my friends again. Dearest Mother, travelling is very pleasant but there is no place like home!

You will see by my letter to John that we have joined the Thompsons and like them very much. He is a great huntsman[3] in Yorkshire, she is a most ladylike agreeable person and would I am sure just suit your fancy. They have asked us to pay them a visit when we go into Lancashire, which we shall be very glad to do.

I have been reading and re-reading your letters all this morning and really I hardly know where to begin. I have so much to say – I am very glad you went to some places that I had seen as I can actually imagine you in the parks that afforded me much pleasure and is just the place for the boys.

I am surprised to hear Basil has taken such a fancy to the sea. I should rather thought it was much to Richard's taste, give him my

---

[1] Mont Blanc - highest mountain in the Alps and of Western Europe that straddles the borders between Switzerland, France and Italy.
[2] Staying at Seaview during the summer of 1844, Helen's family must have visited this newly opened 'theme park' - a steep coastal ravine on the southern point of the Isle of Wight, opened the previous year. Now UK's oldest 'theme park' it was originally, viewed as a health resort. With the winding, sloping pathways through landscaped gardens there was then another attraction displayed that would have delighted Helen's younger brothers – the bones of a whale.
[3] Several men from the Yorkshire family of Thompson were then noted riders, owners and members of the Yorkshire Union Hunt Club formed in 1835.

'Castle of Chillon – it has nothing in itself worthy of attention, except from the interest of Lord Byron's lines'

'... Lake Leman lies by Chillon's walls:
A thousand feet in depth below
Its massy waters meet and flow;
Thus much the fathom-line was sent
From Chillon's snow-white battlement,
Which round about the wave inthralls:
A double dungeon wall and wave
Have made—and like a living grave
Below the surface of the lake
The dark vault lies wherein we lay:
We heard it ripple night and day;
Sounding o'er our heads it knock'd;
And I have felt the winter's spray
Wash through the bars when winds were high
And wanton in the happy sky;
And then the very rock hath rock'd,
And I have felt it shake, unshock'd,
Because I could have smiled to see
The death that would have set me free...'
Extract: Prisoner of Chillon (1816)

Lord Byron was staying at the Villa Diodati on the shores of Lake Geneva during the wet summer of 1816 when he befriended Percy Bysshe Shelley and his future wife Mary Godwin. They were trapped indoors by the rain, where they read and came to imagine fantastic stories. Byron, intrigued by the story of the imprisonment of a 16th century monk Francois Bonivard in nearby Castle of Chillon, wrote his famous poem of that title. He also worked on 'Childe Harold's Pilgrimage' ...whilst Mary, known by her married name Shelley, created her 'Frankenstein'.

'You are a nice young gentleman,
I don't think...
As Mr Bailey Whilom of 'Todgers' would have expressed it '

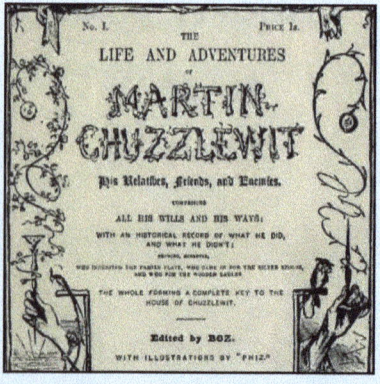

Edward's good sense of humour as seen in his notes and post scripts must have been greatly appreciated by his younger brothers-in-law.

This obvious family joke relating to 'Todgers' from Charles Dicken's novel 'Martin Chuzzlewit' could only have been started after December 1842 when the first of the 19 parts became available.

Edward possibly first entered the Fanshawe circle about that time and his lively urbane humour would have been appreciated by his new young relatives-to-be.

Edward & Helen were married and abroad when the last serialised part was issued in July 1844, but the 'catchphrase' remained in their conversation as they remembered happy family evenings at Parsloes when all took turns to read aloud with Edward probably intoning Bailey's cockney vowels.

If you read the peculiarly spectacular capers acted out by Bailey at Todgers'...you will easily imagine their laughter.

very affectionate love and tell him how much obliged I am for his letter. I shall certainly write to them the first opportunity. I hope they will like Shrewsbury, I have no doubt they will be happy when they are once settled.

I am very glad to hear such good accounts of Aunt Caroline and Aunt Tupper[1] in the letter I received from Aunt Mourant – she gave me a very full and particular account of Aunt C's poor baby she said with a most striking resemblance of its father, even the hair was the same colour and she wished the parents would have seen it. Pray give my love to them all when you write and also to Aunt Eliza, with many thanks for her kind letter which I hope to answer soon.

You would be highly amused with some of the people one meets abroad at the table d'hote. There is one <u>Viennese</u> woman staying at this hotel with her children, she has just married a second time and is expecting another. She comes to dinner every day with a fan which she uses frequently and she tries to look delicate, but as long as she retains her appetite and is so fat I do not think she will excite much pity.

There is also a little girl here who has fallen in love with her cousin and it is the most amusing thing possible to watch her. She does nothing but look in his eyes all dinner time and sigh while he does not care or attend about her one thought.

There are a great number of English abroad this year, there do not seem to be a very great number of ladies and gentlemen.

---

[1] This was an unfortunate situation involving two sisters of Mrs Fanshawe for Caroline who married late, delivered her only child presumably stillborn and at about the same time, Anna Maria safely delivered her eighth child (seven survived to adulthood).

With an air of melancholy - recent is the deaths of Lord Euston[1] and also of the death of the daughter of Lady Leicester[2], her happiness has indeed been of short duration.

It must be a very great relief to you that Aunt Mary has seen Dr Chambers[3]. Mrs Thompson places implicit confidence in him, for after having had the most wretched health for years he quite set her up and now she is as fit and strong as possible. I certainly hope he will be equally successful with Aunt Mary. It is a great comfort to hear that there is nothing the matter with her heart or lungs.

I am very glad you find Annie Lefevre[4] so much improved, she always promised to have the most pleasing manners. Poor Helen's delight must be great to be released from Mr Lindsberg[5] and I hope she is soon enjoying herself at Parsloes, give them all my love.

I laughed very much at your account of Mr Roberts' fright at the idea of sailing at Sea View in the small boat. I think you really right to have been in the party, there must have been so much amusement. You must be quite glad that Mr Baugh[6] has at last accepted the preachership at the Charterhouse as you may still look

---

[1] George Henry Fitzroy, 4th Duke of Grafton (1760 - 1844) continued to use his lesser title Lord Euston after succeeding to the dukedom as before his elevation to the House of Lords, he was a Whig M.P. Whilst at Cambridge he had been a student with his close friend William Pitt the younger. His wife was Lady Charlotte Waldegrave, of Navestock, Brentwood whom he married in 1784 at the old village church.

[2] Lady Anne Keppel (1803 – 1844) 2nd wife of Thomas William Coke, 1st Earl of Leicester - known as 'Coke of Holkham Hall' (1754 – 1842).

[3] The leading physician in London, William Frederick Chambers, KCH (1786–1855) was 'physician in ordinary' to King William IV and Queen Victoria.

[4] Helen's cousin, Anna Maria Shaw Lefevre (baptised Dagenham 1830), daughter of Helen Le Marchant & Henry Shaw Lefevre.

[5] Lindsberg was possibly a tutor or teacher. After their mother died, Helen and her sisters were boarded at school where they were unhappy. Helen left Miss Fryers' school 'The Cedars' in Hammersmith in 1844 when she was 16.

[6] Rev. Foillett Baugh (b.1820), Vicar of Ilford, appointed Preacher at Charterhouse.

upon him as a neighbour and possibly see more of him than you did when he was still at Ilford. Pray remember me kindly to him when you see him. Who is likely to take his place?[1]

I heard from Minnie Carey[2] who tells me they like their new sister Maud more as they know her better, she appears to be extremely amiable and she talks of going to Guernsey for a few days with Caroline and the newly married couple as Aunt Eliza has postponed her visit to the Island for another year. I hope your wish will at last be gratified and that you may then be able to accompany them.

I am surprised you did not find time improved by Miss Masson's instructions, but as you always say it is easier to begin right at first than to unlearn. Your system, there is no doubt is by far the best.

You don't know how pleased I was to see your letters sealed without wax. I quite agree with Papa that it would be dreadfully dismal to have ones wife always draped in black. Poor Mr Le Marchant[3] does indeed seem to be always unfortunate with his children, but I hope the change of air will save his daughter's life.

How is Mrs Moss[4], is there any chance of her recovery?

---

[1] Baugh's successor - Rev'd the Hon Henry W Bertie, Vicar of Great Ilford for 37 years.
[2] As yet unidentified from these 'nicknames' – possibly the new wife of Hewett Carey was 'Maud' from her second name Martha - all are almost certainly connected to Major General Octavius Carey.
[3] The brothers of Mrs Fanshawe were always addressed as Uncle, therefore 'Mr' Le Marchant could only have been one of her many cousins of some degree with shared Guernsey heritage.
[4] The Moss family purchased The Three Mills at Chadwell Heath in 1841 and soon became well established in the parish community. Mrs Anna Moss died in April 1845 at the age of 38 - her funeral took place at St. Peter & St. Paul Church, Dagenham with presumably the Revd T L Fanshawe officiating.

Will you tell John that I have just discovered Col. Thompson is a very old friend of Mr Oswald Smith's? He has known him for years but has seen not so much of him since Mr S's marriage[1].

I have heard from Jemima twice since we have been abroad and that is quite as often as I have any right to expect, considering I have only written to her once and Edward wrote half the letter. I assure you it is very difficult always to find time, especially in Switzerland where the weather is so uncertain that we are obliged to take advantage of every fine moment. No wonder everything looks so fresh when there is rain every other day! The pomegranates[2] (I don't know if it is rightly spelt) flower most abundantly and look so remarkably bright and jaunty; I shall try and get some seeds of some plants in Italy or in France.

Martin, I am sorry to say has not pleased me very much lately and from several things I have heard she is not all she professes to be. She is as thoughtless as any child of three or four years old and the greatest dawdler that ever existed. She and Peter have dreadful squabbles and the most extraordinary change must take place before they ever think of matrimony. I have not the slightest intention of keeping Martin on when we return and I am quite sure from the little experience I have had, that I should much prefer having an English maid about me.

From what Annie says in her letter, I suppose she is staying with you now, pray give her my best love and tell her I will write and

---

[1] Oswald Smith (1794–1863) was married in 1824 to Henrietta Mildred Hodgson (1804-1891).
[2] This exotic fruit was introduced into England during the 18th century but with little success as it only normally grows in Europe around the Mediterranean Sea and not north of the Alps. Excavation at the site of a Roman camp at Vindonissa, Switzerland in 1996 found fragments of pomegranate seeds in storage barrels.

Royal Visitors to the United Kingdom in 1844

Frederick Augustus II, King of Saxony stayed a short time at the Hotel Bel Vue in Brussels. He was 'en route' for England from Dresden making a private visit accompanied only by his personal physician.

He stayed at Windsor as a guest of Queen Victoria & Prince Albert while enjoying some of Society's summer events. He also made visits to Lyme Regis, Oxford, and Cambridge before leaving for the Highlands of Scotland, mostly travelling incognito.

The Highlands received another European royal visitor that year - Prince Frederick, Crown Prince of Denmark. Arriving on the Danish royal yacht at Leith he then travelled via Edinburgh to the Highlands – and on to the Faroe Islands for a geological tour.

At a similar time, Nicholas I Emperor of Russia arrived in London - his visit was not a private visit but a full state visit carried out with all pomp and ceremony.

'How fortunate you were to see the Races this year where there were so many grandees. I should like to have seen the Emperor of Russia, he is not a sort of person one meets with every day. What did you think of him, all the papers say he is a fine man?'

'On the 6th we went with the Emperor and King to the races, and I never saw such a crowd; again here the reception was most brilliant. Every evening a large dinner in the Waterloo Room…
I got to know the Emperor and he to know me. There is much about him which I cannot help liking, and I think his character is one which should be understood, and looked upon for once as it is. He is stern and severe—with fixed principles of duty which nothing on earth will make him change; very clever I do think him, and his mind is an uncivilised one; his education has been neglected; politics and military concerns are the only things he takes great interest in; the arts and all softer occupations he is insensible to, but he is sincere, I am certain…'
                Victoria R. 'Letter to King of the Belgians' – 11 June 1844

Queen Victoria and her ministers laid on lavish entertainment for the state visit of the Russian Czar who staying at Windsor Castle, also enjoyed the company of the King of Saxony. Newspapers reported how Prince Albert, acting on behalf of his wife, carried out the formalities of meeting and greeting the visiting monarchs. A highlight of the visits was Royal Ascot - truly a sport for Kings when on the first day, unaccompanied by Queen Victoria, the three princely gentlemen, attended the races. They were greeted with great cheers - popularly reported in newspapers and recorded in the Annual Register.

The good King of Saxony remains another week with us, and we like him much. He is so unassuming. He is out sight-seeing *all* day, and enchanted with everything.'   11 June 1844
'Our kind and good King of Saxony leaves us to-morrow, after having seen more than anybody has done almost, and having enjoyed it of all things. He is quite at home with us and the children, whom he plays with much.'
Victoria R ' Letters to King of Belgians'   18 June 1844

thank her very shortly. She seems to have been enjoying herself excessively but as usual she abounds in adventures.

I shall go on with my German - and my frame hall chair, I was obliged to leave at Lucerne as we brought as few things as possible, but when I get to Italy I hope to make great progress.

Will you tell me when you write how Aunt Margaret is and her family? I have not heard a word about them since we left so I concluded they must be quite well.

Mind you wear the Polka[1], I am delighted to hear you are getting a little fatter, I shall hope to see you growing quite a <u>corpulent woman</u> when we meet!

I fear this is a very stupid letter but I don't like to tell you everything, else I shall have nothing to advise you when we sit by the fireside - how I wish that time were come!

Goodbye, dearest Mother and with a thousand thanks for your precious letters which are my great delight and with a very large portion of love for yourself, dearest Papa, John, Basil and Richard.

Believe me, ever dearest mother your affectionate daughter

Helen Denison

PS. Don't forget to tell me if you found your wedding ring. God Bless you dearest Mamma!

Edward unites with me in best love to all and many thanks for your kind and interesting letters.

---

[1] Red flannel - a cholera belt, usually a flat strip of flannel (mostly red) or knitted wool about six feet long and six inches wide, worn as a precautionary measure against chills to the abdomen.

Letter to John Gaspard Fanshawe - brother

Lucerne
September 8th (1844)

Dearest John,

We only arrived here yesterday coming by the diligence[1] and are off again by 7 o'clock tomorrow morning to Zurich on our way over the Splugen[2].

So, I have only the time this evening to thank you and dear Mamma for your most affectionate and interesting letters. Which I do most heartily - and only wish I could say all I feel in person but that I hope to do in a very few months and am like yourself, counting the days till my return to dear old Parsloes. I shall have so much to hear and so much to say!

I am delighted you have all been enjoying yourselves so much and are quite well. Your visit to Blendon has I hope, been quite as happy and pleasant as you expected.

We are both of us as well as possible and enjoy this beautiful weather much. It is more settled now than it has been the whole time since we have been in Switzerland. I am by no means sorry to be leaving this country as far as the people are concerned, for a more disobliging, mercenary cheating set never existed. The Germans are infinitely preferable on many accounts and I really think they are the cleanest of the two nations.

Many thanks, dearest John for the interesting account you gave me of your gay doings at Billingbear though I am afraid you must have

---

[1] A solidly built coach with four or more horses - French stagecoach or public conveyance.
[2] The old mountain pass that connects the Hinterrhein valley and Splügen in Switzerland to the Valle Spluga and Chiavenna in Italy.

been up very late to have entered into the particulars of so many days amusements.

For fear I should be pressed for time as I shall have to rise by what hour in the morning, I will begin at once and tell you what we have been doing.

After our return from Champéry (how I wished you could have seen Mont Blanc) we remained a few days longer at Geneva - saw Miss Burdett Coutts[1] who stayed at our hotel two days and then went on to Lausanne.

The day before we left, Mr & Mrs Thompson went by the first steamer to pay a visit to a friend's who lived higher up the lake and were to have come on with us in the afternoon. But the N. E wind (what they call here the Bise[2] set in and it was so enough that one steamer was obliged to put in and the other did not come, so they had to find their way back as they best could. The next day the wind subsided and the lake from being as rough as the sea, became as smooth as a mill pond and we all set off together.

We only remained one day at Lausanne but we drove about the country, saw many remarkably pretty country houses to let and were very much professed in favour of the place. The next day we posted to Neuchatel, where on a clear day there is a very fine view of the Alps - and the following morning we posted from the Thompsons - to our infinite regret, for we never liked any people better! You would like them exceedingly, Colonel Thompson is full

---

[1] Angela Georgina Burdett-Coutts, 1st Baroness Burdett-Coutts (1814 – 1906) - a great philanthropist. She became one of the wealthiest women in England on inheriting £1.8 million in 1837 on the death of her grandfather, Thomas Coutts, the banker.
[2] 'La Bise' the cold, dry wind blowing through the Swiss Plateau from N.E to S.W. that occurs when pressure is built between the Jura mountains and the Pre-Alps, then blows over the western end of Lake Geneva.

of fun and used to amuse us the whole evening with some most absurd stories, his wife is still pretty and has been in particular, very agreeable and most amiable. I was with her from morning till night for six weeks and I always found her the same. They are on their way home and when I saw them setting off, I could not help wishing that we were going also!

We took the opposite direction to Bern[1] in a horrid [wetness] mistook the road and went through some marshes which reminded me much of Marshside. The next morning we went by the diligence at <u>five o'clock in the morning</u>!!! …only fancy, when did you do that last?!! …and reached Lucerne by 5 in the evening. Though it was a long day, anything was better than more vetturino work.

What a house full you seem to have had! Just fancy old Mr Denison all in his glory arranging the books in the library! Edward is now writing to him – if Jemima is with you, tell her with my love, she is a silly little thing not to have sent us a line at Lucerne.

Our plans for the future are to be at Milan in a week[2], where we expect old Hales; then go to Venice, remain there a week or ten days, post on to Florence and Leghorn where we leave the carriage and as we have so short a time for our Italy trip – steam <u>up to Naples,</u> then to <u>Rome</u> and come back through France. Of course, we shall take a peek at Paris on our way.

I shall not forget your [-] pins[3] but shall be on the [que] ball[4] for anything that is pretty. The only purchase I made at Geneva was a

---

[1] Formed as a federation of cantons, Switzerland recognises Bern as the capital.
[2] Distance between Lausanne and Milan by modern roads - 205 miles.
[3] Probably stick pins (tie/cravat pins) fashionable from this period.
[4] Relating to the importance of the 'cue' ball in Billiards – probably a favourite game of John Gaspard Fanshawe.

little broach with a painting of the Jungfrau[1] - all the rest of the mementos were just what one sees in London and are tremendously dear. The Swiss generally make it a rule to ask twice as much for a thing as it is worth.

You must not think us indifferent to your wishes dearest John because we did not call on Eric Smith[2] at Geneva, we did not know his direction till I received your letter yesterday, and we had no means of finding him out.

I am so much obliged to Oddy and Frederick[3] for their remembrance of me, pray say all that is proper and kind in return.

I expect to find you a most accomplished Polka dancer and shall certainly get you to teach me on my return. We could not muster up courage to take lessons at Geneva.

I was so surprised to hear that Aunt and Uncle Somerville were going to Parsloes, I never dreamt of them leaving Guernsey. Give them our love and I am very glad they are both so well.

The accounts you have had of Basil and Richard seem most satisfactory and Papa and Mamma must be much pleased they have taken such good places and I hope they will continue to like Willie[4] and that they have a nice companion.

---

[1] 'Jungfrau' (13,642 feet) one of the highest mountains in the Swiss Alps, located near the town of Interlaken in the Bernese Oberland and close to mounts Eiger and Monch.
[2] Eric Carrington Smith (1828 – 1906), a younger brother of Oswald (Oddy) - both were at Eton with John Gaspard Fanshawe.
[3] Possibly another Eton friend - Frederick Thesiger, 2nd Baron Chelmsford - began a long military career in 1844 and later was noted for action in the African Zulu Wars.
[4] Edward's nephew William Kershaw, pupil at Shrewsbury School from 1843 until 1845. School records show his name as Hanson from 20th June 1844 when he legally took the name and arms of his grandmother's family, owners of Strangeways Hall, Manchester.

Zurich - I brought my letter on with me because I should have a few minutes to spare after tea – we have been in the carriage the whole day and I am very tired. Before I left Lucerne I had to unpack every single thing in <u>all</u> the boxes and put them in again myself. Martin had done it so disgracefully, she has been behaving very ill, so much so that I had very serious thoughts of sending her off and doing without a maid. The Thompson's servants, as well as Peter could not bear the sight of her. She is very deceitful, detested and like the Swiss, much necessary. Peter says he will be civil to her as long as she's with us and really considering how she plagues him, I wonder he is as good natured to her as he is?

So you really are going to have Mr Waldgrave[1] as a neighbour. I hope you will find him as agreeable neighbour as Mr Baugh, and [he] has a wife also, if it is true he is going to be married. Remember me kindly to Mr Baugh and I hope he's now quite well and able to join the christening party.

By the way, did Papa receive the letter I wrote to him from Lucerne? I wish I could [see] him enjoying himself in his garden, tell him I shall look out for some choice plants in Italy.

When you write again tell me how you like the new pony and which of the two old ones you have sold?

Martin has come to tell me the hour, so I must draw this letter to a close as we depart again early in the morning by the steamer. Pray ignore this stupid letter – a whole days travelling does not improve my intellect and I will try to make my next more interesting. Will

---

[1] The Ecclesiastical Gazette made an error in announcing the appointment of the Revd Samuel Waldgrave to the parish of Great St. Mary's Ilford. The December issue contained a retraction and the vicar duly appointed was Revd. Hon. Henry W Bertie, son of the Earl of Abingdon who served the parish from 1844 to 1881 and came to be generally appreciated.

you tell Mamma that I will write to her directly we get over the Splugen, which will be in a week's time and then I will thank her more fully for her last letters?

You need not fear our prolonging our stay abroad – home has too many attractions and I am most anxious to see you again. I hope we shall spend many a happy evening altogether over the little wood fires at Parsloes.

Edward is going to add a few lines - write again as soon as you can and with repeated thanks, a thousand good wishes and very much love to yourself, dearest Papa and Mamma and all other numerous friends in which Edward unites.

Believe me, my very dearest John, and with great love your most affectionately attached sister

Helen Denison

All particulars of your Blendon gaiety will be required!
Give my love to Annie, I believe is with you, Adieu…

Note added to the previous letter by Edward Hanson Denison to his brother-in-law John Gaspard Fanshawe

Zurich
September 9th 1844

My dear John,

You are a nice young gentleman, I don't think – as Mr Bailey Whilom of 'Todgers'[1] would have expressed it - not to write to me! There are you, quietly at home with nothing to do and I weighted down, immersed with business – does not your conscience prick you? Does not the Litany with its charitable prayers for 'all travelling by land and water'[2] remind you every Sabbath of your remissiveness?

You seem to have been having a good deal of fun - how did you like Ascot?[3] I envy your being there - there is nothing in the world I like better than a good race.

By this time too, I picture you to myself, up to your middle among potato tops and where is the vineyard that can be compared with potatoes? With your new Westley Richards[4] resolutely pointed at your neighbour's head!!! Talk of Waterloo and Trafalgar – did ever man confront such danger as I and your father have done?

---

[1] Reference to 'Martin Chuzzlewit' by Charles Dickens - published in nineteen parts from June 1842 – July 1844.
[2] 'We beseech thee to hear us, good Lord - That it may please thee to preserve all that travel by land or by water' - extract from The Litany, The Book of Common Prayer.
[3] Ascot Races - attended by Nicholas I of Russia on his state visit to England in 1844.
[4] Westley Richards founded in Birmingham, opened a shop in New Bond Street in 1815. During the 19th century this company made the rifles used by the British Army and by receiving the patronage of Prince Albert in 1840 (the first of several Royal Warrants), fashionable gentlemen were attracted to these highly prized sporting weapons.

But I hope to find you mended – I conceive the shooting is not first rate in this country – I should think on a clinical computation there cannot be more than three brace of Black Game[1] on the whole chain of the Alps with a stray ptarmigan[2] or two or Alpine Fox[3] – as to the Chamois[4], a man gets about one shot per month after climbing to awful supra marine altitudes and if he kills, he finds himself in possession of flesh like what I should think an old black worn-out tom cat would be.

Send me word of what shooting you have had with all other accounts of your doings and larks – that is a good fellow!

The only place I have chance of taking gun in hand will be at the old shooting quarters of one Julius (<u>song</u> mind after Yankee parody) Cesar – 'that fruity fighter'[5].

Tomorrow we cross or rather start for the crossing of the Alps and hope to get into Italy on Thursday or Friday. We shall find it awfully hot, I doubt not – here it has been as cool as a cucumber.

On the whole we have enjoyed this land of snows and rogues very much - and so nominally depart owing them some very pleasant companions, but I doubt not Helen has told you all about this as well as all our jolly doings, so I will not bother you with them.

---

[1] Black Grouse/Black Game or Black Cock - large game birds in the Grouse family which bred in moor or bog lands close to wooded areas across northern Europe.
[2] Rock ptarmigan - a medium sized gamebird in the Grouse family sometimes called White Game, found in icy regions across northern Europe, including Scotland.
[3] Red Fox.
[4] Chamois - species of goat-antelope native to mountains in Europe.
[5] 15th century Pope Julius II, chose his papal name to emulate the fighting Julius Caesar. He lead his army to defeat the Ottomans and saved the Papal States and is known as the 'Warrior Pope' or the 'Fearsome Pope'.

I have just seen in the paper that the House of Lords have reviewed the Cornish sentence but I cannot believe it – What! – in opposition to the opinion of (<u>juries judges</u>) out of <u>mind</u> are the Noble Lords, mad or were they only <u>drunk as Lords</u>?[1] If true it is enough to make one wish to see them <u>wiped out</u> - in the meantime Lord Broughham's[2] prayer takes it from the before mentioned beautiful form of the Litany and reconciles namely that it may please providence endure them with 'grace wisdom & useless tawdry'[3] which they evidently are lamentably in want of if they have done as the paper says.

My kind remembrances to your Father and Mother and believe me your affectionate brother in law,

E H Denison

I hope to meet old Hales at Milan!

---

[1] Most probably refers to the bill introduced in the House of Lords during 1844 by Lord Brougham ultimately leading to the codification of English Criminal Law.
[2] Henry Peter Brougham, 1st Baron Brougham and Vaux (1778 – 1868) Q.C. was a controversial Whig politician and polymath who served notably as Lord Chancellor. As an original thinker he wrote prolifically and was an early abolitionist.
[3] 'That it may please thee to endure the Lords of the Council, and all the Nobility, with grace, wisdom, and understanding - we beseech thee to hear us, good Lord' - another extract from The Litany.

Letter to Mrs Catherine Fanshawe - mother

Milan
September 23rd 1844

[opens without formal greeting]

Most sincerely do I hope dearest Mamma, you have not thought me unmindful of you or negligent in not having sooner thanked you for your delightful and truly welcome letters I received at Lucerne. Time seems to fly faster than ever and really I have not a second to spare. I will just give you yesterday's occupations as a specimen.

We arrived at Milan a little after 10 o'clock yesterday morning where we found Mr Hales waiting for us. As soon as I had read yours and Annie's most affectionate letters; for which many thousand thanks - we went out and saw the Cathedral[1] which is a gloriously splendid building. If you only could be with us now, how delightful it would be! We then came back to the hotel, took a carriage and spent all the afternoon sightseeing till 5 o'clock when we dined at the table d'hote. Afterwards we went again to see the Cathedral by moonlight - it was so beautiful.

Came home, prepared for the Alps and did not retire till past 12 at night. Each day passes in the same rapid way, only the time perhaps is differently occupied.

I was sorry to hear that you had hurt yourself, you always exert yourself too much but I am very happy you are quite well again. I am looking forward to seeing you at Xmas; quite our <u>comfort</u> so pray do not disappoint me.

---

[1] Milan Cathedral, dedicated to the Nativity of St. Mary - construction began in 1386 but was not fully complete until 1965.

I have such a quantity to tell you that I must begin at once or I shall not get in one half that I want to say. After we left Lucerne we went to Zurich, steamed down the lake and passed our first night over the Splugen staying at Rajaz[1]. Early the next morning we went to Chur[2] both as nasty dirty places as I ever wish to see. I suffered martyrdom from the fleas but fortunately I am become so adapt at catching them that I seldom or ever miss, generally from four to six in a day, all are drowned.

We then went on to the village of Splugen, a very clean little village. It is from Chur to Splugen that the road is so very wonderful and beautiful. After a few minutes drive, we got into the Via Mala, a road cut in the rock and running along the sides of the precipice, looking like a gallery. The rocks on each side are of an immense height and one enormous mass, the ridge is so narrow that in parts the rocks almost meet and scarcely leave room for the Rhine that exists forcing a gurgling treacherous gap. The first part of the [design] is looking back from the entrance to the Trou Perdeu, a tunnel cut through the rock, under which the road passes. The rocks are the grandest and 'sublimest' we could possibly conceive though I fear my[3] poor description will give you no very grand idea of the fineness of the pass. After leaving the Via Mala the scenery as far as Splugen is very wild and desolate. I was enchanted with our day's expedition and was quite sorry when it was over.

The next morning, instead of continuing to Splügen Pass - as the finest part was over, we turned off and went down the St Bernardino[4] which was more convenient for us and wanted to see

---

[1] Spa town known as Bad Rajaz since 1937.
[2] Coire/Chur, 75 miles from Zürich at the meeting-point of the routes from Italy via the alpine passes Lukmanier, Splugen and San Bernardino.
[3] Compare this account to that of the author Mary Shelley who crossed the Via Mala in July 1840 - *'Rambles in Germany and Italy in 1840, 1842 and 1843'*.
[4] San. Bernardino - high pass in the Swiss Alps connecting Thusis and Bellinzona.

the two lakes. We teased our old friend the Minne almost to Lake [Tambosee], for wandering close to the glacier, on which it rises.

The road up to St Bernardino is beautifully made, the only thing we regretted was that before we reached the top we were in the clouds and could not see five yards before us. If it had been fine we should have had a splendid view. When we got down into the pretty and fertile Valley Mesocco on the Italian side, the change of climate was extraordinary. The hills were most magnificently wooded with chestnut, walnut and mulberry trees - and fig trees also growing in the open air, like apple trees. And the vines, instead of being tied up to straight poles in the German and Swiss stiff position, they twine round a sort of trellis work and immense bunches of grapes being with smaller bunches, in the most graceful sequence.

We slept that night at Bellinzona[1] and were in the carriage as the clock struck four o'clock next morning (was that not punishment?) - to be in time for the steamer on Lake Maggiore at 7 o'clock. We went down the lake as far as Laveno and were delighted with the scenery; the mountains all very grand and clothed at the summit with the most lovely verdancy[2].

From Laveno we went to the Borromean Islands[3] belonging to Count Borromean[4] who has a large palace on the Isola Bella. He brought earth to a barren rock in the lake and converted thereby this hard ground into a beautiful garden. It consists of terraces rising one above another to a point and lined with statues. Ascending from

---

[1] Historic town at the junction between St. Gottard Pass, San Bernardino and the Splugen - north-east of Lake Maggoire.
[2] Here the lush green sub-tropical vegetation reflects into the lake as jade green.
[3] Three small islands with a total surface of 50 acres that lie across the lake from the little port of Leveno.
[4] Vitaliano Borromeo – a member of an aristocratic family of merchants, bankers and cardinals who owned the islands from the 16th century.

October 1844 'The Penny Magazine'
Extract from 'Engineering among the Alps'

'The Via Mala, one of the most terrible defiles in the Alps, was the scene of some very skilful engineering on the part of an Italian engineer named Pocobelli. …Travellers used to make a wide detour, clambering over mountains and through valleys, in order to surmount the four miles of distance which forms the Via Mala. Thus it remained till Pocobelli made a capital road through the gorge itself. He pierced the projecting buttresses of rock with galleries or tunnels, a work of great labour from the intense hardness of the rock; and he gained the requisite width of the carriage-road in the face of the rock by blasting a notch as it were in the mountain itself. For more than a thousand feet the road is carried along beneath a stone canopy thus artificially hollowed out; and it is protected on the outer side by a stone wall.

The road crosses the gorge three times, by as many bridges, at spots where the contour of the rocks rendered this course desirable. Between the first and second of these bridges, the chasm assumes such an extraordinary form that the precipices on the one side actually overhang those on the other, on account of the obliquity of the cleft. Beyond the second bridge the road is scooped out of the face of the rock, and the defile is here not more than eight yards wide; but in approaching the third or upper bridge the defile increases in width, and becomes less difficult in its character.

In another, part of the same general pass of the Splügen, the Austrian government has employed the services of an engineer to make a practicable road where nothing but a bridle-path existed before. This is a curious example of the energy which competition induces. The Swiss made a good carriage-road over the Bernardine Pass, which threatened at once to draw off all the traffic from the Splügen Pass; whereupon the Austrians set to work promptly, and made the Splügen road far better than it was before. There are on this new line of road three distinct galleries cut through the solid rock, one of which is six hundred feet long, another seven hundred, and the third more than fifteen hundred, all of them being fifteen feet high, and the same in width. . These galleries are constructed of the most solid masonry, arched with roofs which slope outwards to turn aside the snow, and supported on pillars, or low windows like the embrasures of a battery—a mode of arrangement necessary to protect the road from falling avalanches.'

Edward's planning and research gave Helen opportunities to experience many newly opened sites and forms of transport. During their evenings at hotels, he constantly updated their itinerary by using his travelling library of guide books. Helen having time to reflect and write most of their letters home was clearly excited and impressed by their mountain adventure. Her letters capture this experience well – and may even be favourably compared with the more detailed account of Mary Shelley – another lady of Barking heritage.

'The rocks on each side are of an immense height and one enormous mass, the ridge is so narrow that in parts the rocks almost meet and scarcely leave room for the Rhine that exists forcing a gurgling

The road through the Splugen Pass was opened in 1823 but the route connecting the Swiss valleys of the Hinterrhein and Spluga in Italy had been worn by foot and mule since Roman times. It became an important trade route by the Middle Ages and although well used in succeeding centuries, the path - 'the Via Mala' remained notoriously treacherous.

'It may be imagined how singular and sublime this pass is, in its naked simplicity. After proceeding about a mile, you look back and see the country you had left, through the narrow opening of the gigantic crags, set like a painting in this cloud-reaching frame. It is giddy work to look down over the parapet that protects the road, and mark the arrowy rushing of the imprisoned river. Mid-way in the pass, the precipices approach so near that you might fancy that a strong man could leap across.'
Mary Shelley *'Rambles in Germany and Italy'* July 1840

'I had made an agreement with the conductor that I could use his seat high up on the coach. There I was alone: it was the most lovely post-coach journey I have ever made. I shall write nothing of the tremendous grandeurs of the Via Mala...'   Friedrich Nietzsche *'Letter to his mother'* 1872

'...in time for the steamer on Lake Maggiore.'

Still, we continued to advance toward them until nightfall; and, all day long, the mountain tops presented strangely shifting shapes, as the road displayed them in different points of view. The beautiful day was just declining, when we came upon the Lago Maggiore, with its lovely islands. For however fanciful and fantastic the Isola Bella may be, and is, it still is beautiful. Anything springing out of that blue water, with that scenery around it, must be.
Charles Dickens 'Pictures from Italy' November 1844

'Taken all in all, I should like to live here; here to enjoy the aspect of grand scenery, the pleasures of elegant seclusion, and the advantages of civilisation, joined to the independent delights of a solitude which we would hope to people, were it ours, with a few chosen spirits... English friends arriving down from the mighty Simplon, and Italians taking refuge in my halls from persecution and oppression - a little world of my own — a focus whence would emanate some light for the country around - a school for civilisation , a refuge for the unhappy, a support for merit in adversity: from such a gorgeous dream I was awakened when my foot touched shore, and I was transformed from the Queen of Isola Bella into a poor traveller, humbly pursuing her route in an unpretending vettura. Such, for the most part, has been my life. Dreams of joy and good, which have lent me wings to leave the poverty and desolation of reality. How without such dreams I could have past long sad years, I know not...'

Mary Shelley 'Rambles in Germany and Italy' 1840

'Then the sky clears...it is Isola-Madre, wrapped in its terraces...we land; on the side of the ledge are aloes with their massive leaves and Indian figs sunning their tropical fruit. Alleys of lemon trees run by the walls, and their green or yellow fruit clings close to the interstices of the rocks. With this wealth of beautiful plants, four terraces rise one by one; on the plateau of the isle is a band of green throwing over the banks its masses of leaves, laurels, evergreens, plane-trees, pomegranates, exotics, glycines and full-bloomed clusters of azalea. We walk amid coolness and perfumes . . . the island is a fair garland of pink, blue, and violet flowers picked at morning time, and with butterflies hovering round it. '

H. Neville Maugham 'The Book of Italian Travel 1580 – 1900' (1903)

those terraces flourish most magnificently orange citrons and pomegranates besides aloes, cactuses the complete assortment. In short, trees of tropical countries are growing side by side with those of the northern climates – Scottish pines and firs etc. The terraces are all covered with beautiful flowers. The guide gave me a few, which I have dried and I am going to try to get the seeds of some for Papa. This Isola Bella is a most curious specimen of art - it commands a beautiful view of the lake, as you may imagine.

We then went to Isola Madre a little further off, [that] has more natural beauty than its rival and the views from it are even more beautiful.

In the afternoon we went by the steamer to Locarno[1], full of the most horrid cut-throat looking people I ever saw, and as to filth and dirt, I think it would beat the worst Italian town. There we got into a dirty little one horse carriage to take us to Lugano[2] to get where we had sent Martin on with the carriage. But when we got little more than half way this wretched affair broke down, our springs gave away – fortunately just as we were passing through a village and it was patched up sufficiently for me to ride in it and Edward and Peter walked. We arrived at 10 o'clock and found that the man who had been sent with a very decent carriage to drive us had 'sold us' to a man at Lucerne who gave us the only carriage that could be procured in that dirty little hole.

The lake of Lugano[3] which we passed on our way, is remarkably beautiful, quite as much so as Lake Maggiore but neither of them are

---

[1] Located in Switzerland at the northern end of Lake Maggoire - the sudden expansion in population in this town early in the 19th century, perhaps accounted for the poverty, overcrowding and the behaviour observed by Helen.
[2] Distance of 105 miles from Lucerne to Lugano.
[3] Glacial lake on the border between Switzerland and Italy.

equal to Lake Como about Cadenabbia[1] and Belaggio[2] where we stayed four days and were perfectly enchanted with the spot. We went over two palaces at Bellagio[3], one was very comfortable and had a nice garden but nothing very particular, the space belonged to two bachelor brothers[4] who had spent their energy contriving the most glorious walks in their gardens, commanding the most, lovely views of the lake one could possibly imagine.

In the palace[5] belonging to a Prussian princess at Cadenabbia was a famous statue by Canova of Cupid and Psyche[6] - such a beautiful thing.

We also went to a silk[7] company manufacturing hundreds of wonderful lace, incredibly off their little frame in the cocoon and the finished quality was indeed beautiful.

We then went back to Como and left it in the afternoon for Milan but we were obliged to stop half way for the horses already near

---

[1] On the west shore of Lake Como and already popular with British travellers.
[2] The romance of Lake Como and surrounding towns was enhanced in 1837 when the virtuoso pianist Franz Liszt came to live at Bellagio with his mistress the Comtesse Marie d'Agoult – where he composed the 'Album d'un Voyageur'.
[3] The more important was the Palazzo Melzi d'Eril the home of the Italian politician Francesco Melzi d'Eril, Duke of Lodi & Count of Magenta (1753 -1816).
[4] 'Two brothers now remain of the Serbelloni family – one a general, who served during the wars of the French Empire, the other, a church dignitary. Both childless, and the estates will on their death, be inherited by their sister' *(Mary Shelley 1841)*.
[5] Villa Carlotta was built in 1690 and bought in 1843 by Princess Marianne of Nassau, wife of Albert of Prussia and the grand pink and white house, set in terraced gardens with spectacular scissor stairs, was a wedding gift to her daughter Carlotta.
[6] Since 1824 the original of the sculpture by Antonio Canova, commissioned in 1787 by Colonel John Campbell, has been in the Louvre Museum, Paris - the marble copy at the Palazzo Carlotta was completed under the direction of Canova.
[7] In the early 15th century Ludovico Sforza, Duke of Milan planted mulberry trees around Lake Como. Inevitably silkworms were attracted and since, this area has been traditional for the manufacture of the best quality luxury silk.

'Off course, we have been sightseeing and seen the Cathedral, it is splendid...'

'...by moonlight when the stars seem gathered among those clustered shapes, is beyond anything I had imagined architecture capable of producing.'
P B Shelley, *'letter to TLP Esquire'* 1818

The only redeeming character about the whole being the frequent use of the sharp gable ... which gives lightness, and the crowding of the spiry pinnacles into the sky."
John Ruskin *'Notes'* 1849

'I went daily to the cathedral of Milan, that singular mountain which was torn out of the rocks of Carrara. I saw the church for the first time in the clear moonlight; dazzlingly white stood the upper part of it in the infinitely blue ether...
Hans Christian Andersen *'The Improvisatore'* 1833

'At last, a forest of graceful needles, shimmering in the amber sunlight, rose slowly above the pygmy housetops, as one sometimes sees, in the far horizon, a gilded and pinnacle mass of cloud lift itself above the waste of waves, at sea – the Cathedral! We knew it in a moment.'
Mark Twain – *'Innocents Abroad'* 1869

I climb'd the roofs at break of day;
Sun-smitten Alps before me lay,
I stood among the silent statues,
And statued pinnacles, mute as they.
Alfred Lord Tennyson
'The Daisy' 1851

The Cathedral...an awful failure...the design is monstrous and inartistic.
Oscar Wilde –
'Letter to his mother' 1875

'... the moonlight hour passed in the Piazza del Duomo – beneath the black shadow of the building, then emerging into the clear white light – and looking up to see the marble spires point glittering to the sky, is a pleasure never to be forgotten.' Mary Shelley *'Rambles in Germany and Italy'* 1840

'Lake Como about Cadenabbia and Belaggio where we stayed four days and were perfectly enchanted with the spot.'

'Surely on earth there is no pleasure...so great as lingering, during the soft shades of an Italian evening, surrounded by all the beauty of an Italian landscape, sheltered by the pure radiance of an Italian sky – and then to skim the calm water towards one's home; while the stars gather bright overhead, and the lake glimmers beneath...'
Letter from Cadenabbia (1840)
Mary Shelley

'From my window here in Bellaggio, I have a view of the other side of the lake now, which is as beautiful as a picture... three or four gondolas lie idle upon the water—and in the burnished mirror of the lake, mountain, chapel, houses, groves and boats are counterfeited so brightly and so clearly that one scarce knows where the reality leaves off and the reflection begins!'
The Innocents Abroad (1869)
Mark Twain

died up and could not have taken us on, and as Milan is so full from a meeting of business men that is being held there, that we thought very probably we should arrive late at night and find no rooms.

We arrived at Milan next morning, where Mr Hales had very kindly procured us rooms. I like him exceedingly, he is so very friendly and good natured. He often talks to me of Papa and says he should like above all things to meet him again for to use his several expressions, he says 'he took an amiable fancy to him'.

Of course, we have been sightseeing and seen the Cathedral, it is splendid - but a little print which I intend buying will give you the best idea of it. There are besides some very handsome and curious old churches but the Arco del Pace[1] - the continuation to the Sempione Road along which Napoleon intended making his triumphant entrance into the city - is magnificent, all of marble and at the top are some remarkably spirited bronze horses.

If it is fine on Monday we shall drive over to the Certosa di Pavia[2].

We shall leave Milan on Tuesday; be three days getting to Venice where we shall stay the week or ten days then go on to Florence. As we have so short a time for the rest of Italy we think of leaving the carriage at Leghorn[3] and going by the steamer to Naples[4] and then travel to Rome in some several days.

---

[1] 'Arco Della Pace' – (Arch of Peace) completed in 1838 stands at the Porta Sempione, the city gate of Milan.
[2] Certosa di Pavia - one of the largest monasteries in Italy (built 1396–1495) displays masterpieces of the 15th century. Sited on the border of a hunting lodge of the Visconti family it began as a Carthusian monastery, then was occupied by other orders until 1843, when it was reclaimed by the Carthusians.
[3] Livorno (Italian) – major sea port, west of Florence on the Mediterranean Coast.
[4] By road today - approximately 350 miles.

Now I have given you the account of our proceedings as far as Milan, I am only too glad to enter into the family particulars which are always most interesting to me.

I was indeed much shocked to hear of the death of Mr W Fry[1]; we saw the death of his child in the papers, it is a most melancholy event and I most sincerely sympathise with his poor wife[2]. Pray let me know in your next how she bears up in her misfortune. I should think there was no doubt that John Fry[3] would retain the house.

I perfectly recollect that Mr Nugent, quite a young man and very gentlemanlike. What an awful thing to be taken off so suddenly and away from all his friends.

Poor Harry Gray's[4] case does indeed seem to be very hopeless, it is a great blessing that he is sensible and has been spared ever so long [a] time to think of a future world. Possibly by this time he may be no more and it was only about a year ago that his wife was almost given over and now she is well and her husband then so strong and hearty, taken. It certainly is a lesson to us all to prepare ourselves!

Talking of the dismals, Minnie Carey, who I heard from here, tells me that they found Uncle Jack looking considerably ill and that he now talks in a very different strain to formerly.

---

[1] William Storrs Fry (1806 – 1844) a son of Elizabeth Fry (1780 – 1845), the Quaker social reformer who had a cottage on Dagenham Breach and is buried at Barking. Her visits to the area were frequent between 1826 and 1833, and she was 'on intimate terms with the Rev. T L Fanshawe and Mrs Fanshawe and often drank tea at the vicarage' *(History of Dagenham - J P Shawcross)*.

[2] Sally Juliana Pelly, daughter of Sir John Pelly, Governor of the Hudson Bay Company 1822 – 1852 and Governor of the Bank of England 1841-1842.

[3] John Gurney Fry (1804 – 1872) lived at Warley Lodge, Brentwood in Essex – eldest son of Elizabeth Fry.

[4] Henry Gray (died Jan. 1845) & his wife Esther (both born 1786) farmed at Lodge Farm, Dagenham.

I am very anxious to hear if the Hewett Carey's have been to you and what you think of his bride - <u>any little particular</u> will be most interesting?

I am very glad you enjoyed Mr Denison's and Jemima's visits and that you like her better; more as you know her. I understand for it is that she most heartily enjoyed her visits to Parsloes and will be delighted to repeat them as soon as she can. If Aunt Caroline and Uncle Somerville are with you, pray give them our very best love, I should very much liken to have been there. If you think it would be any comfort to her, since she has lost her poor baby, will you tell her from me that Mrs Thompson who we have been travelling with, was confined last year, after being married <u>thirteen</u> years and her baby died just the same as I think Aunt Caroline's and now she is expecting another, so there is no reason why Aunt should despair.

Mrs Croft[1] seems to be losing no time[2], pray give them my love. I am glad you thought Grace[3] improves and am greatly obliged to her for wishing to hear about me but I am afraid she can only hear through you for with all the [will] in the world, I could not find time to write to her. Lady Croft[4] is a wonderful old lady.

---

[1] Mrs Charlotte Croft, wife of Rev. Richard Croft, Rector of North Ockendon, Essex was the daughter of Lt. Col & Mrs Russell of Stubbers at North Ockendon who were close friends of Helen's parents.
[2] In 1842 Mrs Croft gave birth to a son and another was born the following year. Helen's comment must relate to news that the lady was again expecting a child - a third son, Thomas Denman Croft was christened in April 1845.
[3] Grace (died 1898) was the Rev. Croft's niece, she was the daughter of Sir Thomas Elmsley Croft (died 1835).
[4] Grace's grandmother, Lady Margaret Croft, was a sister of Thomas Denman, 1st Baron Denman of Dovedale, Lord Chief Justice (1832 – 1850). She was the widow of Sir Richard Croft (died 1818), the obstetrician who had attended the ill-fated Princess Charlotte of Wales.

When I hear of many friends going to dine [at] old Parsloes it makes me long more than ever to be one of the members. I look forward to the winter evenings I hope to spend with you all as my greatest pleasure.

The accounts of Basil and Richard seem most satisfactory - Edward heard from Willie who said they were both doing very well and he liked them very much.

Will you give my love to the Lefevres? I do indeed pity poor Helen being left all alone especially after so much gaiety but I am extremely [pleased] you all think her so much improved.

I quite long to see the library again, you give such a flourishing account of it. I cannot quite fancy Papa taking to it altogether - and will Uncle Henry[1] continue there or make the dining room his sitting room? After all these alterations, has he yet heard from Mrs Partridge, and how she's getting [on]?

Tell Papa we did not forget his birthday and wish him many, many years of health and happiness – and you, to enjoy them with him.

John, I hope is as successful with his gun, as he anticipated. Tell him not to forget to write me, Annie accuses him of being troubled with a lazy fit and not reading any last letters!!!

How did you advance the frescoes and the statuary? We have been seeing some beautiful frescoes of Leonardo da Vinci, one the famous one of The Last Supper[2]. Although very much damaged, it still

---

[1] Henry Fanshawe, surviving older brother of Helen's father who had not inherited Parsloes on the death of the eldest brother John in 1843. The estate passed directly to Helen's father - whilst Henry retained the right of accommodation at Parsloes.

[2] 'The Last Supper' by Leonardo Da Vinci, painted in 1494/8 on the wall of the refectory of the Dominican convent of Santa Maria delle Grazie, Milan.

retains a great deal of its original beauty, the face of our Saviour is perfect but I have no space to prolong subject.

We were not so fortunate as to meet John De Lancy[1] and I fear now we have no chance.

Love to Julia Grant and Annie with many thanks for her interesting letter, which I shall not fail to answer in a day or two.

By the way, I want to know why are you still calling my husband Mr Denison? He says he cannot allow it and would have written himself to beg you to desist but he had to go out on the horses with Mr Hales. Pray call him Edward for the future, dearest Mamma I assure you it sounds a vast deal better and would suit us both infinitely.

You really are good in writing so frequently, all I offer you is that if you knew the value of your letters, you would not grudge me one minute spent of your precious time that you devote to me. With plenty of love to dearest Papa, Johnnie, Annie and etc., and a very large portion for your precious dear self, always - which Edward joins.

Believe me your most affectionate daughter

Helen Denison

Remembrance to the servants!!

---

[1] A relative from the Le Marchant family from Guernsey – wife Grace De Lancy previously mentioned.

Letter to Mrs Catherine Fanshawe - mother

Florence
October 15th 1844

My dearest Mamma

I have this instant finished reading yours and Aunt Caroline's most interesting letter and send you a thousand thanks.

It was extremely kind in Aunt Caroline devoting her time to me. I shall write to her in Guernsey which I suppose she has reached by this time. I am very sorry that Uncle Somerville's illness was the cause of their remaining longer, but I am very glad that he was not suffering from one of his serious attacks.

Aunt Caroline has quite delighted me with the account she has given me of you and the rest of the family. She says she has not seen you looking as well and strong for a very long time. Pray keep up your very good looks for my return, which I [am] looking forward to most sincerely. I shall be so delighted to see you all again, dearest Mamma and I hope we shall spend many a happy day together. I am quite envious of all your visitors, but there are only two months more, which is something to comfort me.

You will be glad to hear that I am a great deal better, indeed I may say quite well again, and so is Edward. He and Mr Hales seem as happy as the day is long, though the latter is full of all sorts of crotchety noises and fancies he will not live six months. Papa will tell you what a fat healthy looking man he is.

We spent yesterday, our first day at Florence in the picture gallery then Tribuna[1], a room where all the most precious frieze statues and

---

[1] Tribuna of the Uffizi - the octagonal room designed for Cosimo I de Medici in 1584 which housed the most important antiquities of the Renaissance period.

pictures are - occupied us a long time. They really are so exquisitely beautiful that we could not bear to leave and I have knocked myself up, but I rested well in the afternoon and in the evening was quite fresh for the opera 'Euricine'[1] the new one, the same one we heard at Milan only a different Ballet. It is remarkably pretty, I have some thoughts of buying the music.

The daily occupation is to go every morning to see pictures and in the afternoon we generally take a drive. The outside of the Cathedral[2] here is the most beautiful thing you can imagine. It is quite a different style to the one at Milan and is certainly a most imposing looking building. The dome[3], the first that was ever made is the largest in the world and the <u>body</u> is different marbles and is certainly new from anything we have yet seen. It is so grand and at the same, so <u>very pretty</u> if one may use such an expression, that one might really fancy it more a toy. I have not yet been inside but I hope to do so today.

We were just a week coming from Venice to Florence, ten days going over the Apennines[4] which was rather tedious, the scenery is not to be compared with that one sees crossing the Alps, but though not so grand in many parts it is pretty and the air reminded me very much of the air of Stockgrove.

---

[1] 'Eurydice' was the first 'true' opera. Composed by Jacopo Peri it was first performed in December 1602 at the Pitti Palace, Florence. Probably by 1844 the more 'evolved' version was performed entitled 'Orpheus and Eurydice' written during the 18th century by the German composer Christoph Gluck.

[2] The construction of the Cattedrale di Santa Maria del Fiore begun in the 14th century, but Helen would not have seen the decoration of the exterior as it was not completed until 1887.

[3] Masterpiece of the 15th century architect and builder Filippo Brunelleschi.

[4] 'The Backbone' of Italy – a series of mountain ranges stretching 900 miles from the Maritime Alps to Sicily.

We stayed at Bologna[1] a day extra for we could get no horses, and was really very glad of the time. In the gallery[2] there are some remarkably fine pictures and Edward and I went to take up our station there for the whole morning. Mr Hales very soon got tired for he is not a very great advocate of paintings and he spent his time in the botanical gardens[3].

By the way, will you tell Papa that I did find a quantity of the Spina Christi[4] in the hedges on our way to Bologna - we stopped the carriage and Edward has some. I thought as the seed was quite open he might be glad of the chance to try and make a few more plants.

I was delighted to hear he is so well and is enjoying such excellent sports. It will be an untold pleasure to hear his merry laugh again, I often think of you all, and talk of you and shall be truly happy when I can talk to you in person. I shall have plenty to tell you and plenty to hear after so long an absence and shall trouble you with a quantity of questions!

I shall not forget your promised story of the Miss Buttons - they seem to be strange beings! I was much shocked to find from your letter of this morning, how poor old Mrs Birch[5] was no more. I

---

[1] Etruscan capital of the Emilia Romagna region.
[2] A collection of sacred altarpieces then in the Academy of Fine Arts –including work by Giotto, Raphael, Parmigianino, Tintoretto & Titian – today they are housed in the Pinacoteca Nazionale di Bologna.
[3] The Botanical Gardens of Bologna University are among the most important in the world. Began in 1568 by Ulisse Aldrovandi, the father of natural history; he collected and taught with vast numbers of specimens and the remains of his important Herbarium are still in the university archives.
[4] Ziziphus Spina-Christi - common name 'Christ's Thorn' - is native to the dry and arid areas of the Levant and grows widely around Jerusalem. By tradition this species is believed to be the thorns worn by Jesus Christ at his Crucifixion.
[5] Death of 78 year old Esther Birch, wife of William Birch Esq. of George Lane, Wanstead – 19th Sept.1844 (*The Gentleman's Magazine*). William Birch was a subscriber to religious publications which may account for the family connection.

always liked the old lady very much and should have liked to have seen her some more, but she is now much happier and freed from all suffering. Her poor husband is much to be pitied, being left alone, especially at his advanced age. He must feel her death most deeply for they were so attached to each other, but let us hope that he will not linger very long after her. I shall be glad to hear when you write again, that his sadness after this loss as well as when you last saw him. How desolate his little cottage must appear now that the poor old lady is gone and when he goes it will have lost all its character. Let us pray it is having been the residence of two such a kind and good old couple. I suppose you are now comforted as we have not heard from him for such a long time. I was most afraid she would not be well.

Tell John, with my love, I should be very glad to have a letter from him again and trust he really must find time to send me even a few lines! I am very glad he is in such good health and spirits I shall certainly get him to teach me the Polka when not fully occupied with Aunt and Uncle Denis and Mr Denison – give them all our very best love, not forgetting all the children - and give me an account of their visits and did you find little Powder Puff[1] much altered by being deprived of his locks? I am sorry Jemima cannot be of the party but am glad it is not illness that has deprived her of the pleasure.

I am getting quite ready to return from here and have heard from Mrs Thompson who has written to tell me on her safe arrival in England that Oswald Smith's father has been down into Yorkshire to attend the funeral of old Mr Sykes, a friend of theirs.

---

[1] Helen must be thinking of her first cousin Henry Denis Le Marchant (later 2nd Bt.) who was born 15 December 1839. His only brother Francis Charles, born in 1843 would have been too young to lose his 'baby curls'.

The weather with us has [been] very unsettled the last few days, but we have been most unfortunate, the day we left it blew a complete hurricane and the sea which is generally quite <u>stupidly</u> calm, was so rough that both Edward and Mr Hales were not at all sorry to find themselves safely on shore, not to mention <u>myself</u>.

The letters are just today going from Florence to England so I think this will reach you as near on your birthday[1] as possible. I wish dearest Mother, I could be with you to tell you how much health and happiness I trust is yet in store for you. But as it is impossible, unfortunately for me, to be at dear old Parsloes and Florence at the same time, you must rest assured that I shall not forget you or anything relating to you – and picture Edward and I to yourself on the 20th at dinner time - drinking your health with a bumper!

I suppose you are in daily fear of hearing that Uncle Gostling is ordered off[2], you will be quite sorry to part with them again but I most sincerely hope, the climate will agree with Aunt Mary and children. Pray give them all my very best love and tell Aunt how sorry I am not to have seen her but I do hope it will not be long before we meet.

Your news told me how you liked the frescoes at Westminster Hall[3]. We see such quantities of these that they cease to be a novelty and now we are become quite fastidious.

Since I wrote in the morning we have been to see the pictures in the Duke's Palace[4]; such a splendid collection of all the best artists.

---

[1] The birthday of Mrs Catherine Fanshawe - 20th October.
[2] Col. Charles Gostling waiting orders for his next posting with the Royal Artillery.
[3] The Palace of Westminster destroyed by fire in 1834 was being rebuilt and a competition held for the interior decoration resulted in an exhibition in Westminster Hall from July to November 1844. Displayed were 140 competing entries of 'cartoons' for the frescoes proposed to be permanently installed.
[4] 16th century Uffizi Palace built for Cosimo de' Medici, Grand Duke of Tuscany.

There was one of Raphael of the Madonna & Child and St John the Baptist[1] which is the most perfect thing I have seen. There were many others of Raphael's, all splendid paintings. One or two also of Masaccio's[2] and all the great painters. You have no idea how much the love for picture seeing grows on you and these pictures, basically speaking are no different from what appears in the London exhibitions, the National Gallery of course, excepted. I shall certainly be never best satisfied 'till you have been to enjoy these beautiful works of art!

Tell John nothing would delight him so much - only he must put up with a few inconveniences and I am extremely glad to hear from Aunt Caroline that he has a great wish to commence his travels. If we had been staying longer, I should say he had better come and join us. But I do not think we shall remain here above ten days, as we want to spend as much time in Rome as possible. As to Mr Hales, he is disgusted with Italy – he says there is no place like Paris and he thinks he shall go back to it.

We dined this evening for the first time at the Table d'Hote all very hungry - and fancy our dismay on finding nothing for the three first dishes but bad soup, <u>figs</u>! and Bologna sausages full of garlic, and some little birds that came up intended for Ortolans[3] but which proved to be nothing but <u>really little robins</u> – so much for the Italian

---

[1] 'Madonna of the Goldfinch' (1506) has recently been brought back on display in the Uffizi Gallery after a 10 year programme of restoration.
[2] The Uffizi Gallery still displays two painting by Masaccio – 'Madonna and Child' (1424) & 'Virgin and Child with St. Anne' (1424/5)
[3] Eating Ortolan (tiny birds) was an ancient rite of passage for French gourmets. The birds, captured alive were force-fed, drowned in Armagnac then roasted whole. All of the bird was eaten, including bones and the diner draped a linen napkin over his head to preserve the aromas. Some said it was to hide from God... (*Extracted summary from 'The Wine Spectator'*)

cookery! But we must not complain for we get excellent dinners in our own rooms.

Aunt Caroline tells me Uncle Henry has returned from Mrs Partridge looking too well and robust - I suppose the effect of his good living! He has been about a long time and I suppose has now come home to treat you with a little display while he has an attack of the gout. I am very glad you confirm he is recovering from the fever and hope now it will not spread further in the family.

I hope poor Mr William Fry is going on pretty well and is supported under his heavy life.

Annie still keeps with you so I am in great hopes of finding her in England on my return.

I cannot say that I was surprised to hear that Mr Penny[1] had turned Roman Catholic for he seemed such an eccentric fellow that such a step was not all improbable but I am very sorry he has, for it certainly will confirm people in their fears that the high church party are carrying things so far that this will too frequently be the result.

My time and paper are fast drawing to a close, dearest Mother and so must my letter, though nothing would give me more sincere pleasure than continuing my chat with you.

You cannot be afraid of my finding dear old England dull, the Continent has many attractions which are all very agreeable for a little time, but there is no place like home and no pleasure like that of returning to all the friends of one's childhood.

---

[1] William Goodenough Penny – an Anglican curate and graduate of Christ Church Oxford was part of The Oxford Movement who converted to Catholicism in 1843.

Goodbye, dearest Mamma and with much love to dear Papa, John and the boys, Annie and a very large portion for yourself, my dearest. Edward unites, not forgetting many other friends.

Believe me ever your most affectionately attached daughter

Helen Denison

Will you give my love to Miss Farquharson and ask Annie to address the same to Sophy Tuppy[1] and tell her I am very sorry not to have time to write in her?

---

[1] Linked to Annie – Sophie Tuppy must have been a member of the Tupper family – but not a sister.

Letter to John Gaspard Fanshawe - brother

Rome
November 19th
(Post marked 21st November 1844)

My dearest John,

We arrived last night after a most far expressed journey from Naples and found old Hales waiting for us having arranged everything most comfortably for us at the Hotel. This morning Edward is so full of business of one sort and another - looking out for a carriage and horses for the time we stay here, the bankers etc. that I know he will not be able to write for several days. So I am making use of a few spare minutes to thank you again for your most kind and truly welcome letter we received at Naples.

I am delighted to hear that you are all so well and that dear Papa has returned from the North in such excellent health and spirits. I must now tell you how much I long to see you all again and to share in all your music and merriment. It would indeed be charming if we could have been home in time to have spent the New Year altogether at Parsloes, for you will believe me – there is no place where I should so much like to spend it.

As it is, I think we shall have to be contented to pass it at some little pokey place by the wayside, but you may rest assured that wherever, we are we shall not fail to drink the health of all our dear friends with every wish for their health and happiness in a bumper of whatever such liquid we can procure. We shall be with you in thought though absent in person. In eight weeks more, I do hope we shall meet the 2nd week in January. If we are fortunate in our journey, is the time when we expect to reach England.

If it is fine weather, I think we shall most probably leave this about the 6th and sail to Marseilles instead of posting. We shall then be a fortnight getting to Paris. Edward has had a spring seat made for me at Naples, which is the greatest luxury you can conceive on some of those bad roads…

The last week we spent at Naples we were making excursions. We first went to Pompeii[1] which is interesting in the extreme. The streets of tombs, the first we saw, is a most melancholy aspect from being deserted and in ruins, but it is itself exactly like one of ours, very narrow with the Roman pavement on which we could perceive distinctly the rut that had been worn by the chariot wheels.

The houses are generally speaking small, seldom any windows and painted over outside red and yellow. You first enter in past cloisters into which open some small rooms that were used by the family as bedrooms. The centre is an open yard court - you then go into a hall, some more cloisters, the dining room and a little bit of a garden, which we should not think worthy of the name. The ground is all mosaic work, sometimes also of large pieces of different coloured marbles, and the walls covered with frescoes, but the most valuable of these have been taken to the museum[2] at Naples.

The Forum must have been a splendid place – it is full of the most beautiful marble columns, and the principal of the temples is the Temple of Isis[3]. The baths are in excellent presentation and show the luxury and riches of the inhabitants of this little town. I hope to give

---

[1] Pompeii was first 're-discovered' in 1592 when architect Domenico Fontana digging an underground aqueduct came across ancient walls with paintings and inscriptions.
[2] Museo Archeologico Nazionale di Napoli.
[3] Roman temple dedicated to the Egyptian goddess Isis, discovered during excavations in 1764. The temple is small and almost intact and has inspired many artists including J M W Turner - and Mozart is reputed to have written 'The Magic Flute' following a visit in 1769.

you a better and more interesting account however when I see you and truly wish you could have been with us, you would have enjoyed it beyond measure.

Aunt Caroline told me when she wrote that you were very anxious to commence your travels; whenever you do, which I hope will be before long, you really must come to Italy and I am sure you will be as much delighted with it as I am.

We then went over to Salerno[1] and Positano[2] to see the remains of their Grecian temples[3], quite different from anything we have yet seen. The columns were of a red sandy-looking sort of stone, very hard. The roofs are entirely gone but none of the pillars – of which there are two rows, the outer one forms a court round the temple.

The drive was through a very wild country, we met several droves of buffaloes, very ugly animals and all the men looked like brigands. They carried long guns but fortunately for us they were all peaceably disposed! About sixteen years [ago] there was a most shocking murder on that road. Mr & Mrs Hunt[4] (once great friends of Dr Roskilly[5]), a young married couple on their wedding tour were

---

[1] Salerno on the Amalfi coast, was a centre of culture from the 9th century to the middle ages and the 'Schola Medica Salernitana' was the leading centre of medicine in Europe: *'...students went to study in Arabia and Spain and they returned to their native town to dispense, among crowds of rich and noble patients, the treasures of their skills'* - Mary Shelley (1843).

[2] When they sailed west the Ancient Greeks and Phoenicians used Positano as a beautiful safe port and the name derives from Poseidon, God of the Sea.

[3] These are the remains of Irnti – left by the Etruscans trading with the Greeks at nearby Paestum.

[4] Caroline Isham and Thomas Welch Hunt, Squire of Wadenhoe of East Northampton were married 9th February 1824.

[5] Dr John Roskilly (1788 – 1864) – an eminent physician who practiced in Naples treating mainly English travellers, many were celebrated personalities and among them was the poet Percy Bysshe Shelley who in 1819 was treated for hepatitis.

'The daily occupation is to go every morning to see pictures and in the afternoon we generally take a drive. The outside of the Cathedral here is the most beautiful thing you can imagine...'

'I propose to build for eternity'
- Filippo Brunelleschi

I have seen the Venus, I have seen the divine Raphaels, I have stood by Michael Angelo's tomb in Santa Croce. I have looked at the wonderful Duomo. This cathedral...it struck me with a sense of the sublime in architecture. At Pisa we say, 'How beautiful!' here we say nothing; it is enough if we can breathe.

The mountainous marble masses overcome as we look up, we feel the weight of them on the soul. Tessellated marbles (the green treading its elaborate pattern into the dim yellow, which seems the general hue of the structure) climb against the sky, self-crowned with that prodigy of marble domes. It struck me as a wonder in architecture. I had neither seen nor imagined the like of it in any way.

Elizabeth Barrett Browning
'Letter to Hugh Stuart Boyd' (1847)

'All this brightness and yellowness was a perpetual delight; it was a part of that indefinably charming colour which Florence always seems to wear as you look up and down at it from the river, and from the bridges and quays. This is a kind of grave radiance – a harmony of high tints – which I scarce know how to describe. There are yellow walls and green blinds and red roofs, there are intervals of brilliant brown and natural looking blue...'

Henry James 'Italian Hours' (1873)

'I love my native city more than my own soul'
Machiavelli 1527

'Pompeii...the streets ... exactly like one of ours, very narrow with the Roman pavement on which we could perceive distinctly the rut that had been worn by the chariot wheels'.

Sudden eruption of Vesuvius in 79 AD buried Pompeii under ash and lapilli and the city lay without rediscovery until 1689. The next century, a Bourbon King initiated the first of many scientific excavations that continue today. 19th century British travellers and tourists were increasingly attracted to the site after the publication of *'The Last days of Pompeii'* (1832) by Edward Bulwer, Lord Lytton - a novel that brought to life the ill-fated city and gave names to the inhabitants.

'You may ramble about and lose yourself in the many streets. Bulwer, too, has peopled its silence. I have been reading his book, and I have felt on visiting the place much more as if really it has been once more stirred into life, now that he has attributed names and possessors to its houses, passengers to the streets. Such is the power of the imagination...' Mary Shelley *'Rambles in Germany and Italy'* 1843

Stand at the bottom of the great market-place of Pompeii, and look up the silent streets, through the ruined temples of Jupiter and Isis, over the broken houses with their inmost sanctuaries open to the day, away to Mount Vesuvius, bright and snowy in the peaceful distance; and lose all count of time...
Charles Dickens *'Pictures from Italy'* 1846

'When one considers the distance of this town from Vesuvius, it is clear that the volcanic matter which overwhelmed it could not have been carried hither either by any sudden impetus of the mountain, or by the wind. We must rather suppose that these stones and ashes had been floating for a time in the air, like clouds, until at last they fell upon the doomed city. ' Johan von Goethe
'Letters from Switzerland and Travels in Italy' 1881

They were not lazy. They hurried in those days. We had evidence of that. There was a temple on one corner, and it was a shorter cut to go between the columns of that temple from one street to the other than to go around—and behold that pathway had been worn deep into the heavy flagstone floor of the building by generations of time-saving feet! They would not go around when it was quicker to go through. We do that way in our cities.
Mark Twain *'Innocents Abroad'* 1869

'The drive was through a very wild country, we met several droves of buffaloes, very ugly animals and all the men looked like brigands.'

'The plain extending from Battipaglia to Paestum is tenanted by wild horses, buffaloes, swine and sheep, guarded by fierce dogs...'
John Murray's Guide to Southern Italy (1865)

Edward was wise to keep the tragedy of Caroline (Isham) Hunt away from Helen's imagination – she too had been a clergyman's daughter enjoying her bridal tour with her new husband and although the tragedy was twenty years in the past, this wild open country remained notoriously dangerous. Despite warnings of brigands roaming the open plain to Paestum, Thomas Hunt naïvely failed to conceal his valuables at an hostelry and they were targeted and on the lonely road, set upon by villains. Possibly by resisting and not handing over all he carried, Thomas Hunt sealed the couple's fate. Helen tells this tragic story of misplaced bravery correctly - the couple died with a single bullet passing though Thomas and entered his wife. The shocking news quickly resounded back to Naples and local outrage caused the nest of criminals to be rounded up and executed in April 1825 but Helen's comments show the dramatic story was repeated as a cautionary tale long after as a warning to the many travellers from northern Europe.

'Turning away to Pæstum yonder, to see the awful structures built, the least aged of them, hundreds of years before the birth of Christ, and standing yet, erect in lonely majesty, upon the wild, malaria-blighted plain—we watch Vesuvius as it disappears from the prospect, and watch for it again, on our return, with the same thrill of interest: as the doom and destiny of all this beautiful country, biding its terrible time.'   Charles Dickens *'Pictures from Italy'*

While in the progress of their long decay, Thrones sink to dust, and nations pass away.   *7th Earl of Carlisle, 'On the Ruins of Pæstum' (1821)*

'Sorrento, one of the sweetest spots on the Continent! The drive is lovely, through orchards of orange trees, figs and vineyards...'

'As the old woman and young girl emerged from the dark-vaulted passage that led them down through the rocks on which the convent stood to the sea at its base, the light of a most glorious sunset burst upon them, in all those strange and magical mysteries of light which anyone who has walked that beach of Sorrento at evening will never forget.'
Harriet Beecher Stowe
'Agnes of Sorrento' 1861

'Now spread the night her spangled canopy,
And summoned every restless eye to sleep.'
Torquato Tasso
(Born 1544 - Sorrento)

'At every moment the senses, lapped in delight, whisper – this is Paradise... Here the poets of Italy tasted the sweets of those enchanted gardens which they describe in their poems – and we wonder at their imaginations; but they drew only from reality – the reality of Sorrento. '
Mary Shelley
'Rambles in Germany and Italy' 1843

'Do you know a land where the lemons are considered flowers? In the green leaves golden oranges shine, a quiet wind blows from the blue sky, quiet is the myrtle, serene the laurel. Do you know it well? There, there, I would like with you, my love to go!'
Johann von Goethe *'Mignon'* 1786/87

'You may have the universe if I may have Italy'   Giuseppe Verdi

Sorrento and Naples are beautiful – people have not been exaggerating. The air here is a mixture of mountain and sea air. It is very soothing for my eyes; from my terrace I look down first on a big green tree garden (which stays green in winter), beyond that the very dark sea, beyond that Vesuvius.
Friedrich Nietzsche *(Selected letters)* 1876

returning from Paestum[1] to Naples and in a small wood, not far from the former place were attacked by brigands. Mr Hunt stooped down, whither to get the money or the pistols is not known, however the robbers shot [and] killed Mrs Hunt who had turned before her husband. The ball passed through her and also killed Mr Hunt who died almost immediately – she survived a few hours. Is it not a melancholy account? I am very glad I did not know the last story when we passed the spot or I should have been terribly frightened.

The next day we went in a boat along the coast to Amalfi, remained there a short time and returned to Salerno in the afternoon. The scenery was remarkably fine and bold, very rocky and the green weeds blended most beautifully with the such yellow tint of the cliffs.

We then returned to Naples and the next day set off to Sorrento[2], one of the sweetest spots on the Continent! The drive[3] is lovely, through orchards of orange trees, figs and vineyards. The hotel was remarkably comfortable, very nice rooms looking divinely over the sea. Directly underneath the windows in the evening when it was dark, we watched the poor men fishing with a fire at the end of their boats to attract their prey – principally lobsters we saw fished. If we had only known what a delightful comfortable spot this was we certainly should have made it our headquarters instead of Naples for all our expeditions, but our time would not allow of our remaining longer than one night.

---

[1] An area of Salerno, site of the Greek temple of Athena.
[2] Beautifully located on the Bay of Naples with views of the Isle of Capri and the volcano Vesuvius – Sorrento attracted early tourists and remains popular today.
[3] Known later as the 'Amalfi Drive' this scenic, breathtakingly beautiful coastal road when experienced by horse drawn carriage must have been even more lovely.

You would be highly amused with the Neapolitans, the fishermen are called Lazzaroni[1] and are peculiar to themselves. They drive about in a one horse gig all at once, [which] is a very common number, and go a tremendous pace. Besides this they are the very dirtiest people and the greatest rogues, but undoubtedly Naples is by far the more truly busy town we have been in yet in Italy, and there is not that air of desolation about it that one generally sees.

The grand resort is Chiaia[2] or Quay, where one meets some extraordinary objects, wishing, thinking, [they] are great swells[3]. We saw some of the royal family and were in great hopes the Duc D'Aumale[4], who is to be married to the Princess of Salerno, would have arrived before we left. The palace on the opposite side of the street to our hotel was being prepared for him and he is to be here any time and to be married on the 25th. We heard there seems to be very grand doings in the mansion.

Edward has had a letter from his father saying that as there was no law existing why Papa should not hold the land in Wyersdale - the plans were altered and Papa occupies the farm himself. This is just the same as Mamma mentioned in her last. I hope the land will be more productive than they think and that the little trips into Lancashire to see the property will afford you all much pleasure.

---

[1] A name was not only used to describe fishermen but also generally for the poor lower working classes in Naples.

[2] This district is still the most exclusive and fashionable in Naples.

[3] 'A fashionably dressed person or dandy, or a person of social prominence' – Swell was probably already in common parlance but had not appeared in literature until Charles Dickens wrote Martin Chuzzlewit (published 1844). Helen using the expression with her brother, demonstrates how younger people were starting to update and modernise language through popular culture. (The same expression was used by Basil Fanshawe writing from Crimea in 1855).

[4] Henri Eugène Philippe Louis d'Orléans, Duke of Aumale (1822 – 1897) was King Louis Philippe's 5th son. Married on 25th November 1844, his bride was Princess Maria Carolina of the Two Sicilies.

We have been very much surprised to hear of Mr Livesey's[1] intention of taking a wife unto himself and only hope the lady will prove to be Miss Caroline Denison. Edward is accordingly pleased that he has chosen such a nice amiable person and thinks it an excellent step. Tell me when you write if you have [heard] anything about it and whether it really is true.

I suppose you will soon be going to Billingbear and hope you and Papa will have good sport. Remember me most kindly to Mr & Mrs Le M Thomas.

Wednesday morning - Since writing yesterday, we have seen nearly all Rome – we drove to all the principal places within the town and I think I may say that we have been to no place yet that has come up so much and even more to my imagination than Rome!

One cannot go twenty yards without some old ruin bearing witness to their previous greatness. The Coliseum, the Baths of Caracalla[2] and lastly St Peter's are so gigantic, and St. Peter's so gorgeous that it requires more than one bird's eye view before one can realize them.

When Edward writes, which will be <u>very shortly</u> we shall have seen more and therefore I shall have time to give you an account of those splendid buildings.

---

[1] Joseph Livesey - a witness to Helen & Edward's marriage, was a school friend from Eton (both pupils of Bishop Chapman 1826/29). His home was Stourton Hall, Lincolnshire and he was High Sheriff for his county in 1853. He married Sara Maria Welby in 1850 but both died in 1854.
[2] Rome's second largest public baths (thermae) built during 2nd century AD in the reigns of Septimius Severus and Caracalla. Mosaics of athletes exposed by the excavations of Count Egidio di Velo in the 1820's are now in the Vatican Museum.

Have you seen in the papers the death of Mr Sutton (who came down to Parsloes on the 7th May)? Uncle Mr Manners Sutton[1], poor old gentleman, he has only been ill a short time and his death is a dreadful blow to all his family.

It is quite astonishing the number of people whose deaths we have seen in the paper this year who were known to Edward and Mr Hales.

Yesterday was the first day of the hounds meeting and there was a most shocking accident. A Mr Bertie Matthew[2] who was at Eton with Edward, went out hunting, he was a very bold horseman, and was jumping a very high [gate] and the horse knocked his knees against the wood, hurled Mr Matthew [and] fell upon [him]. The poor man was killed on the spot. He has been staying three years at Naples and has now three sisters who were staying with him. This melancholy accident has put quite a damper on us all for Mr Hales knew him also and was talking to him a few days since.

Have you seen any account of the inundations at Florence? The Arno has overflowed its banks and when Mr Hales left there, water was in the streets and in the piazzas, and in parts was more than 12 feet deep[3]. To give you an idea the Grand Duke and Duchess[4] went

---

[1] Rev. Thomas Manners Sutton (1795 – 27 October 1844), chaplain to his brother Charles Manners Sutton 1st Viscount Canterbury - Speaker of the House of Commons. The Speaker's first wife Lucy Denison was distantly connected to Edward's family. Significantly by the middle of the 19th century, members of the families of Fanshawe, Le Marchant, Denison, Lefevre and Manners Sutton served alongside of each other in many roles at Westminster.
[2] Bertie Bertie-Mathew (1811 – 1844) was very well known to Edward as throughout their time at Eton they were taught together, in the class of Revd James Chapman (later Bishop of Colombo 1845 -1861).
[3] Florence suffered its greatest floods during the years 1333, 1844 and 1966 – all occurring within the first days of November.
[4] Leopold of Tuscany (1797 – 1870), Grand Duke from 1824 to 1859 and his 2nd wife, Maria Antonia of the Two Sicilies.

to see what mischief was done, had his two leaders[1] washed away or drowned. The damage done is <u>very</u> great and the losses are to a very great extent.

Mr Webb[2] and his friend are this day there now but we expect they will come to Rome just in time to see before we leave.

I want a long account of the opening of the Royal Exchange[3] and how you must have enjoyed the different scenes much – Mamma told me you went…

I hope my dear John, I shall be with you very soon to check your drop in spirits. There is one thing I have yet to say, that I hope you will follow my good advice and don't think of being a bachelor! I have not time or room to expatiate[4] any further on this important subject but shall leave this for another occasion.

I was just going to enclose Mamma a few lines thanking her for her last letter and with repeated thanks for yours with all the news.

---

[1] 'The leaders' are the pair of horses at the front beyond the shafts. They have no power to brake, relying upon the pair called 'the wheelers' closest to the vehicle.
[2] Probably Christopher Webb Smith a former official of the East India Company who settled in Florence in 1842. An ornithological artist, he collaborated to produce two books with his friend and relative Sir Charles D'Oyly (see Webb Smith Collection Cambridge University). He also worked on a 'critique' of the 300 paintings in Florence's Pitti Gallery from 1849 to 1860 which unfortunately never reached publication as it was lost when the steamer Black Prince sank close to Portugal.
[3] The opening of the 3rd building of the Royal Exchange, on the original Tudor site at the junction near the Bank of England - constructed by the architect Sir William Tite. The formal opening by Queen Victoria was on 28th October 1844 and trading commenced 1st January 1845. Among the traders were the brokers of Lloyds who for the next 150 years continued to carry out business in the building.
[4] To speak or write about in detail.

With most affectionate love from myself and Edward to yourself and <u>also</u> to Annie. Believe me my ever dearest Gaspard, your most affectionate attached sister

H Denison

P.S.

Please direct your next to Paris with the number for the size of your gloves! I hope you will like the coral pin[1] which I got as nearly like Oswald's as possible.

Love to Annie and tell her I have long thought she must be deranged and the circumstance of the scarlet cloaks at Stockgrove has confirmed me in my opinion - Jemima has been delighted with her visit to her.

---

[1] Probably a cravat pin decorated with red coral as jewellery from Naples frequently included coral where it was regarded as a symbol of good luck.

'I want a long account of the opening of the Royal Exchange and how you must have enjoyed the different scenes much – Mamma told me you went...'

'I had the happiness of receiving your kind letter... while I was dressing to go to the City for the opening of the Royal Exchange. Nothing ever went off better, and the procession there, as well as all the proceedings at the Royal Exchange, were splendid and royal in the extreme. It was a fine and gratifying sight to see the myriads of people assembled—more than at the Coronation even, and all in such good humour...'
Queen Victoria 'Letter to her uncle the King of the Belgians' 29th October 1844

Each new exchange building had a splendid royal opening!

'Unto which place, on January 23, 1570, Queen Elizabeth came from Somerset House through Fleet Street past the north side of the Bourse to Sir Thomas Gresham's house in Bishopsgate Street, and there dined. After the banquet she entered the Bourse on the south side, viewed every part; especially she caused the building, by herald's trumpet, to be proclaimed 'the Royal Exchange,' so to be called from henceforth, and not otherwise.'
John Stow 1631

'Sir W. Pen and I back to London, and there saw the King with his kettle-drums and trumpets, going to the Exchange, which, the gates being shut, I could not get in to see. So, with Sir W. Pen to Captain Cockes, and thence again towards Westminster; but, in my way, stopped at the Exchange, and got in, the King being nearly gone, and there find the bottom of the first pillar laid. And here was a shed set up, and hung with tapestry, and a canopy of state, and some good victuals, and wine for the King, who, it seems, did it.'
Samuel Pepys October 1667

'Yesterday was the first day of the hounds meeting and there was a most shocking accident...'

Bertie is buried in the Non-Catholic Cemetery in Rome at the base of a ruined tower of the Aurelian wall and close by is the grave of the poet Percy Bysshe Shelley who drowned in the Gulf of Spezzia in 1823.

Originally, the owner of Bertie's plot reserved the space for Shelley's widow Mary Shelley, who returned to England. She next visited Rome in 1843 when it is assumed she indicated it was no longer her wish to be buried in Rome.

This prestigious plot then became available to Bertie's sisters who settled permanently in Rome after inheriting their brother's considerable fortune. Purchasing the plot, they then commissioned this magnificent memorial.

Bertie Bertie Mathew and Edward were at Eton together in the class of the Rev'd James Chapman. After service in the Hussars, Bertie had been living in Rome with his three sisters where he was well known as an excellent rider and huntsman.

Helen's report compares well to those held in Rome that add his neck was broken in the fall.

This accident caused wide concern in Papal and local circles as hunting had only recently been permitted but with the persuasion of Prince Livio Odescalchi and other Roman noblemen hunting was continued.

In today's foremost hunting club - 'Circolo della Caccia' hangs a painting by Massimo d'Azeglio depicting Bertie and his horse in their tragic last leap –

'The fall of Bertie Mathew, Esquire English, Master Prince Odescalchi outside Porta Salaria on 19 November 1844.'

'Nothing of him that doth fade
But doth suffer a sea-change
Into something rich and strange'
Percy Bysshe Shelley - 1792-1822

Letter to Rev'd Thomas Lewis Fanshawe - father

Paris
December 24th 1844

My dearest Papa,

We are much enjoying our first evening in Paris over a comfortable wood fire which brings to our minds most forcibly the cherished one you are all probably now looking towards. I can assure you the happiness we are now experiencing from having arrived so far on our journey safe and well, can only be surpassed by the pleasure we are anticipating in meeting all our dear friends in England in so very short a time.

Most sincerely do I hope this will find you all quite well & as merry and happy a party as ever assembled on Christmas time. I must not [forget to] say, that tomorrow we shall not fail to drink the health of all and wish you every good wish that it is possible to conceive, my dearest father.

After resting one day at Avignon[1] when Edward wrote to John, we again set off on our journey and have never stopped since, except for the night, till we arrive here this afternoon by the train from Orleans[2].

We have been most fortunate in the weather, the last few days very cold but only one rainy day. The roads were in a dreadful state and we generally spent from ten to twelve hours in the carriage. I am none the worse for any journey and after we have been to church[3]

---

[1] Distance between Avignon and Orleans is approximately 420 miles. Rail travel for this stage was not yet possible as the earliest section of the line northward from Avignon to Lyons, 'Chemin de fer de Lyon a Méditeranéé' was opened in 1852.
[2] Railway line between Orleans and Paris opened in 1843 when the Paris terminal was the Gare d'Austerlitz.
[3] The Anglican church of St George in Paris, then sited at 10 Rue Marboeuf.

tomorrow morning we shall begin to see all there is to be seen. The shops are all so tastefully arranged and are filled with so many tempting things, I really don't know how I shall resist them all.

I am sure if you ought to go to Rome to see antiquities then you ought to bring Mamma to Paris to restock her wardrobe but as it is an impossibility for her to come now, mind you let me know if there is <u>anything</u> that I can get for her, or any of you.

I must say very dearest father, I think you have been most incorrigibly idle in not writing me a single line since I left England. I certainly shall not let you off so easily when I get home! You have not followed the excellent example Mamma has set you. But I shall <u>scold you</u> well for it when I see you!!!

I hope to hear from Mamma in a few days. There were no letters except from Stockgrove when Peter went to the post this afternoon, but I am daily expecting the letters to arrive which I stupidly neglected to call for in Genoa. We asked the Captain who brought us to Marseilles to forward them to Paris.

Jemima tells me that Lucy Hewett is going to be married to one of her cousins. I am most curious to know if this is really the case and who the gentleman is – is it Charles Carey[1]? I really hope whoever she has chosen will make her a really happy woman – and from what I know of her I think they are most fortunate in having such a person as their wife. I shall not write to congratulate her until this piece of news has been confirmed by one of you. So don't forget to tell me when you write.

---

[1] Charles Carey, son of Peter Carey and Julia Hewett, married his mother's niece, Louisa (Lucy) Hewett daughter of Sir George Hewett on 3rd April 1845. (Mrs Fanshawe was first cousin to the groom via her maternal uncle, Peter Carey).

You know that Mr Denison has taken [Solong] Lodge - so I shall not tell you any of the particulars.

To return to ourselves, I must take you back to Marseilles and give you an account of a very pleasant afternoon we spent with a Mr and Mrs Mechlenburg. He is an Englishman whom Edward met in times of his last wanderings and travelled with in Spain. He has now settled at Marseilles and married a French lady – a remarkably nice and agreeable person. With all her beauty and fragrancy she is as nothing so homely a woman as possible to now meet. We dined with them at xxx o'clock and had a most excellent dinner, served completely in the 'French' style. Their five children were also in this party – with cheeks so rosy and fat you would have thought they must be English instead of French. From their youngest of (baby....) years old, to their oldest of 14 they all behaved most [impeccably] and would have been a credit to any English mother. We have heard the sound of family voices all summer and something that Edward considers perfection, is children when a look from their parents to be quiet sufficient.

Mrs Mechlenburg and I had a long chat entirely in French, for she doesn't speak a word of English – after the first few minutes we got on most capitally, much better than I ever imagined and the conversation never flagged and I really enjoyed myself very much.

We could not see much of the town of Marseilles for the snow[1] was two feet deep on the ground & when the thaw came it was by far too wet to walk out.

I admired the pretty little French caps of the girls and women and though their sabots[1] are not quite so ornamental, still they have a very picturesque effect.

---

[1] Snow in December is not unusual at Marseilles.

By the way, I must not forget to tell you that I got you & Uncle Denis some splendid cones of those celebrated & beautiful trees, the Roman Pine[2] and can show you a picture of the tree when we get home. I am quite sure you will admire them exceedingly and will think them highly reminiscent to the place. I only wish I had known about the <u>fir cones</u> a little sooner & I would have got you some of those also. But it was too late, I could not get any at Rome or in Italy.

I expect you will have a great deal to show me in your garden and in the hot greenhouse[3] and the various improvements you made in the summer.

It does seem such an age since I left you all, I cannot tell you how more than delighted I shall be to meet you again.

Basil & Richard are home with you and next week you will be having all our party from Stockgrove - though absent, dearest Papa, my thoughts will be constantly with you & I shall console myself with imagining how you are spending your times & picture to my mind all your happy countenances.

I suppose the gamble at Papa Joan[4] will be played tomorrow and on New Year night. Mind you write me a full and particular account of

---

[1] In France and the Low Countries, wooden clogs covering the whole foot were worn by the working classes from the 16th century onwards.

[2] Pinus Pinea - called Stone Pine, produces edible pine nuts. In Italy it is this species of pine with its umbrella structure which creates the Italian renaissance landscape characteristic of numerous paintings.

[3] Hot greenhouses, necessary to grow foreign varieties of the plants brought back from continental travel were high fashion in 1844 - many greenhouses were actually conservatories which extended home space into the garden.

[4] A popular Victorian card game played with a board for three to eight players. It was often played in clergyman's homes but originated in France some centuries before where it was called 'Nain Jaune' - (Yellow Dwarf). 'Papa Joan' refers to the legend that Pope John VIII was a woman. As this was contrary to the doctrine of the Catholic Church, the English title may originate from Protestant propaganda.

all that is going on. You must remember, thinking to tell trifling incidents is doubly precious and interesting to those at a distance.

Jemima tells me that Mamma mentioned not having been well in one of her letters. I hope it was nothing of any consequence and that [she] is quite happy and well and even as <u>energetically stout,</u> as she was fearful of becoming.

Give Basil and little <u>chimney sweeper</u> Dick my very best love and say I am delighted to hear the masquerade ball at Shrewsbury went off so well. I long to see them again and hear how they have enjoyed their first half year at a public school.

It is getting late and as a good night's rest will be very acceptable after all late fatigues, I shall say farewell for the present. Wishing you all many, many years of health and happiness and with most affectionate love to yourself, dearest Mamma, Johnny, the boys, Annie – in which Edward unites.

Believe me ever your truly attached daughter

Helen Denison

Ask them to write to me once more - a letter is too precious to lose.

Letter to Revd Thomas Lewis Fanshawe – from Edward Hanson Denison

Paris
December 24th (1844)

My dear Vicar,

From the length of Helen's document she must have given you many details of our travels so it will suffice for me to tell you how thankful I feel that we have accomplished this (at this time of the year) formidable journey, so well. She has stood her journey admirably, indeed I never saw her look better – and this after eight days real hard work is saying a good deal!

I am very sorry we cannot join your hospitable board this time, but it was not on the cards unless we had gone to Rome and <u>never known</u> our enthusiastic countryman. What a comfort it is to get to this X'tian town – 'Old Hales' says it is the only place for a gentleman to live in. I almost agree with him, at all accounts at least I think it is the only place for a gentleman <u>to rue</u> in. I used to think France quite a lost country but now believe there is some hope of its salvation. To give you a proof, I observed 2 or 3 post boys on the road, ride without <u>stirrups.</u> Now, if this is not a symptom of their overcoming prejudice and so of national reservations – I don't know what is!

We stay here a week or ten days, during which time we mean to give ourselves up to gastronomic indulgence and celebration and not do as a benighted friend of mine did – come to this Eden of cooks and eat beefsteak and drink his half-pint of sherbet. It is only proper to add, for the credit of England - that the gentleman was of Scandinavian origin!

Wishing you and yours every happiness and good mince pies!

I remain your affectionate son-in-law   EHD

Letter to Mrs Catherine Fanshawe - mother

Hotel Bristol[1]
Paris
Dec. 31st (1844)

Your most welcome letter my dearest mother, I received yesterday morning and most truly glad are we to hear you [are] all so well and spending this joyous season so happily and merrily.

It is impossible to regret more than I do, not being able to join your party but I live in hope and am consoling myself with the thought of meeting all those who are dear to me so soon. Our entertainments are certainly very different to yours but I can assure you it is a great treat to hear of all the English games that are going on even though we cannot join in them. I should enjoy seeing all the merry happy faces that are now assembled at Parsloes.

We have been to the opera or theatre every holiday excepting Tuesday[2], and on Saturday last, the great treat of hearing Rachel[3] it was her first appearance this season, she personated Roxane in Racine's play of Bajazet[4] and certainly acted most splendidly. I was delighted with her, she made what would otherwise have been a very stupid thing, most interesting. If Peter can get us good places we shall go again this evening.

Last time we had also the good fortune to see most of the Royal Family, the young Duchess D'Aumale who is just married, was also there - a fine pretty looking woman.

---

[1] Hotel Bristol - sited at 3 & 5 Place Vendôme was 100 metres from the present site of the Hôtel Ritz.

[2] Christmas Eve.

[3] 'Rachel' stage name of the celebrated French actress Elisabeth Félix (1821–1858) known for her performances in the plays of Racine & Moliere.

[4] A tragedy in 3 acts first performed at the Hôtel de Bourgogne Theatre, Paris in 1672.

We have been once to the Italian Opera and heard the Beatrice di Tenda[1] in which Persiani[2] and Ronconi[3] are the principal performers. Both the singing and the music are beautiful.

The letter you wrote to me at Marseilles I am sorry to say missed - at all events it had not arrived at the Post Office when we left. I fear from what you say you have been suffering from a low fever[4]. <u>I do hope</u> you are quite well and strong again dearest Mother, and that you do not now feel any bad effects from it. Poor Helen Lefevre must have been much weakened by it. A low fever is a nasty thing at all times, especially with one so naturally delicate as she is, but I trust she is quite recovered and is enjoying her Christmas and New Year with her sisters and cousins at Heckfield. Pray give them my best love and also to their father.

I hope Mr Foster's[5] illness is not likely to be serious or of long duration. I shall be glad to hear that he is relieved, it must be so very melancholy for him.

By the way, I must correct one great mistake you make in your letter though no doubt Mr Denison has already; as you seem to have understood from me that Valley Lodge had been taken <u>for us</u>,

---

[1] Beatrice di Tenda – a tragic opera by Vincenzo Bellini, from a libretto by Felice Romani.
[2] Fanny Tacchinardi Persiani (1812 – 1867) a soprano associated with the work of Rossini, Donizetti, Bellini, and Verdi.
[3] Giorgio Ronconi (1810 – 1890) - baritone with a brilliant stage presence who in 1842 successfully created the original title role in Verdi's 'Nabucco' at La Scala, Milan.
[4] Presumably equates to the modern medical term 'low-grade fever' when the body's natural reaction is for the temperature to rise while fighting bacterial and viral infections or respiratory illnesses.
[5] Helena LeFevre's stepmother, Elizabeth Emma Foster who died in childbirth during April 1842 was the daughter of Rev. John Foster (died 1838). Although the 'Mr Foster' mentioned was not her brother, he could have been an older male relative known to Heckfield's hostess who also had 'Foster' connections.

instead of Mr Denison having taken it <u>for himself </u>- you remember the lease of Stockgrove is up in (June). He has kindly asked us to take shelter under his roof this next year and we shall be most glad to accept his offer. I shall not fill up my letter with an account of the house as I know Jemima will furnish you with the every particular much better than I can. Edward is very glad his father has taken the house, it seems likely to suit him and he still remains in the same neighbourhood. I suppose all the Stockgrove party arrived yesterday and are, I hope quite well. Pray give them our affectionate love.

I am very curious to hear your opinion of little Mary[1]. Judging from her letters she must be uncommonly clever, or should I say, she was wanting in spirits. It will be a great treat to her having so many young people to play with…

I am surprised to hear that Charles Gostling[2] has not topped Basil - he may be a tall man after all!

We shall leave Paris next Wednesday the 8th, go by railway to Rouen[3] – have two long days posting and reach Boulogne[4] on Friday evening in time to cross over on Saturday. We shall remain the Sunday at Dover or Folkestone and come up to Town on Monday.

---

[1] Letitia Mary Gostling baptised Woolwich August 1837, daughter of Colonel Charles & Mary (Le Marchant) Gostling - 10 years younger than her older sister, had two younger sisters.

[2] Son of Charles & Mary Gostling, baptised Dagenham 1828 was less than a year older than his cousin Basil. Charles Gostling served with the East India Company in Madras, where he married Selina A.M.C Stonehouse - he died in 1857 aged 29.

[3] The Paris to Rouen section of the 'Ligne Paris–Le Havre' opened on 9 May 1843 and was served by Gare de Rouen Saint-Sever on the left bank of the Seine.

[4] The only regular sea crossing to England at this time was via Calais or Boulogne. There were no rail links through from Rouen to Boulogne or even from Paris to the ports. This was only possibly after the line opened in 1846, from Paris to Lille in Belgium, was extended further to connect to the ports.

The idea of being in England so soon is delightful and our visit to Parsloes is a constant topic of conversation. I shall write to you again the moment we arrive in England, if not before but really we are now so very little in [during] the day it is difficult to find time to write anything to be a connected letter.

I need not tell you how tempting the shops, and as to the Madamoiselles they are so engaging it is next to impossible to resist. I expect to come home quite ruined but I comfort myself with the idea that one does not come to Paris every day!

I shall have much to tell you when we meet and no doubt you will enjoy talking of a place you visited some years ago. The Place de la Concorde[1], which Edward tells me is new since you were here is remarkably handsome, and the Church of St Madeleine[2]... but I shall leave all this till we meet.

I am exceedingly glad to hear of Lucy Hewett's[3] engagement to Charles Carey[4] and am going to write to congratulate and most sincerely do I wish her every happiness.

---

[1] The Place de la Concorde only reverted back to this original name given in 1795 following the July Revolution of 1830. Therefore we can assume Mrs Fanshawe visited Paris whilst it was called Place Louis XV or later Place Louis XVI and changes she might have noticed were the Luxor Obelisk - installed in 1836 and the fountains added in 1840.

[2] North of the Place de La Concorde, 'The Madeleine Church' was designed as a temple to the glory of Napoleon's army and since has remained important in national life. The funeral of Frederic Chopin, the composer was held at this church in 1849.

[3] Louisa Julia Hewett (born 1817) daughter of Col. Sir George Henry Hewett and Louisa Majendie.

[4] Married in 1845 this couple were first cousins as the bride's father and the groom's mother were brother and sister. Then as Charles Carey's father was Mrs Fanshawe's uncle - Lt Col. Peter Carey, they too were first cousins.

I had not heard of poor Minnie's attack of jaundice in the summer, I am very sorry for her, poor girl but I hope she will soon get strong again.

Tell Aunt Tupper with my best love, that I congratulate her on Gassy's[1] success. We saw by the papers that he passed his examinations. I shall be delighted to see her, it is quite an unexpected pleasure for her remaining in England in the winter!

Both Edward and myself have got colds from which I hope you are all quite free. I manage without Martin very well and the little inconvenience I feel from being without a maid is fully compensated for by the comfort of having got rid of such a disagreeable women and Mrs [Bachieling] the mistress of the Hotel, very kindly lends me hers whenever I want her.

I hardly like asking you to write to me again at Paris, though as you will know dearest Mother nothing would give me more sincere pleasure. If however, you should find a few minutes to spare amongst your hundred occupations, do send me a line and direct to the <u>Hotel Bristol</u>, Place Vendome, Paris - and <u>don't prepay</u> your letter.

I must say goodbye now, for the carriage is waiting and so is Edward - to go to the Louvre. We have been once and seen the Gallery of Pictures[2]; certainly a very fine collection. There are some

---

[1] Another of Helen's 1st cousins - Gaspard Le Marchant Tupper (1826- 1906) son of Anna Maria (Le Marchant) & Daniel Tupper. 'Congratulations' relate to his first commission in the Royal Artillery taken up in 1845. After long service, he retired as Lt General and Colonel of the Regiment receiving the Companion Order of the Bath in 1905. Gaspard was also a talented artist, and his watercolour paintings and sketches of the Crimea, the West Indies and other locations of his service now hang in private and public collections.

[2] Grande Galerie.

beauties of Raphael and other great painters but I must say I cannot admire the modern French style or colouring[1].

Once more, goodbye and with most affectionate love to <u>all</u> (your party is now too successful to enumerate) and wishing you all <u>every happiness,</u> in which Edward joins.

Believe me ever dearest Mother,
Your truly attached daughter

Helen Denison

PS. Please tell Jemima we have this instant received her kind letter, for which Edward and I are much obliged.

---

[1] Possibly referring to the 'French Romantic School' in vogue at the time - the leading artist was Eugène Delacroix (1798 – 1863) whose work was mostly bought directly by the state and includes 'The Massacre at Chios'.

Appendix I

1832

Letters to Parsloes
Written from school at Brighton

Helen Fanshawe

(6 years of age)

(Addressee on the reverse of letter)

Mrs Fanshawe
Dagenham, Essex

> Brighton
> 5th June (1832)

My Dear Mamma

I am very much obliged to you for sending us such a nice letter.

I am glad to hear that you will come to see us when our [w]hooping cough[1] is gone away.

I was rather afraid of the sea when I came to Brighton but I am not now. I have got a nice bit of seaweed in our trunk.

We are reading Mrs Markham's[2] history about the Saxons and the Normans.

I am very sorry that I cannot go home and see you all.

Your affectionate child

Helen Fanshawe

---

[1] Whooping Cough (Pertussis) - a highly contagious bacterial disease that starts with cold symptoms before severe coughing fits develop with high-pitched whoop sounds. As children are at greater risk from this illness, fortunately since the early 1950s vaccination has kept it under control.

[2] 'A History of England from the First Invasion by the Romans to the End of the Reign of George III' (1823) by *'Mrs Markham'*, nom de plume of Mrs Elizabeth Penrose (1780 – 1837) a popular writer of history books for young readers in England and America. She was a daughter of Edmund Cartwright, inventor of the power loom.

St John's Wood
22nd June 1832

Madam,

I brought these with me to town – lessening the postage. Helen was anxious you should have hers and from here the double postages will not be so much more than the single from Brighton.

I shall be here till Wednesday. If you should be in London perhaps you would feel it a satisfaction to see me.

The children were quite contented and entered into the pleasures of the other ones pastimes with them in a very amicable manner.

They received your letter on Sunday and I was glad you were reading their answers as is on the same day.

The enclosed letter of Kate's[1] is awkwardly folded. It was finished while I was packing and made by someone else, far too deep at the sides.

We shall soon I hope, see you at Brighton.

Believe me, very dear Madam.

Yours very sincerely

P Ravenscroft[2]

On the reverse of the letter – addressee **Mrs Fanshawe**

---

[1] Catherine Fanshawe - Helen's elder sister.
[2] The 1840 local edition of the directory Pigot & Co., includes Mrs Priscilla Ravenscroft at 124 Marine Parade, with the property listed as a school in Brighton, Sussex. The census for the following year shows 'P Ravenscroft' – Schoolmistress aged 40, residing at Portland Place, Brighton.

(No Addressee)

I wish you my dear Mamma many, many happy returns of the day.

May all the blessings you now enjoy long be preserved to you, the only one I could wish added to them is, that you may have one more obedient child and <u>that</u> child I trust will be myself. Today I shall try and begin well and this day next year I hope you will find my promises and wishes were sincere, and that I shall be able to sign myself then, more truly than now

Yours affectionate child

Helen Fanshawe

Monday October 20th 1835

Appendix II

1899 - 1902

Letters from Helen Denison

An extract

Gordon & Fanshawe family letters
1846 – 1985 (Volume One)

Published by John Gordon in 2008
(*private circulation to members of the families*)

Letter from Helen Denison to her nephew, Evelyn J Fanshawe.
(Black-edged paper)

Little Gaddesden
Gt. Berkhampstead
Oct. 27th [1899]

My dear Evey,

It was very good of you to write and give me the first news of the wedding, and I am so very glad it all went off so well and so cheerily. I thought I would wait to thank you till Violet and Huntly had been here when I could give you the latest news of them.

They came yesterday to lunch and remained all the afternoon, unfortunately it rained all the time so we could not show them the gardens etc., and they could not drive home thro' the Park, but the afternoon passed very pleasantly. I never saw Violet looking better, and she seemed so happy and so gratified with all the kindness she had received from friends and relations, and at so many of them being present. I know it is [the] beginning of a very happy life for her.

We liked Huntly very much, he was most agreeable, plenty to say for himself and had a nice kind face and manner, and seemed very proud of his wife. They are greatly enjoying being at Beechwood[1], and even the rain does not spoil their pleasure – there is so much to see in the house to interest them.

I am very glad May[2] and Edgar[1] were there as well as yourself and I am sure Violet would have been very much disappointed if they

---

[1] Beechwood at Markyate, Hertfordshire, home since 1628 of the Sebright family with parklands laid out by Capability Brown during the 18th century.
[2] Muriel Mary Fanshawe (born 1891), daughter of Basil Thomas and granddaughter of John Gaspard Fanshawe.

had not gone. It was a very good arrangement for your Father and Mother staying at Terry's so that they could thoroughly rest before returning home. Mabel seems to have arranged everything capitally and Violet said 29 Rutland Gate looked lovely with the decorations.

I hope Mabel will not be quite knocked up after all the fatigue. Please tell your Mother with my best love I will write to her in a day or two. I can fancy Edgar's delight at the novelty of the whole thing.

My cold is better but very slow in going. We are looking forward to seeing the account of the wedding this evening in the 'Lady's Field'. Best love to you and May and the rest of the family.

Ever dear Evey,

Your very affectionate Auntie

H. Denison

---

[1] Edgar Sydney Waldo Fanshawe (born 1891), son of Evelyn and grandson of John Gaspard Fanshawe.

Letter from Helen Denison to her niece Mrs Violet Gordon

Kingsmear[1]
S. Devon
Sept. 18th [1900]

My warmest congratulations dear Violet on the safe arrival of your little son, and may he prove a great happiness and blessing to you both.

I trust you are going on well and will regain your strength speedily.

I should have written sooner to offer my congratulations, but have been ill in bed from a chill and it was only on Saturday that the Doctor gave me leave to come here, thinking the change would be the best thing, so I started yesterday morning.

Beyond being very tired, I am none the worse for the journey. Dorina[2] begs me add, how glad she is to hear of your little boy's safe arrival.

Excuse a longer letter today and with best love and good wishes for yourself and love to Baby.

Ever you very affectionate Aunt

H. Denison

My kindest remembrances to your husband.

---

[1] This must be an error by the transcriber of the Gordon & Fanshawe letters - a village called Kingsmear does not exist in South Devon. From more detailed information of Helen's family now available we must assume Helen was staying with her newly widowed daughter-in-law Anna Dora Denison at Kingswear near Dartmouth.

[2] Presumably the family's name for Anna Dora.

Letter from Helen Denison to Huntly D. Gordon
(Black-edged paper)

> Little Gaddesden
> Gt. Berkhampsted
> Sept. 5th [1902]

Dear Huntly

I must send you a few lines of warmest congratulations over the safe arrival of another little son[1], and the well doing of both him and dear Violet. I trust the good accounts will continue and you will have no cause for anxiety on account of either.

My Brother has shown me the lovely Photo of little Douglas[2]. He must be a beautiful boy and I hear he is charming in all ways, so that you have every reason to be very proud of him. He has such a good expression and most intelligent.

I am glad to tell you my Brother is looking much better since he came here, when I was really shocked to see him. He looked so ill and feeble – but now he can walk without his stick and enjoys being out.

With my best love to Violet and wishing her a speedy recovery.

Believe me

Yours sincerely

H. Denison

---

[1] Strathearn Gordon born September 1902.
[2] Douglas John Gordon born September 1900.

Letter from Helen Denison to Mrs Barbara FB Fanshawe[1]
(Black-edged paper)

Little Gaddesden
Gt. Berkhampsted
Sept. 5th [1902]

Dearest Bab,

I am so glad to hear the good news about Violet, and hope she will [have] no drawback to a speedy recovery. If No. 2 is as fine and engaging a child as No. 1 they will be most fortunate. The Photo of little Douglas is beautiful, and the little fellow must be a wonderful child, so handsome and intelligent and such a good expression, no wonder they are proud of him.

Fan[2] is looking much better and says he feels much stronger. At present he does not seem up to eating joints but seems to like rissoles[3] and little dishes which perhaps your cook could manage. I wish he could have stayed longer but we have people coming next week. He will return on Monday by 10.18 train from here, and we will see him off. I think it would be better if Lionel[4] could meet him at Bletchley, in case he has the stairs to go up. Tell me how you think he is. Fan is quite cheerful and ready to joke now – I hope you may be able to come with him next time.

Ever dearest Bab most affectionately yours

H. Denison

---

[1] Barbara Fanshawe (nee Coventry) wife of Helen's older brother John Gaspard Fanshawe.
[2] John Gaspard Fanshawe.
[3] Chopped meat or vegetables, worked into balls and fried.
[4] Lyonell Fanshawe born 1866, the youngest son of John Gaspard Fanshawe.

Appendix III

1840

*Letter to from Revd. Thomas Lewis Fanshawe
to his elder daughter
Catherine Sophia Fanshawe*

1840

My dear Kate,

You may perhaps be surprised at seeing my handwriting but as tomorrow you will enter upon your eighteenth year I cannot refrain from offering some council & advice – consider my dear child, you have now arrived at an age fully to appreciate all the kindness & improvement we have been able to bestow on your education. Examine carefully your own heart & see if there is not much to be striven against, and got the better of & humbly beg the assistance of God's holy spirit to enable you to arouse to more diligence & activity & to enable you to subdue & conquer a temper which at present appears to be the greatest impediment to your improvement – having discovered the evil seeds, take courage & eradicate them <u>at once</u> –

Hearing from your Mamma, you wished for a pencil case, I have great pleasure in presenting you with one & hope you will accept it as a birthday present.

From your ever, very affectionate Father

T L Fanshawe

Saturday evening

Appendix IV

Letters of Condolence

Catherine Fanshawe
Died 3rd May 1841
(18 years of age)
Buried Dagenham

Letter to Rev'd Thomas Lewis Fanshawe from Rev'd W Erle[1]

My dear Fanshawe

I am heartily sorry for the affliction that has come upon you & Mrs Fanshawe and send you both my sincere condolence.

The incipient occupation of my course of life almost debars me from social communication but it would give me sincere pleasure to see you & Mrs Fanshawe at any time here and introduce Mrs Erle.

I beg you both to accept the kind regards of an old friend.

Yours, dear Fanshawe

Faithfully

W Erle

20 Bedford Square
1st May 1841

Letter to Mrs Catherine Fanshawe from her sister Anna Maria Tupper

---

[1] Rev'd Walter Erle (1791-1870) - older brother of Lord Chief Justice Sir William Erle PC QC FRS (1793 – 1880).

[1841? entered in pencil – possibly by JGF]
Melrose – Thursday

My dearest Catherine

It is I am sure pointless for me to express how sincerely Dan[1] & myself sympathise with you as the mourning parents at Parsloes. No one can feel so heavily as those who have been called to the same trial and many tears flow from you.

Your loss is very great but how sweet my dear brother & sister is the [other turn] of your child's gain. With all your love would you have ensured, dear Kate the sweet peace she now enjoys. That fearing of separation is hotter to flesh & blood but would you recall her? No, I can sense you would neither of you call back that purified spirit to this world of cares, if you could.

You have indeed been spared a great deal in the closing sense. The xxxx is the first burst of grief from xxxxxxxxxx, it is so comforting to think in the place of death the assurance from dear Kate's hope that she could resign the prospect of her life without regret and look forward without fear to the awful change from time to Eternity. We should indeed to heed to these solemn meanings and I pray they may be sanctified to us. Your fair flower just coming to perfection, cut down and so very little but suffered so early, we little thought how soon this dear girl was to follow her infant cousin –

How thankful you must feel my dear Catherine that you were able to nurse her to the last, and that you held sweet converse together on the one thing needful, encouraging her much spirit to look to the

---

[1] 'The Guernsey Star of Tuesday says Daniel Tupper Esq., received yesterday his commission as Receiver-General of the Island, and was this morning sworn into office. We believe that his appointment has given very general satisfaction.' *The Atlas 20 June 1840.*

merciful Saviour who binds the broken soul, who is a friend ever present and ever willing to secure all who come unto him.

Had dear Kate lingered, it is probable her sufferings would only have been increased and the agony of seeing one you so tenderly loved, daily dying would have been additional sorrow.

I hope dear Catherine, your own health will not have suffered from the constant fatigue and anxiety you have undergone and that your Tom bears up under his bereavement. It is these moments we regret the distance which prevents one being useful to our friends but I am comforted to know Caroline [is] with you and I am sure nothing will be wanting in her wish to sympathise and console but, of how little avail – I grief much how it's cruel and it's better not checked, time is the best soother of our griefs and the hopes of a blessed reunion at no very future day. [The most supporting familial insides affliction?]

I will no longer intrude on your sorrows at this moment, I am aware how firstly my very poor expresses all my heart would dictate at this moment. Dan begs most affectionately to be included in every expression of sympathy for you and Tom, and believe me –

My dearest Catherine,

Your attached sister

Anna Maria Tupper

Letter to Revd Thomas Lewis Fanshawe from Revd (T.L) Bayliff

My dear Fanshawe,

I arrived in town this morning and on looking at the newspaper was truly deeply grieved to notice the melancholy loss you had sustained.

On my last visit to Parsloes I indulged a hope that a short time would restore your daughter to her former health and I have been looking forward to a visit to you that I might congratulate you and Mrs Fanshawe on her recovery. The shock has therefore been most unexpected and most sincerely do I sympathise with you in your loss. I trust however you have all been prepared for it, and it will please God to support you both under so painful a trial.

I am fully aware that nothing can compensate for your loss nor can you want to grieve, for religion does not forbid our sorrowing, but I am quite sure you have too deep a sense of the value of religion to derive no consolation from it – and you have the gratification of reflecting that for your beloved daughter the change is gain for she has always evinced that sincere piety and resignation which alone are evidences of faith in Him who bids us look forward to death without fear and to contemplate the end of our worldly career as the entrance to endless happiness.

You will too I am sure, learn to find comfort in this thought and the memory of her, who is now no more, will be cherished with holy gratitude – for by all whom she was known she was loved and her virtues and piety will long live in their memory and be an example worthy of imitation.

I have written hastily to you but I could not allow a post to pass without attempting, however imperfectly, to express my sincere sympathy in your loss. I am also <u>very</u> anxious to know how your poor wife bears the trial - if any would write me to tell me.

With my kindest regards to all,

Believe me

Your sincere friend

(T L) Bayliff

(Thetford)

April 29th 1840

Returning Home

Helen and Edward Denison returned to England in January 1845 with little more than three months to settle into their home before the birth of their first child. Yet Helen Jemima's arrival on the 6th May seems to have been perfectly timed to be celebrated with her parent's first wedding anniversary the next day.

Although the letters offer no real clues to anticipate the baby's birth, news of Helen's condition probably reached the new grandparents before the young couple returned. Perhaps it was communicated on one of the few missing pages of the letters or more probably, in one of the personal notes intended only for Mrs Fanshawe - the more natural thing for any daughter to do.

Expected births were then rarely confirmed or announced until after two months into pregnancy, and away from her family, Helen may have wanted only to share her news once it was confirmed by a doctor. Edward probably knew Mr Roskilly was available for consultation at Naples and when in a letter that doctor's name is mentioned, there is an implication that Mrs Fanshawe already knew of the name.

So if it is assumed Roskilly was consulted early in November 1844, that would account for Edward choosing to change their itinerary and adapt the transport for the journey home …'*I think we shall most probably leave this about the 6th and sail to Marseilles instead of posting. We shall then be a fortnight getting to Paris. Edward has had a spring seat made for me at Naples, which is the greatest luxury you can conceive on some of those bad roads…*'

Settling in

Once back in London, the 'honeymoon' must soon have become a memory as Helen and Edward settled at 32 Thurloe Square, Brompton. They soon eased themselves into Victorian domestic and social life and on Wednesday 4th June, their daughter was christened at St Luke's Church in Chelsea. When a son was born in 1847, they obviously had more time to plan, and Joseph Basil was brought to Dagenham to be christened by his grandfather, Revd Thomas Lewis Fanshawe.

Details of those births and that of Helen's third child Edward Fanshawe Denison born on 30th January 1849 were easily found in public registers, but tracing the professional activities of Edward during those years has not been simple.

Documents show Edward's profession as 'barrister-at-law' and although sometimes described as 'not in practice' he held an appointment as a magistrate for Middlesex. Possibly his professional situation was very fluid for with access to substantial independent means from land and property he had no urgency to build a legal practice. Most likely, he spent time managing his father's investments and acquisitions, handling the legal work entailed. Through open public records, there are details of the family's rental income and rate obligations which show gradual transfers of property into a trust in Edward's name.

Obviously, not all their properties were for commercial purposes and Tyne Hall at Bembridge on the Isle of Wight was occupied and enjoyed by all the Denison family and the house and that area close to the sea, came to play a central part in their life events. One of the first noted occasions shared at Bembridge was on 13th September 1849 when

Edward's niece Jemima Kershaw married William Oswell at the nearby church of St Helen.

The established family

About this time Helen and Edward took a long tenancy on a large country house at White Hill, Little Gaddesden in Hertfordshire. Situated away from London with good access to the City, they were joining friends already established nearby and Little Gaddesden proved to be a haven for the family over many years. Through the 1851 census the family are first recorded as resident, when Edward listed as head of the household was followed by Helen and their children 'Nellie', 'Joe' and 'Ned'. Also at home was sixty-seven year old Joseph Denison; they were all looked after by seven living-in servants.

Helen's third son, born later that year received the fashionable names of Albert Charles. Normally referred to as 'Charlie', he too was christened by his grandfather - although not at the font of Dagenham Church, but in the parish church at Little Gaddesden.

October 1853 was a time for all Helen's family to celebrate as her brother John Gaspard, then twenty-nine and no longer 'adverse' to the wedded state; married Barbara Coventry[1] of Earls Croome, Worcestershire. Within a year, Helen's children had a baby cousin, and as heir to the Parsloes estate he was appropriately christened with the old family name of Evelyn.

By June 1855 all the family's concern shifted to more serious matters when the reality of Britain's involvement in the war in Crimea came close to home. With extreme cold weather all across Europe during the previous winter, it had been

---

[1] Granddaughter of 7th Earl of Coventry.

exceptionally harsh in Crimea. Great losses were sustained by the allied troops who were ill-equipped for the conditions and fresh soldiers were being despatched. Among them was Helen's twenty-five year old brother Thomas 'Basil' Fanshawe.

Basil had already served eight years with tours of duty in the West Indies and North America in the Duke of Wellington's 33rd Regiment. He had risen to the rank of captain but this posting brought his first experience of war. Arriving at Sebastopol, he spent the first night on duty with his company in the battery where they found themselves under direct attack. That experience and others equally harrowing, were shared in letters to his family and through his general comments we also know of the contemporary activities of those at home…*'I am very sorry to hear Edward and Helen leave Parsloes, evidently too long in one spot is not their maxim'*… he also thanks Edward and Helen for sending a gift of beer that he shared with the fellows of his mess.

During September 1855, Basil wrote to Helen and Den[1] … *'I am very sorry to find you have determined on leaving Parsloes, but hope you will be fortunate in the choice of your new residence. I am glad you are not going away immediately – Edward, I am told is shooting with the Gov'r[2] this year, how I should like to be with them or rather with you all, but of that, I see no chance for the present'…'Tell Edward, the Light Division races come off on the 3 of next month. I will write to him. There are numbers of quail about & I mean to have a turn at them someday, they are very fat & would be a great addition to the table'* … proof of the bond these men had formed through shared sporting interest.

---

[1] Presumably Basil's name for his brother-in-law.
[2] Governor – a respectful affectionate term used by public schoolboys when speaking of or directly addressing their father.

Basil's letters tell us that Helen and her family were still at Parsloes in January 1856 and also that they had left by March, probably for Bembridge - which would fit Basil's plan for his journey home...*'If we disembark at Portsmouth or Plymouth it will be quite handy for Helen and Edward.'*...

Happily, Basil returned safely home from Crimea and so for a while no more of his informative letters were retained.

Life changes

Very soon after, Helen and Edward must have been caught up in the changes and decisions being made when her father retired. Thomas Lewis Fanshawe was never a robust man but as he approached sixty-five his health rapidly began to fail. Supported by his very capable wife, he had served his parish for more than forty years but within weeks of retirement he died - 5th March 1858.

The family then experienced another sad loss in the way that so often happens in sequences - for less than two months later on 28th April 1858, Edward's father Joseph Denison died at Bembridge.

There were many affairs to arrange for both families but pressing was the need for Mrs Fanshawe to be settled into a suitable home. Fortunately they found 15 Gloucester Street, Warwick Square where she lived happily for her remaining years – it was only streets from Helen and Edward's London home, then 33 Wilton Place, and also John Gaspard's at 22 Chester Terrace, Eaton Square.

As Mrs Fanshawe established her widowed life, her younger unmarried sons were travelling in the colonies; Basil with his regiment in India until 1861, and Richard who sailed to New Zealand to take up land surveying and went on to make it his permanent home. Yet, Mrs Fanshawe continued to help her numerous relations and by enjoying her family and friends, kept her life full and active – whilst she observed how her daughter's life was changing.

The first change came in 1860 for as Joe reached fourteen he was off to Rugby School and then two years later Ned followed. Through the register of Rugby School, we discover the house at Bembridge was considered the family home, although the London 'townhouse' was always maintained even though the lease on the house at Little Gaddesden may then have come to an end.

The 1861 census might have clarified the situation of their residence but unfortunately Helen, her children and Mrs Fanshawe cannot be traced… perhaps they were visiting family or friends or even abroad?

By chance, Edward has been found on that census, although staying in an unexpected place that was only revealed while searching for Basil Fanshawe. On census night Basil is found as a 'visitor' at the Aldershot Barracks of the 49th Regiment of Foot and immediately beneath his entry is recorded another 'visitor' - described as a 'gentleman' named Edward Denison.

Basil's entry must be correct as it states 'Captain 33rd Regiment age 33' but noticeably unusual for both, neither man has his correct full name. It can only be imagined that these census entries were added in haste as the two 'visitors' were included at the end of a long list of soldiers without rank. They were probably not consulted when added by the Army clerk anxious to make numbers and books tally in regulation order.

Regimental records confirm 'the 33$^{rd'}$ was then in India which implies Basil had been on home leave and his return would be facilitated with the next regiment to be 'shipped' out. With embarkation underway, Basil's older brother-in-law 'Den' must have accompanied him to the barracks to help transport the extensive baggage.

The next time we discover Helen and Edward is in 1863 when after a gap of twelve years, they again became new parents. Their daughter Katherine Alexandra[1], obviously named for her grandmother also received the name of the fashionable new royal princess.

That same year must have been a social family time for all Helen's family as Basil had returned with his regiment. He was able to spend time in Bath where he met and courted Emily Gosselin. They were married the next year and at their wedding on the 8th March, as they planned their own new life, so Edward might have been thinking how to celebrate his fiftieth birthday in a few months.

Edward's summer birthday on 1st July was to be celebrated at Bembridge, but fate intervened and the day that should have been happy and full of family joy brought a tragedy – it was the day of Edward's death.

Although officially recorded as 2nd July 1864, family history insists Edward Hanson Denison actually died on his birthday. It is not clear if death was sudden - he may have suffered an stroke earlier, as on his death certificate the cause is simply stated as 'paralysis'.

Changed status

For Helen and the children the shocking reality of Edward's death can only be imagined. Possibly an older close male relative was not nearby who could help … but perhaps Denis Le Marchant took some control from London? Or

---

[1] Princess Alexandra, daughter of Christian IX of Denmark married the Prince of Wales (Edward VII) in 1863.

perhaps it was just coincidence that the person despatched to record Edward's death was Francis Gerard St. George Tupper, Helen's twenty year old cousin, employed in Uncle Denis' parliamentary office? Co-incidentally that young man was 'the baby' mentioned in the letters as having been born to 'Aunt Tupper'[1] three weeks before Helen's wedding.

Through her mourning[2] Helen must have realized it was only six years since her mother became a widow and now her own life had changed in this dramatic way when she was only thirty-eight. With three maturing sons to guide towards careers and two daughters to launch, she had serious responsibilities.

Her two older sons were near to finishing their time at Rugby, but Charlie, still not thirteen was not due to start at the school for another year. Perhaps Charlie or even Helen could not face that separation as he never went to Rugby. The family returned to live in London and possibly he attended another public school closer to home.

In addition to family concerns Helen had the responsibility to administer Edward's estate which was made complicated by the fact that he had been his father's sole executor with probate still unresolved at the time of his own death. Fortunately, probate for Edward's estate was granted to Helen without delay on 8th November 1864 enabling her to apply for letters of administration for Joseph – granted 30th May 1866. These personal family papers have not been explored but many properties shown in open records are held in the Edward Hanson Denison Trust - mostly located at prime sites in central Manchester - resulting in substantial income.

---

[1] Letter 5th June 1844.
[2] Mourning for a widow was normally two years.

At home, Helen had the company of her youngest daughter Katherine and the eldest, nineteen year old Nellie. When the boys finished their schooling, all decided against university, opting for apprenticeships in transport and engineering, or in Charlie's case, the army. Old Joseph Denison would have applauded such modern ideas as they certainly pleased 'Uncle Basil' who kept watch from distant outposts of the Empire…*'I think Joe is very wise in looking out for something to do and not leading an idle life. I wish Ned could find something and Evy…'*[1]

A few months after his father's death, Joe at the age of seventeen became a pupil of the civil engineer John Wright. He worked three years on the Carmarthen & Cardigan Railway before travelling north to continue his training on the Doncaster and Gainsborough Line. Joe was industrious, and with his ability soon recognised he was to achieve a very successful career. Travelling to the vast territories of North & South America he supervised and constructed rail networks and today the name of Joseph Denison is found among those listed as pioneers of railway and marine engineering.

Helen must have been satisfied to know her sons had plans and ideas and their success enabled her to concentrate on her daughters, especially Katherine who was the only child of Edward's not to have a memory of him. No doubt for companions Katherine had her young cousins living nearby in John Gaspard's family but her other cousins, the children of Basil were not so conveniently close. Their early years were spent in India and later they grew up at home with their mother in Bath where they were educated. Under India's heat, Basil was alone as he served many of the remaining fourteen years of his army service.

---

[1] Letter from Lt. Col. T B Fanshawe - Kamptee, India 1876.

A grown up family

Military careers were of course, the tradition of Mrs Fanshawe's own family, with many officers of rank serving in different regiments...' *as I am sure considering your military turn that will interest you much'*... After her father, perhaps the most successful was her brother, Lt. General Sir John Gaspard Le Marchant (1803–1874) who was Lt. Governor of Nova Scotia and Governor of Malta[1].

When his eldest daughter Emily married on 9th March 1865 it was a society event and included among the family guests would have been Mrs Fanshawe and Helen the bride's eldest first cousin, accompanied by her daughter Nellie.

Emily had made a good match - her bridegroom was William Romilly, son of the Master of the Rolls, the Whig politician John Romilly. Soon after the wedding Emily became pregnant with her son, John Gaspard Le Marchant Romilly who was born only days after her first wedding anniversary – but sadly Emily died sixteen days later.

Basil's letters from India, show that Mrs Fanshawe was close to Emily's family, although nothing is known of who raised the motherless child. However, public records reveal the marriages of Emily's two younger sisters around 1870 and those occasions may have provided Emily's widower with opportunities to socialise with Helen's daughter Nellie. Perhaps their relationship began in that way or maybe a courtship was simply planned by the families. Marriage was the outcome and Nellie's wedding took place at St George's, Hanover Square, on 6th November 1872. Two years later, on the death of his father, William succeeded to the title 2nd Baron Romilly.

---

[1] GCMG KCB - Nova Scotia 1852–58 and Malta 1858-64.

Meanwhile, Helen was experiencing the next period of change. Gradually her children were leaving home – at eighteen Charlie enlisted in the army and during May 1870 was gazetted a Lieutenant in the 100th Regiment of Foot, The Leinster Regiment.

At the time of the 1871 census, the family had left Bembridge and those resident at home lived at Wilton Place. Joe was absent in Brighton supervising the construction of a new tramway. Nellie was home but soon to be married, and Ned, recorded as resident was coming and going using the family home as his base. Therefore effectively, from this time onwards, Helen was alone with Katherine and her governess with nine other servants living-in.

Following Nellie's marriage Helen's family pattern remain the same for the next decade. Joe was in demand for his expertise in building road, railway and tram tracks and frequently travelled to South America and the United States - he could accept many exciting opportunities for he was a single man.

Inevitably, Charlie, as a soldier in Queen Victoria's army was posted to India and embarked with his regiment for Bengal in 1877. The year before, his uncle, Lt. Col. Basil Fanshawe anticipated the event writing from his command at Kamptee, India ... *'I wonder where the 100th will go to on arrival in this country? Nowhere near us, I expect - how does Charlie like the idea of coming out?'*

Basil's letters from India inform us about Ned's activities at that time ... *I hope Ned will have more success than has hitherto attended his efforts with the machine for raising ships. How hard it seems to get employment...'* and those efforts came to fruition in 1880 when he and Joseph became partners in 'Simpson &

Denison' - producing engines and machinery for yachts and electricity generation.

The younger members of the family were not the only members of the family busy, for when the 1871 census was taken Mrs Fanshawe was staying with her old friends, the Bramfills at Stubbers near Upminster. Basil's letters from India tell us her life was generally full as she enjoyed her small London home. She welcomed many guests and visiting friends and when Basil planned his journey home to England in 1877, he was looking forward to bringing his children to stay with their grandmother who hoped to show them London.

Mrs Fanshawe was more than eighty and had lost most of her contemporaries (including her brother Denis) but still she seemed to keep looking forward.

In her prime

'Helen is getting streaked'... Basil tells us, but if she was a little grey, she was just entering her prime. Her own mature life was now well established and she often travelled to the Isles of Scilly where she was a guest of the Smith-Dorrien family[1] - an extension of the familial link between the Denison, Smith and Le Marchant families, explained by their mutual connections to Smiths Bank of Nottingham.

The Smith-Dorrien family also owned a substantial estate at Little Gaddesden - known to Basil ...*'his quarter Ashlyn's Hall used to be A1 for shooting & fishing but I suppose it is altered like other good quarters'*... and that connection might explain why early in their marriage, Helen and Edward chose to live at

---

[1] Thomas Algernon Smith-Dorrien-Smith (1846 – 1918), Lord Proprietor of the Isles of Scilly from 1872 until his death – who continued the development of the Tresco Abbey Gardens started by his uncle. He is reputed to have conceived the plan to export flowers from the Islands.

Little Gaddesden and also why Helen returned when ready to take another country house.

She settled at Marian Lodge[1] ... *built by Lady Marian Alford some thirty years ago. It is now tenanted by Mrs. Denison, under whose care soft cloth[2] is woven, some of which is sent yearly to the queen'*.... Although it is not clear when Helen's tenancy began, it was probably before July 1881, as Mrs Fanshawe's death was recorded while staying with Helen in the area at The Cell, Markyate Street.

Just a few months prior to Mrs Fanshawe's death the 1881 census confirms she was still lived independently at 15 Gloucester Street. Added by only an elderly cook and a housemaid all was as normal for she was enjoying a 'visitor,' a younger member of her family[3] - so the charming Mrs Fanshawe finally leaves us with one last reminder of her abiding generosity and kind hospitality.

Helen at fifty-five had effectively become the family's matriarch with only her daughter Nellie married - all of her sons were single and as yet she was not a grandmother.

Edward then thirty-two, was joined with Joe in a business venture at Dartmouth in Devon where they began to achieve success under the partnership of Simpson and Denison marine engineers – an interest that must have pleased Helen as Edward's enthusiasm for the sea had first taken them to the Isle of Wight.

By 1883 they had successfully registered patents that brought improvements to steam boilers and the business partnership lasted until 1887 when it was mutually dissolved. The work

---

[1] A History of the County of Hertford Vol.2 Victoria County History, London, 1908 – (Marian Lodge has since been renamed Denison House).
[2] Unconfirmed - but may have been linen cloth.
[3] Alice Carey - 2nd cousin and a granddaughter of Col. Peter Carey.

continued successfully under Simpson so it must be assumed Edward received a substantial financial settlement allowing him to remain settled in Dartmouth with his wife Anna Dora Cumberbatch whom he had married in 1883.

Little is known of Anna Dora except this account told in The Western Gazette 31st July 1885 when she was twenty-eight ...*'A lady on Fire – Narrow Escape' On Monday a very exciting scene was witnessed in Dartmouth harbour. Mrs Edward F Denison was proceeding from Kingswear towards Sandquay in a steam launch, when her hat was blown into the water. Mrs Denison endeavoured to reach it, and in doing so her dress caught fire through her getting too close to the engine. A volume of flame immediately burst forth, but Mrs Denison sprang overboard, and the water at once extinguished the fire. Being a fairly good swimmer she struck out for the shore. In the meantime six or seven boats put off to rescue Mrs Denison, and she was soon landed...* Anna Dora appears to have been intelligent, resourceful and perhaps good fun. As a couple they enjoyed Dartmouth's sailing community, particularly as Edward took on the role of honorary secretary of the Royal Dart Yacht Club.

New realities

At the age of forty, Joe also married and his wedding to Annie Louisa Campbell took place at Dartmouth in January 1889.

With two young daughters-in-law, Helen must have felt hopeful that she would soon be a grandmother but optimistic feelings for her family were dashed two months later. News of her daughter Nellie's death was received - she was only forty-three and died whilst a guest of a distant relative, Lady Grey Egerton of Oughton Park - which surely must imply her death was unexpected.

After seventeen years of marriage and raising her stepson, unfortunately for Nellie there had been no children of her own and there was further tragedy two years after her death, when her widower William, Lord Romilly died at his London house in Egerton Gardens in a very dramatic fire.

Fortunately there was happier news - Annie who was with Joe in Canada, had a son on 2nd January 1890. Called Archibald Campbell, after his Campbell grandfather - at last with this boy the family name of Denison had the chance to continue. Whilst still in Canada, a daughter was born to complete the family the following year - named Helen Alice Denison.

The 1891 census shows Helen with Katherine settled at Little Gaddesden with a full staff of servants but that year, Charlie retired from the Leinster Regiment with the rank of Lt. Colonel. He was still only forty and unmarried and took himself back to Bembridge on the Isle of Wight. He bought a cottage known at Balure and must have been full of plans but his retirement by the sea was short as his death was recorded in 1896.

Losing her children in such an untimely way, Helen must have sought solace and comfort in planning and working her large garden. Similar to many Victorians she was fortunate to find honest countrymen ready to be employed as gardeners and among those men were some of the best of England's dedicated professional gardeners.

The plants in Helen's garden at Little Gaddesden flourished under the attention of Mr Arthur Gentle, who was her head gardener from 1895 and by working together for many years, he was able to concentrate on producing prize winning new varieties of Sweet Pea. He entered competitions at national level and won many medals that are proudly retained by his descendants together with the prestigious 'Sydenham Cup' won outright after winning the contest for three consecutive years.

As Helen's life revolved around the seasons of the garden and her friends at Little Gaddesden her sons were often abroad. Joe with Annie was mainly in the Americas, and Ned and his wife were frequent travellers in Europe - but sad news never kept far away…

When Ned and Anna Dora were in Rome early 1899, he was suddenly taken seriously ill. With difficulty, Anna Dora managed to bring him back to London, hoping that more specialist medical treatment might save him but that was not to be and Ned died in June that year - aged only fifty-one,.

As Ned's father Edward had died at a similar age and also Charlie, his younger brother, it must be speculated that perhaps today's modern medical practices could have prevented at least one of those early deaths. Money and connections were of little help without the knowledge of the importance of simple regular heart and blood pressure controls and the relevance of inherited familial medical history.

The 20th Century

Entering the 20th century at the age of seventy-four Helen was left with only her eldest son and youngest daughter. Soon she outlived all her brothers with Basil dying last in 1905.

Yet she could still view the new century with optimism by centring her thoughts on the lives of her grandchildren. We know from her family correspondence[1] during the period 1899 – 1902 that she remained in regular contact with the

---

[1] See Appendix II.

family of her brothers. In particular she was taking an affectionate interest in the new babies born to her young newly married niece, Violet Gordon[1].

The census of 1901 paints an equally pleasant picture as staying with Helen without her parents was ten year old, Helen Alice Denison. That little girl's older brother Archie was a boarder at 'Sandroyd' prep school near Epsom, but must have spent school holidays at Little Gaddesden as Joe was still working abroad (although he was in England for the census - temporarily lodging alone at Bembridge, although not at Balure the cottage inherited from Charlie).

In 1904 Archie went on to Harrow School where he remained until 1907. Then starting his military career at the Royal Military College at Sandhurst he passed out in 1908. In the tradition of his Campbell ancestors he was gazetted into 'The Black Watch', 2nd Battalion, The Royal Highlanders but Helen could be equally proud - he was keeping up the military traditions of the Le Marchant family.

Similar to many of his family, Archie served in India. While stationed at Sialkot he attended the Delhi Durbar of December 1911 and was honoured to be selected to carry the regimental colours in the guard of honour for the newly - crowned King George V and Queen Mary.

In the same year, back at Little Gaddesden the household expanded for Joe and Annie came to live with Helen and Katherine. Helen was then eighty-five but her standards in the house were being maintained for she still retained nine servants. Mr Gentle was keeping her gardens looking beautiful and with his family living nearby, he brought his

---

[1] Youngest daughter of John Gaspard Fanshawe who was the grandmother of John Gordon.

fifteen year old son into the garden, hoping to pass on his skills.

Yet old age could not protect Helen from the sadness of losing relatives, and the next year Joe's wife Annie died at the age of only forty-one, leaving Joe a widower at sixty-five.

The Great War

Early in the summer of 1914 and only weeks before the start of the Great War, Joe's daughter, Helen Alice married Graham Marshall Walker of Easton Gray, Malmesbury in Wiltshire – whilst her brother Archie was still in India.

By November 1918 Archie had arrived with his regiment in France - they landed at Marseilles and as they moved north, the Black Watch became engaged in action.

At the Battle of Neuve Chapelle during March 1915, Archie sustained a slight wound and was 'mentioned in despatches' for his gallant conduct.

Later the same year the regiment engaged in the Battle of Loos - and on 25th September, Archie, who was bravely leading his men, lost his life from a single shot to the head.

His father received a letter from Lt. Col. A. S. Wauchope, the commanding officer ...*'You know how greatly I always cared for and admired Archie, both as a man and as a soldier. He was in peace and war a splendid young Officer. Of his action on the day of the battle I can only say that it was wonderful, and I would like all his friends to know how well he did, and all friends of the Regiment to know the General's and everyone's praise'*... words that perhaps gave some comfort, but were little consolation for the loss of an only son.

One of Archie's brother officers wrote...*'I feel I must write a few words as to how Archie Denison fell. Every N.C.O. and man who was near him speak of the gallant way in which he led his men in the attack, always in the front, frequently standing on the parapet directing operations, encouraging his men on, apparently fearless. It was in front of his men bombing up a trench that he was sniped, shot through the head and killed instantaneously. It was almost up to the limit of our objective that he fell, and to have reached such a point, in the words of the General to the men yesterday, will be an endless glory to them. His dash and courage, at the same time his coolness, to keep his men together, to penetrate so far, must have been wonderful. Unfortunately all the Officers who were killed were well behind the German lines, so, on account of the withdrawal later, are left where they fell.'*[1]

Twenty-five year old Archibald Campbell Denison is among the brave soldiers who have 'no-known grave' but his sacrifice is commemorated on the Loos Memorial at Dud Corner Cemetery, Loos-en-Gohelle in France. He is also included among the fallen on the First World War Memorial at Harrow School but perhaps the most poignant memorial is the personal commemoration on a bronze plaque raised by his father at Holy Trinity Church, Bembridge. The regimental colours of the Black Watch hang above the plaque, together with Archie's personal sword - beneath all there is a small bronze plaque Joe Denison – his father.

After the loss of his only son, Joe retired to 'Balure' at Bembridge and perhaps Helen, without hope for the continuity of the Denison male line, retired to her garden. If she spoke of Archie with Mr Gentle, then war was to prove a brutal leveller for within seven months the gardener's own second son Bertie Gentle also died in action.

---

[1] From the citation accompanied by Archie's photograph included in the archives of Harrow School WW1 Memorial.

Helen survived only another two years, dying at Little Gaddesden on the 10th July 1917 at the great age of ninety-one.

As her older and only surviving son, Joe was left to arrange his mother's affairs. He obtained probate by early November and then only days after, quietly at his cottage close to the sea, Joe's life came to an end.

Only the beginning and not the end

Helen's youngest child Katherine never married and died in 1938 - almost a century after her parent's marriage with their bridal tour.

Her sister-in-law Anna Dora, Ned's widow of forty years passed away the year after and having remained close to her husband's niece Helen Alice she left her the legacy of her estate.

Fortunately, that younger Helen, who was the sole link to the Denison & Fanshawe families had a son and he in turn had a son and a daughter. Now it is their modern day descendants that inherit this story for although the name of Denison disappeared along with Helen Alice's own married name, nevertheless Edward and Helen and all their many ancestors await their interest.

The small rural community of Dagenham where Helen Fanshawe was born has become a sprawling dormitory town on the edge of Greater London. Her travels that began in horse drawn carriages and ships with sails, progressed onto the first trains across newly laid railway tracks and then to ships with steam engines. Helen's generation enjoyed the sight of the first photographic images and witnessed the first of the moving pictures and possibly near to the end of her life, she travelled by car.

When Helen visited new exhibitions in London, did she speak and reminisce of the wonders she had seen in the galleries and museums of Europe? Did she tell how she and Edward crossed the Alps by carriage? Or speak of who she saw and met? Did she pass any of those stories on?

Without a portrait of Helen our knowledge of fashion and style allows us to visualise how she might have looked when those stories were told, and we know much of how she thought - but perhaps what remains most opaque, is sound and clarity of her voice.

Deirdre Marculescu

2023

The Vicarage
Dagenham Village,
Essex

Marian Lodge, Little Gaddesden, Hertfordshire
Postcard published by Wm F Piggott Leighton Buzzard, (1905 or earlier)

The burial plot at Brompton Cemetery of Helen & Edward with their son Charlie and his sister Katherine. Mrs Catherine Fanshawe also shares the plot.

Captain
Archibald Campbell Denison
1890-1915
2nd Battalion Royal Highlanders
The Black Watch
Died at the Battle of Loos, Flanders

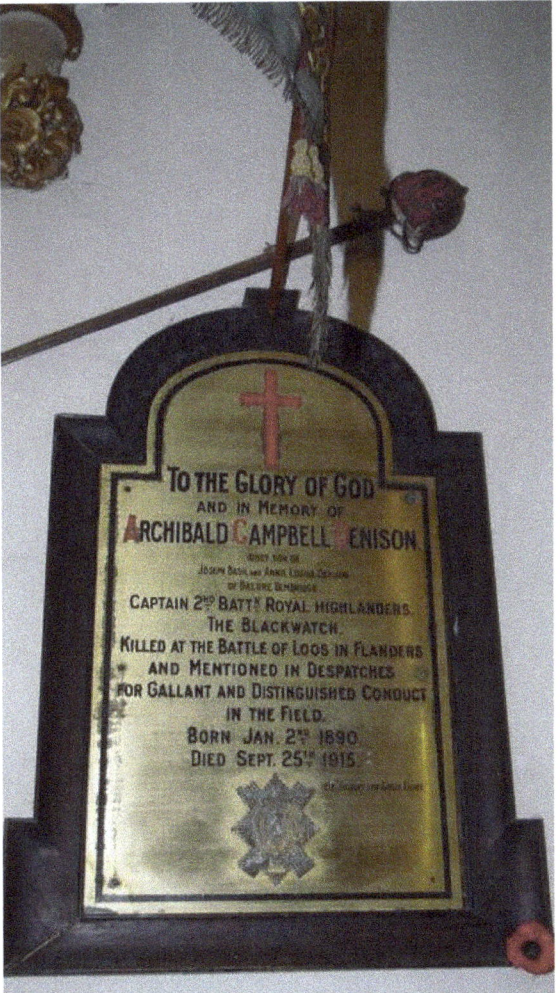

To commemorate the life of Capt. Denison a bronze memorial plaque is displayed in the Holy Trinity Church Bembridge, Isle of Wight- Above hang his personal sword and the colours of the Black Watch.

Beneath is another smaller plaque with the inscription: 'In loving memory of Joseph Basil Denison of Balure, Bembridge 1846 – 1917'

Illustrations & Acknowledgements

The majority of images included were sourced via Wikimedia Commons and classified as within the public domain - the exceptions are listed below:

Page 16
SER Crest & map, painting: http://www.southeasternandchathamrailway.org.uk/.

Page 40
Montem: 'The Illustrated London News'.

Page 87
Photograph of Blendon Hall: Blendon Archaeological & Historical Research Group - Blendonhall.com/about/blendon. Portrait of Oswald A Smith, pewter tankard & scorebook: online sale catalogue dated July 2019 - www.sothebys.com.

Page 90
Image of Denis Le Marchant – Valence House Museum.

Page 106
The Races: 'The Illustrated London News'.

Page 145
Portraits of Thomas Hunt & Caroline Isham Hunt: Courtesy of Peterborough Museum & Art Gallery – Peterborough.

Page 154
Information has been extracted from the article *'Bertie Bertie-Mathew's death while hunting in the campagna'* - the newsletter of the *Friends of the Non-Catholic Cemetery in Rome* 35 (2016), 6-7. The author N Stanley-Price whilst granting permission gave generous advice and supplied the photograph - both are much appreciated.

Page 206

The central picture 'House & garden at Little Gaddesden' are from the family collection of Ms Caroline Dix a direct descendent of Mr Arthur George Gentle the Head Gardener of Helen Denison. We were delighted to meet her when she travelled from the USA to visit Valence House in 2016 and now very pleased to have this opportunity to include part of her own family's story with that of the Denisons.

Photographs: Dagenham Vicarage & Denison Graves at Brompton Cemetery - author's own.

Page 207

Archibald Campbell Denison photograph:
www.harrowschool-ww1.org.uk/DOCS/DENISON_AC.pdf.
Plaque at Bembridge, I.O.W:
www.iwm.org.uk/memorials/item/memorial/21711.

Hopefully all sources are included but in view of the wide use of many of the images over many years, copyright it is not always apparent. If we have omitted or failed to obtain prior permission our sincere apologies are offered in advance.

Historical resources & selected further reading

A Handbook for Travellers on the Continent: being a guide through Holland, Belgium, Prussia and Northern Germany (5th Edition) – *Published by John Murray Albemarle St, London (1845). Online access – Google Books*

Boyes, Michael
A Victorian Rector & Nine Old Maids - *Phillimore (2005)*
Dying for Glory – the adventurous lives of five Cotswold brothers - *Phillimore (2006)*

Crowne, William
A true relation of the remarkable places & passages observed in the travels of the Rt. Hon. Thomas, Lord Howard - *(1637)*.

Dickens, Charles
Martin Chuzzlewitt - *(1844)*
Pictures from Italy – *(1846)*.

Duff, David
Hessian Tapestry, The Hesse family & British Royalty
David & Charles Ltd (1979)

Fanshawe, Colonel Thomas 'Basil'
Sebastopol to Dagenham - Crimea War letters - *Valence House Publications (2016)*
Abyssinia 1868, Expedition letters - *Valence House Publications (2018)*
Fanshawe's Indian Summer - letters from Kamptee, India
Valence House Publications (2019)

Fanshawe, H. C.
The History of the Fanshawe Family – *Andrew Reid & Co. (1927)*
The Memoirs of Ann Lady Fanshawe - *John Lane Company (1907)*

Ferris, Paul
Les Remèdes de Santé D'Hildegarde de Bingen – *Marabout (France 2002)*

Gordon, Strathearn
'The Family Book' (extracts) unpublished - *Fanshawe Collection, Valence House Archives.*

Hayle, Joanne
The Royal Race of 1818 – death of Princess Charlotte - *Amazon (2015)*

Le Marchant, Sir Denis
Memoirs of the late Major General Le Marchant 1766 -1812
Republished by Spellmount Ltd (1997).

Le Marchant, Major-Gen. John Gaspard
Private letters to Katherine Le Marchant (Fanshawe) 1811/12 *unpublished transcription - Fanshawe Collection, Valence House Archives.*

Noel Jackson W
Saint Mary the Virgin, Great Ilford – notes on the history
Church Publication (1967)

Shawcross, J.P
A History of Dagenham - *Valence House Publications (Republication 2016).*

Shelley, Mary
Rambles in Germany & Italy in 1840, 1842 & 1843
Reprinted by Lighting Source – also online access.

Wilson, A.N
The Victorians - *Hutchinson (2002).*

Wilson, F. M. G
A Strong Supporting Cast, the Shaw Lefevres 1789 - 1936
– Athlone Press (1993)

Index

Aachen Cathedral: 10, 32, 34.
Albert, Prince Consort: 36, 38, 40, 105-106, 114.
Aldershot Barracks: 190.
Antwerp: 4, 9, 23, 27-28, 30, 78.
Ariadne statue: 71, 73.
Arundel, Lord (1636): 63.
Aumale, Duke & Duchess: 148, 161.
Bacharach: 54-55, 63.
Balure: 199, 201, 203.
Barking Church *(St Margaret's)*: 37.
Battle of Salamanca: vi.
Baugh, Foillett Revd: 26, 42, 92, 102-103, 112.
Bayliff Revd T.L *(& family)*: 25, 82, 85, 96, 183-184.
Beguinage: 3, 5.
Bembridge: 79, 186, 189-191, 195. 199, 201, 203.
Bertie Matthew, Bertie: 150, 154.
Bertie, Henry W Revd.Hon *(Vicar Gt. Ilford)*: 103, 112.
Billingbear: xxii, xxiii, xxiv, xxv, xxix, 11, 24-25, 41-42, 66, 78-79, 108, 149.
Binnie & Richardson: 81.
Birch family: 134–135.
Black Gang Chine: 98.
Black Watch: 201-203, 207.
Blendon Hall: 80, 85, 87, 108, 113.
Boisragon, Henry, Dr: xii-xiii.
Boisragon, Mary Annetta: xii-xiv.
Bologna: 134.
Bonn: 35-36, 43.
Bonynge, Sarah *(née Parkinson)*: xii-xiii.
Boughton, Henry MP: 116.
Bowes-Lyons, Elizabeth *(Queen Consort)*: 80.
Brickhill: 79, 86, 89.
Bronte, Charlotte & Emily: 8, 15.
Bruges: 2, 3, 17-19, 22-23, 30.

Brussels: 2, 4, 8-9, 13, 22-23, 30-31, 35, 105.
Burdett-Coutts, Angela: 109.
Byron, Lord: 39, 97, 99.
Campbell, Annie Louisa *(see Annie Louisa Denison)*.
Canova, Antonio: 124, 126.
Carey, Hewett Revd: 24, 65, 129.
Carey, Mary *(wife of Major Gen. J G Le Marchant)*: 65, 92.
Carey, Peter Lt. Col. *(family)*: 24, 65-66, 92, 103, 128, 156, 164, 197.
Casinos: 64, 72.
Chaia: 148.
Charlemagne: 32, 34.
Chester Terrace: 189.
Chillon: 97, 99.
Chobham Place: xxv, 41.
Coblenz: 43, 45-46, 82.
Cologne: 20-21, 30, 32, 35-36, 48, 52.
Como, Lake: 124, 126.
Croft Elizabeth, Lady & family: 70, 129.
Croft, Richard (Rector – North Ockendon): 70, 129.
Croft, Sir Richard: 70, 129.
Cross Keys Public House: i.
Cumberbatch, Anna Dora *(see Anna Dora Denison)*.
Dagenham Idol: iv.
Dagenham Parish Church: i, iii, xiii, 11, 28, 37, 49. 103, 186-187.
Dagenham Vicarage: i-ii, xiv, 128, 206.
Dagenham Village: i-iv, xii-xiii, xiv, xxi, xxv, 10-11, 17, 28, 37, 40-41, 48-49, 60, 66, 70, 102-103, 128, 163, 168, 179, 186-187, 204, 206.
De Lancey, *(family)*: 81, 131.
Denison, Albert Charles *(Charlie)* 187, 192-193, 195, 199-201.

Denison, Anna Dora *(née Cumberbatch)*: 174, 198, 200, 204.
Denison, Annie Louisa: 198-202.
Denison, Archibald Campbell Capt: 199, 201-203, 207.
Denison, Edward Fanshawe *(Ned)*: 186-187, 190, 192-193, 195, 197-198, 200, 204.
Denison, Helen Alice *(see Helen Marshall Walker)*.
Denison, Helen Jemima 'Nellie' *(See Helen Jemima, Lady Romilly)*.
Denison, Joseph *(Mr Denison)*: xv-xviii, xx, xxiii, xxv-xxvii, 10, 26, 81, 89, 110, 129, 135, 157, 162-163, 187, 189, 193.
Denison, Joseph Basil *(Joe)*: 186-187, 190, 193, 195, 197-204.
Denison, Katherine Alexandra: 191, 193, 195, 199, 201, 204.
Denison, Sarah: xv, xviii.
Denman, Lord Chief Justice: 129.
Dickens, Charles: 100, 114, 122, 144-145, 148.
Dover: 13-14, 16, 44, 47, 57, 60, 163.
Dr Roskilly: 142, 185.
Drachenfel: 36-37, 39, 68.
Duke of Wellington's 33rd Regiment: 25, 188.
Dumas, Alexandre: 50-51.
Duncombe family: 58, 79.
Durer, Albrecht: 7.
Easton Gray: 202.
Elizabeth Stuart *(The Winter Queen)*: 74, 77.
Erle, Walter Revd.: 180.
Eton College: vii-viii, xiii-xiv, xviii, xix, xxi, xxiii, xxvi, 38, 40, 80, 87, 95, 111, 149-150, 154.
Fanshawe Gate: 15.
Fanshawe John (1773-1843): vii.
Fanshawe, Ann Gascoyne Mrs: xi.

Fanshawe, Barbara (née Coventry): 176, 187.
Fanshawe, Catherine née Le Marchant *(Mamma))*: v, vi, xxiii, xxvii, 9, 11-13, 23, 28, 30, 41, 43, 46, 50, 52, 60, 62, 66, 68, 70, 72, 78, 81-82, 85-86, 96, 107-108, 111, 113, 117, 131-132, 136, 139, 148, 151, 153, 156, 159, 161, 180, 168, 170, 178.
Fanshawe, Catherine Sophia: ix, 3, 177–184.
Fanshawe, Edgar S W: 173.
Fanshawe, Emily: 191.
Fanshawe, Evelyn J.: x, 172-173, 187.
Fanshawe, Henry (Uncle Henry): vii, 92, 130, 138.
Fanshawe, John Gascoyne: xi, xii.
Fanshawe, John Gaspard: ii, v, vii-viii, ix, xx-xxii, xxvi, 2, 13, 22-23, 29, 40, 42, 47-48, 50, 58, 65-66, 70, 81, 87, 98, 104, 108, 110-111, 114, 137, 140, 172, 176, 187, 189, 193, 201.
Fanshawe, Mary Annetta *(see Mrs Mary Annetta Boisragon)*.
Fanshawe, Mary: xi, xii,
Fanshawe, Richard *(Dick)*: v. xxvi, 26, 59, 69, 81, 85, 92-93, 95, 98, 107, 111, 130, 158-159, 189.
Fanshawe, Thomas (2nd Remembrancer): x.
Fanshawe, Thomas Basil *(Basil)*: v, xx, xxv-xxvi, 25-26, 41, 49, 59, 65, 69, 81, 85, 92-93, 95, 98, 107, 111, 130, 148, 158 -159, 163, 190-196, 200.
Fanshawe, Thomas Lewis Revd *(Papa)*: iv, vii, xiii, xiv, xxvi, xxvii, 2, 10-13, 16, 22, 24-26, 29, 32, 36, 41, 43, 47, 60, 66, 69, 81-82, 93-94, 96, 103, 107, 111-113, 123, 127, 130-132, 134, 139-140, 148-149, 155, 158, 160, 177, 180, 183, 186,189.

Fanshawe, Violet *(see Mrs Violet Gordon)*.
Fanshawe, William (1583-1634): vii.
Farquharson, Harriett: 25, 42, 139.
Florence: 110, 127, 132-133, 136, 143, 150-151.
Foss v Harbottle 1843: xviii, xxvii.
Foulis, Henry Revd Sir: 79.
Frankfurt: xix, 10, 26-27, 38, 41, 46, 48, 50, 52, 60-62, 64, 70-73, 75.
Frederick, Crown Prince of Denmark: 105.
Fry, Elizabeth *(& family)*: 128, 138.
Gascoyne, Bamber: xi.
Geneva & Lake: 41-42, 67, 81, 96-97, 99, 109-111.
Gentle (family): 199, 201, 203.
Ghent: 2-3, 5-7, 17, 21.
Goethe, Joseph von, 9, 56, 61.
Gordon, Douglas J.: 175.
Gordon, Huntly the Hon.: 172, 175.
Gordon, John; ii, 171, 201.
Gordon, Strathearn: 175.
Gordon, Violet: ii, 172-176, 201.
Gosselin, Emily *(see Emily Fanshawe)*.
Gostling Charles: 163.
Gostling, Charles, Lt. Col. RA.: 11, 136.
Gostling, Letitia Mary: 163.
Gostling, Mary (née Le Marchant): 11, 24, 47, 69, 85, 102, 136, 163.
Graham, James Sir: 58.
Grant *(Vicar of Romford)*: 66, 131.
Gravesend: 47, 69.
Gray, Henry *(Lodge Farm)*: 128.
Grey-Egerton, Lady: 198.
Guernsey: xiii, xiv, xxiii, 11, 25-26, 41, 51, 67, 81, 86, 88, 91-92, 103, 111, 131-132, 181.
Hales: 110, 116-117, 127, 131-132, 134, 136-137, 140, 150, 160.
Hanson, Joseph: xv-xvi, xxiii.

Hanson, Sarah *(see Mrs Sarah Denison)*.
Harrow School: 201, 203, 207.
Heckfield Place: xxiv, 12, 162.
Heidelberg: 56, 77.
Heidelberg: 56, 77-78.
Holy Blood, procession of: 22.
Homberg: 61-62, 64.
Hugo, Victor: 1, 50-51, 63.
Hunt, Thomas & Caroline: 142, 145, 147.
Isola Bella: 119, 122-123.
Kent, Duchess -Princess Victoria: 69.
Kershaw, Jemima Elizabeth *(See Mrs Jemima Elizabeth Oswell)*.
Kershaw, Jemima: xv, xxiv, xxv.
Kershaw, Joseph: xv.
Kershaw, William *(Willie)*: xvi, xxvi-xxvii, 111, 130.
Kershaw, William Capt.: xv, xxiv, xxv, 79.
Kursaal: 72, 76.
Landseer, Edwin: 59.
Last Supper *(da Vinci)*: 130.
Lausanne: 97, 109-110.
Le Marchant, Denis, Sir *(Uncle Denis)*: vii, xiii-xiv, xxi, xxv-xxvii, 40, 46-47, 66, 81, 86, 90, 135, 191.
Le Marchant, Eliza: 26, 101, 103.
Le Marchant, Emily *(see Emily Romilly)*.
Le Marchant, John Gaspard Lt. Gen, Sir: 48, 194.
Le Marchant, John Gaspard, Major. General: vi, xiii, xxvii.
Le Marchant, Lady Margaret (née Taylor): 48, 107.
Le Marchant, Sarah *(Aunt Eliza)*: xxi, 41, 48, 66, 81, 101.
Le Marchant, Thomas Col.: 66, 86.
Le Pelley – Seigneur of Sark: 24.
Lefevre, Anna Maria Shaw: 102-103.

Lefevre, Charles Shaw, Viscount Eversley: xxiv, 12.
Lefevre, Helen Shaw: 11, 82, 96, 103, 162.
Lefevre, Helena (née Helena Le Marchant): 11, 102.
Lefevre, Henry Shaw *(Uncle Henry)*: vii, xxi, xxii, xxiv, 11, 65-66, 82, 96, 102, 150.
Lefevre: Elizabeth Emma *(née Foster)*: xxii, 162.
Lincoln's Inn: xiii, xviii-xix, 44.
Little Gaddesden: 172, 175-176, 187, 190, 196-197, 199-201, 206.
Livesey, Joseph: 149.
Loos Memorial: 203.
Louvre: 124, 165.
Lucerne: 82, 84-85, 91, 94, 107-108, 110, 112, 117-118, 123.
Lugano, Lake: 123.
Maggiore, Lake: 119, 122-123.
Manchester: xv-xviii, xx, xxvi, 25, 60, 192.
Marquis of Anglesey's Leg: 31, 33.
Marshall Walker, Graham: 202.
Marshall Walker, Helen Alice: 199, 202, 204.
Martin *(servant)*: 10, 13, 24, 83, 85, 104, 112, 123, 165.
Martin Chuzzlewit: 100, 114, 148.
Memling - St Jan's Altarpiece: 18-21.
Milan: 117, 124-125, 127-128, 130, 133, 162.
Milner, John & family: 48.
Montem: viii, 38, 40, 80.
Moss family *(Three Mills)*: 66, 103.
Mourant, Sophie 'Aunt' (née Carey): 41.
Murray's Travel Guides: xix, 2, 13, 25, 72, 145.
Naples: 75, 110, 127, 140-148, 150, 152, 185.

Napoleon Bonaparte: 8, 127.
Nicholas I, Tsar: 80, 105-106, 114.
Oswell, Jemima Elizabeth: xv, xxi, 79, 104, 110, 129, 135, 152, 156, 159, 163, 166, 187.
Oswell, William F: 79, 187.
Oxford Movement, The: 138.
Oxford University: v, vii, xii, xxiii, 105, 138.
Paestum: 142, 145, 147.
Papa Joan: 158.
Paris; 75, 76, 110, 124, 137, 141, 152, 155-156, 160-161, 163-165, 185.
Parkinson, Mary *(see Mrs Mary Fanshawe)*.
Parsloes: i-iii, v, vii-viii, xi-xv, xxi, xxvi, 9, 22, 49, 71, 81, 86, 100, 129-130, 136, 150, 164, 183, 187-189.
Peel, Robert Sir: 47, 58.
Pell, Eliza: 78.
Pierre/Peter *(servant)*: 10, 13, 35, 67, 69, 78, 83, 85, 104, 112, 123, 156, 161.
Polka: viii, 72, 76, 112, 135.
Pompeii: 141, 144,
Potts, Henry & Cecilia: 60-61, 71-72.
Powder Puff: xxi, 135.
Prussia, King of: 6, 68.
Queen Adelaide: 32.
Queen Victoria: 36, 38, 49, 69, 76, 80, 102, 105-106, 151, 153, 195, 197.
Raphael: 134, 137, 143, 166.
Ravenscroft, Priscilla: 169.
Ripple Marsh: iv.
Rippleside: 17.
River Moselle: xix, 38, 45, 53-54.
River Rhine: 20, 35-39, 44-45, 50-55, 57, 63-64, 68, 76, 83, 118, 121.
River Thames: iv.
Rome: 20, 110, 127, 137, 140, 149, 151, 154, 156, 158, 160, 200.
Romford Bank: 66.
Romford: iv, 4.

Romilly, Emily: 194.
Romilly, Helen Jemima, Lady *(Nellie)*: 185, 187, 194-195, 197-199.
Romilly, John Gaspard Le Marchant *(3rd Baron)*: 194.
Romilly, William *(2nd Baron)*: 194.
Romilly. John *(1st Baron)*: 194.
Rothchild family: 61, 71, 75.
Royal Exchange *(opening)*: 151, 153.
Royal Military College Sandhurst: 201.
Royal Military College: vi.
Rubens, Peter Paul: 23, 28.
Rugby School: 190.
Rusholme Park: xv - xvii, 26.
Ruskin, John: 125.
Russell family of Stubbers: 70, 129.
Saxony, King Frederick Augustus II: 4, 106.
Seaview: xxiii-xxix, 92, 98.
Shelley, Mary: 99, 118, 120-122, 124-126, 142, 144, 146, 154.
Shelley, Percy Bysshe: 99, 125, 142, 154.
Shrewsbury School: xxvi, 26, 59-60, 81, 101, 111, 159.
Simpson & Denison: 197.
Smith Sarah *(Mrs Sarah 'Eliza' Le Marchant)*.
Smith, Eric Carrington: 111.
Smith, Oswald Augustus *(Oddy)*: 80, 85-87, 111.
Smith, Oswald: 80, 86-87, 104-105.
Smith, Payne & Smith Bank: 87.
Smith-Dorrien family: 11, 196.
Somerville, Caroline (née Le Marchant): 11, 41, 48, 60, 65, 80, 82, 94, 101, 103, 129, 132, 138, 142, 182.
Sorrento: 146-147.
Splugen: 108, 113, 118-121.
St Bernardino Pass: 118-119.

St John of Bletso *(family)*: xxii, xxiv-xxv.
St John, Augusta the Hon.: xxii, xxiv.
St. John, Jemima *(see Mrs Jemima Kershaw)*.
St. Ursula Shrine: 20.
Stockgrove: 10, 26, 86, 89, 133, 152, 156, 158, 163.
Strangeways Hall: xvi, 111.
Strasbourg: 56.
Sutton, Thomas Manners Revd: 150,
Thesiger, Frederick: 111.
Thomas, John: xxii, xxiii, xxv, 11, 25, 66.
Thomas, Le Marchant: xxii-xxiii, xxv, xxvii, 11, 47.
Thomas, Margaret Le Marchant: xxii-xxv, 79.
Thompson Capt & Mrs: 96, 98, 102, 104, 109, 112, 129, 135.
Thurloe Park: xx, 186.
Trinity College, Cambridge: xiii, xviii, xix, 80.
Tupper Anna-Maria *(Aunt Tupper)* (née Le Marchant): 11, 41, 180, 182, 192.
Tupper, Anna-Maria *(Annie)*: viii, 11-12, 24, 31, 41, 47, 65, 78, 104, 113, 117, 130-131, 138-139, 152, 159.
Tupper, Daniel: 11, 26, 41, 80, 165, 182.
Tupper, Eliza *(See Mrs Eliza Le Marchant)*.
Tupper, Francis Gerard St. George: 41, 192.
Tupper, Gaspard Le Marchant: 67, 80, 165.
Tyler, Fred: 11, 26, 48.
Van Eyck, Hubert & Jan: 3, 6-7.
Vaughan, Charles R, Sir: 79
Vaughan, Margaret *(see Margaret Le Marchant Thomas)*.

Via Mala: 118, 120-121.
Victoria Park Co.: xvii, xviii.
Wagner, Richard: 39.
Warwick Square: 189.
Waterloo: 10, 27, 30-31, 33, 114.
Weaver's Friend, The: xvi.
Wellington, Duke of: 2, 33.
Westley Richards: 114.
Westminster Hall Frescos: 136.
Whitbread *(Brewers)*: xxii-xxiv.
Wiesbaden: 50, 61-62, 64, 72, 76.
Wilton Place: 189, 195.
Wyersdale: xi, 92, 148.

The Archives & Local Studies Centre at Valence House, has for many years been the hub of historical research for the London Borough of Barking & Dagenham and among the vast archives is 'The Fanshawe Collection' relating to the Fanshawe family resident in the borough from Tudor times.

Year on year Fanshawe family members continue to deposit their documents and papers allowing the staff & research volunteers to make new discoveries. Each generation with a different story to tell helps to build a picture that reflects the history of our nation.

Currently, the volunteer Fanshawe researchers Deirdre Marculescu and Rosalind Alexander are slowly working to bring the lives of the late 18th and 19th centuries to public attention and they are helped by Derek Alexander, Valence volunteer computer expert. The legacy from our 2016 grant from the Heritage Lottery still makes this possible along with encouragement from Valence staff and fellow volunteers. Most of all, we are inspired by the interest and enthusiasm of John Gordon whose main justification for donating family treasures is that as historical resources they will be used and enjoyed by a wider audience.

www.ingramcontent.com/pod-product-compliance
Lightning Source LLC
Chambersburg PA
CBHW040240130526
44590CB00049B/4043